高一同學的目標

1.「用會話背7000字①」書＋CD　280元

以三個極短句為一組的方式，讓同學背了會話，同時快速增加單字。高一同學要從「國中常用2000字」挑戰「高中常用7000字」，加強單字是第一目標。

2.「一分鐘背9個單字」書＋CD　280元

利用字首、字尾的排列，讓你快速增加單字。一次背9個比背1個字簡單。

3. rival

rival [5] (ˈraɪvl̩) n. 對手
arrival [3] (əˈraɪvl̩) n. 到達　　}都有 rival
festival [2] (ˈfɛstəvl̩) n. 節日；慶祝活動

revival [6] (rɪˈvaɪvl̩) n. 復甦
survival [3] (səˈvaɪvl̩) n. 生還　　}字尾是 vival
carnival [6] (ˈkɑrnəvl̩) n. 嘉年華會

carnation [5] (kɑrˈneʃən) n. 康乃馨
dona___ (dəˈneʃən) 捐贈　　}字尾是 nation
don___

3.「一口氣
把大學____　　　　　　　　　　　後，
會說英語，又習考試

例如：

> What a nice surprise! (真令人驚喜！)【常考】
> I can't believe my eyes.
> (我無法相信我的眼睛。)
> *Little did I dream of seeing you here.*
> (做夢也沒想到會在這裡看到你。)【駒澤大】

4.「一口氣背文法」書＋CD 280元
英文文法範圍無限大，規則無限多，誰背得完？
劉毅老師把文法整體的概念，編成216句，背完
了會做文法題、會說英語，也會寫作文。既是一
本文法書，也是一本會話書。

1. 現在簡單式的用法

I *get up* early every day.	我每天早起。
I *understand* this rule now.	我現在了解這條規定了。
Actions *speak* louder than words.	行動勝於言辭。

【二、三句強調實踐早起】

5.「高中英語聽力測驗①」書＋MP3 280元

6.「高中英語聽力測驗進階」書＋MP3 280元
高一月期考聽力佔20%，我們根據大考中心公布的
聽力題型編輯而成。

7.「高一月期考英文試題」書 280元
收集建中、北一女、師大附中、中山、成功、景
美女中等各校試題，並聘請各校名師編寫模擬試
題。

8.「高一英文克漏字測驗」書 180元

9.「高一英文閱讀測驗」書 180元
全部取材自高一月期考試題，英雄
所見略同，重複出現的機率很高。
附有翻譯及詳解，不必查字典，對
錯答案都有明確交待，做完題目，
一看就懂。

高二同學的目標——提早準備考大學

1. 「用會話背7000字①②」
   書+CD，每冊280元

「用會話背7000字」能夠解決所有學英文的困難。高二同學可先從第一冊開始背，第一冊和第二冊沒有程度上的差異，背得越多，單字量越多，在腦海中的短句越多。每一個極短句大多不超過5個字，1個字或2個字都可以成一個句子，如：「用會話背7000字①」p.184，每一句都2個字，好背得不得了，而且與生活息息相關，是每個人都必須知道的知識，例如：成功的祕訣是什麼？

11. What are the keys to success?

Be *ambitious*.	要有<u>雄心</u>。
Be *confident*.	要有<u>信心</u>。
Have *determination*.	要有<u>決心</u>。
Be *patient*.	要有<u>耐心</u>。
Be *persistent*.	要有<u>恆心</u>。
Show *sincerity*.	要有<u>誠心</u>。
Be *charitable*.	要有<u>愛心</u>。
Be *modest*.	要<u>虛心</u>。
Have *devotion*.	要<u>專心</u>。

當你背單字的時候，就要有「雄心」，要「決心」背好，對自己要有「信心」，一定要有「耐心」和「恆心」，背書時要「專心」。

背完後，腦中有2,160個句子，那不得了，無限多的排列組合，可以寫作文。有了單字，翻譯、閱讀測驗、克漏字都難不倒你了。高二的時候，要下定決心，把7000字背熟、背爛。雖然高中課本以7000字為範圍，編書者為了便宜行事，往往超出7000字，同學背了少用的單字，反倒忽略真正重要的單字。千萬記住，背就要背「高中常用7000字」，背完之後，天不怕、地不怕，任何考試都難不倒你。

2.「時速破百單字快速記憶」書 250 元

字尾是 try，重音在倒數第三音節上

entry [3] ('ɛntrɪ) *n.* 進入【No entry. 禁止進入。】
country [1] ('kʌntrɪ) *n.* 國家；鄉下【ou 讀 /ʌ/，為例外字】
ministry [4] ('mɪnɪstrɪ) *n.* 部【mini = small】

chemistry [4] ('kɛmɪstrɪ) *n.* 化學
geometry [5] (dʒɪ'ɑmətrɪ) *n.* 幾何學【geo 土地，metry 測量】
industry [2] ('ɪndəstrɪ) *n.* 工業；勤勉【這個字重音常唸錯】

poetry [1] ('po‧ɪtrɪ) *n.* 詩
poultry [4] ('poltrɪ) *n.* 家禽　　字尾 y 表「集合名詞」
pastry [5] ('pestrɪ) *n.* 糕餅

3.「高二英文克漏字測驗」書 180 元

4.「高二英文閱讀測驗」書 180 元
全部選自各校高二月期考試題精華，英雄所見略
同，再出現的機率很高。

5.「7000字學測試題詳解」書 250 元
一般模考題為了便宜行事，往往超出7000字範圍
，無論做多少份試題，仍然有大量生字，無法進
步。唯有鎖定7000字為範圍的試題，才會對準備
考試有幫助。每份試題都經「劉毅英文」同學實
際考過，效果奇佳。附有詳細解答，單字標明級
數，對錯答案都有明確交待，不需要再查字典，
做完題目，再看詳解，快樂無比。

6.「高中常用7000字解析【豪華版】」書 390 元
按照「大考中心高中英文參考詞彙表」編輯而成
。難背的單字有「記憶技巧」、「同義字」及
「反義字」，關鍵的單字有「典型考題」。大學
入學考試核心單字，以紅色標記。

7.「高中7000字測驗題庫」書 180 元
取材自大規模考試，解答詳盡，節省查字典的時間。

TEST 1

Read the following passage and choose the best answer for each blank from the choices below.

Global warming, deficiencies in the world's natural resources, loss of rain forests, mass __1__ of animals—these are just a few of the dangers __2__ the stability of our environment. If we are to salvage the world we live in, action needs to be taken and it needs to be taken immediately. __3__ that the environment is becoming increasingly unlivable, many people are __4__ to "go green." From celebrities to your neighbor next door, people around the world are becoming more __5__ of the fact that it is the duty of every individual to conserve the environment.

1. (A) distinction   (B) extinction
   (C) sanction   (D) negotiation

2. (A) contributing   (B) maintaining
   (C) threatening   (D) sustaining

3. (A) Believed   (B) Seen   (C) Regarding   (D) Fearing

4. (A) opting   (B) popping   (C) tending   (D) taking

5. (A) conscious   (B) ignorant
   (C) characteristic   (D) sensitive

TEST 1 詳解

Global warming, deficiencies *in the world's natural resources*,

loss *of rain forests*, mass <u>extinction</u> *of animals*—these are just a few
　　　　　　　　　　　　 1

of the dangers *threatening the stability of our environment.*
　　　　　　 2

全球暖化、全世界天然資源短缺、雨林消失、大量動物<u>滅絕</u>——這
些只是一些<u>正威脅著</u>我們環境安穩的危險因素而已。
　　　　 2

* *global warming* 全球暖化　　　deficiency[6] (dɪˈfɪʃənsɪ) *n.* 缺乏
natural resources 天然資源　　 loss[2] (lɔs) *n.* 喪失
rain forest 雨林　　　mass[2] (mæs) *adj.* 大量的
stability[6] (stəˈbɪlətɪ) *n.* 穩定

1. (**B**)　(A) distinction[5] (dɪˈstɪŋkʃən) *n.* 差別；特質；卓越
　　　　　 (B) *extinction*[5] (ɪksˈtɪŋkʃən) *n.* 滅絕；絕種
　　　　　 (C) sanction[6] (ˈsæŋkʃən) *n.* (國際) 制裁
　　　　　 (D) negotiation[6] (nɪˌgoʃɪˈeʃən) *n.* 談判；協商

> extinct (ɪksˈtɪŋkt) *adj.* 絕種的
> extinction (ɪksˈtɪŋkʃən) *n.* 絕種
> distinct (dɪsˈtɪŋkt) *adj.* 不同的
> distinction (dɪsˈtɪŋkʃən) *n.* 差別；卓越
> distinctive (dɪsˈtɪŋktɪv) *adj.* 特殊的
> distinguished (dɪsˈtɪŋgwɪʃt) *adj.* 卓越的
> instinct (ˈɪnstɪŋkt) *n.* 本能
> instinctive (ɪnˈstɪŋktɪv) *adj.* 本能的

2. (**C**)　(A) contribute[4] 〔 kən'trɪbjut 〕 v. 貢獻；捐獻；投（稿）
　　　　(B) maintain[2] 〔 men'ten 〕 v. 保持；維持
　　　　(C) ***threaten***[3] 〔'θrɛtn̩ 〕 v. 威脅
　　　　(D) sustain[5] 〔 səs'ten 〕 v. 支撐；維持

If we are to salvage the world we live in, action needs to be taken

and it needs to be taken *immediately*. ⌈*Fearing **that** the environment*
　　　　　　　　　　　　　　　　　　　　3

is becoming increasingly unlivable, ⌉ many people are <u>opting</u> to "go
　　　　　　　　　　　　　　　　　　　　　　　　　　4

green." *From celebrities to your neighbor next door*, people *around*

the world are becoming *more <u>conscious</u>* of the fact ⌈***that** it is the duty*
　　　　　　　　　　　　　　5

of every individual to conserve the environment.⌉

如果我們要<u>挽救</u>我們所居住的世界，就必須要採取行動，而且要馬上進
行。由於<u>害怕</u>環境日漸變得不適合人類居住，許多人<u>選擇</u>開始「做環
　　　　　3　　　　　　　　　　　　　　　　　　　　　　4
保」。從名人到你隔壁的鄰居，世界各地的人正逐漸<u>意識</u>到一項事實，
保護環境是每一個人的責任。
　　　　　　　　　5

　　* salvage[6] 〔'sælvɪdʒ 〕 v. 搶救【 salvation[6] n. 拯救 】
　　immediately[3] 〔 ɪ'midɪɪtlɪ 〕 adv. 立刻
　　unlivable 〔 ʌn'lɪvəbl̩ 〕 adj. 不適於居住的
　　go green 做環保
　　celebrity[5] 〔 sə'lɛbrətɪ 〕 n. 名人
　　duty[2] 〔'djutɪ 〕 n. 責任
　　individual[2] 〔ˌɪndə'vɪdʒuəl 〕 n. 個人
　　conserve[5] 〔 kən'sɝv 〕 v. 節省；保護

salvage[6] v. 搶救
= save[1]
= rescue[4]

3. (**D**) (A) believe[1]〔bɪ'liv〕*v.* 相信

   (B) see[1]〔si〕*v.* 看見

   (C) regard[2]〔rɪ'gɑrd〕*v.* 認爲

   (D) *fear*[1]〔fɪr〕*v.* 害怕

   Fearing that the environment is…，是由 *Because many people fear* that the environment is…簡化而來的分詞構句。

4. (**A**) (A) *opt*[6]〔ɑpt〕*v.* 選擇【option[6]〔'ɑpʃən〕*n.* 選擇】

   (B) pop[3]〔pɑp〕*v.* (意外地) 出現；發生

   (C) tend[3]〔tɛnd〕*v.* 易於；傾向於 < *to* >

   (D) take[1]〔tek〕*v.* 拿　　take to 喜歡

5. (**A**) (A) *conscious*[3]〔'kɑnʃəs〕*adj.* 知道的；察覺到的

   be conscious of 知道；察覺到 (= *be aware of* = *know*)

   > 【比較】
   > { conscious[3]〔'kɑnʃəs〕*adj.* 知道的；察覺到的
   >   consciousness *n.* 意識
   > { conscience[4]〔'kɑnʃəs〕*n.* 良心
   >   conscientious[6]〔ˌkɑnʃɪ'ɛnʃəs〕*adj.* 有良心的；負責盡職的

   (B) ignorant[4]〔'ɪgnərənt〕*adj.* 無知的 < *of* >

   (C) characteristic[4]〔ˌkærəktə'rɪstɪk〕*adj.* 有特質的；特有的
   n. 特質；特性

   be characteristic of 是…特有的

   (D) sensitive[3]〔'sɛnsətɪv〕*adj.* 敏感的 < *to* >

TEST 2

Read the following passage and choose the best answer for each blank from the choices below.

Spanish authorities __1__ a massive invasion of jellyfish along the country's eastern coast over the coming days and advised bathers of the best ways to treat stings.

Over the past month, __2__ of jellyfish have plagued many coastal areas __3__ from the northeastern region of Catalonia down to Murcia and Andalucia in the south, __4__ temporary bans on bathing on many beaches.

The latest alert, posted on the Interior Ministry's website, was __5__ after coastal guards said they had spotted new banks of jellyfish several kilometers off different areas along the coast in recent days.

1. (A) laid off   (B) rooted out
   (C) warned of   (D) dropped in
2. (A) herds   (B) packs   (C) schools   (D) flocks
3. (A) stretched   (B) stretching
   (C) expanded   (D) expanding
4. (A) led to   (B) leading to
   (C) resulted from   (D) resulting from
5. (A) entitled   (B) edited   (C) performed   (D) issued

TEST 2 詳解

Spanish authorities <u>warned of</u> a massive invasion *of jellyfish*
1

along the country's eastern coast over the coming days ***and*** advised

bathers of the best ways *to treat stings*.

　　西班牙當局<u>預先通知</u>，未來幾天，西班牙東部沿海會有大規模的
　　　　　　　　1

水母入侵，並建議游泳者治療水母叮咬的最佳方式。

* Spanish〔'spænɪʃ〕 *adj.* 西班牙的
authorities[4]〔ɔ'θɔrətɪz〕 *n.* 當局
massive[5]〔'mæsɪv〕 *adj.* 大規模的　　invasion[4]〔ɪn'veʒən〕 *n.* 入侵
jellyfish〔'dʒɛlɪ,fɪʃ〕 *n.* 水母　　eastern[2]〔'istən〕 *adj.* 東部的
coast[1]〔kost〕 *n.* 海岸　　coming[1]〔'kʌmɪŋ〕 *adj.* 即將來臨的
advise[3]〔əd'vaɪz〕 *v.* 建議；勸告　　bather〔'beðə〕 *n.* 游泳者
treat[2]〔trit〕 *v.* 治療　　sting[3]〔stɪŋ〕 *n.* 螫；刺痛

1. (**C**)　(A) lay off 解僱　　　　　　(B) root out 根除
　　　　　　(C) ***warn of*** 預先通知　　(D) drop in 順道拜訪

Over the past month, <u>schools</u> of jellyfish have plagued many
2

coastal areas *<u>stretching</u> from the northeastern region of Catalonia*
3

*down to Murcia **and** Andalucia in the south*, <u>leading to</u> temporary bans
4

on bathing on many beaches.

　　過去一個月裡，水母<u>群</u>侵襲了從加泰隆尼亞東北地區往下<u>延伸</u>到南
　　　　　　　　　　2　　　　　　　　　　　　　　　　　3
部的穆爾西亞和安達魯西亞的許多沿海地區，<u>導致</u>在許多海灘游泳的暫
　　　　　　　　　　　　　　　　　　　4
時禁令。

* plague[5] 〔 pleg 〕 v. 使苦惱；煩擾　　coastal[5] 〔'kostl̩ 〕 adj. 海岸的
　 northeastern 〔ˌnɔrθ'istən 〕 adj. 東北部的
　 region[2] 〔'ridʒən 〕 n. 地區
　 Catalonia 〔ˌkætə'loniə 〕 n. 加泰隆尼亞【西班牙東北部的自治區】
　 Murcia[3] 〔'murθjɑ 〕 n. 穆爾西亞【西班牙東南部自治區】
　 Andalucia[3] 〔ˌændə'lusjɑ 〕 n. 安達魯西亞【位於西班牙南部地區】
　 temporary[3] 〔'tɛmpəˌrɛrɪ 〕 adj. 暫時的　　ban[5] 〔 bæn 〕 n. 禁令

2. (**C**)　(A) herd[4] 〔 hɝd 〕 n. (牛、象) 群
　　　　　　　　a herd of cattle/elephants　一群牛/象
　　　　　　(B) pack[2] 〔 pæk 〕 n. (狼) 群
　　　　　　　　a pack of dogs/wolves　一群狗/狼
　　　　　　(C) *school*[1] 〔 skul 〕 n. (魚) 群
　　　　　　　　a school of fish　一群魚
　　　　　　(D) flock[3] 〔 flɑk 〕 n. (鳥、羊) 群
　　　　　　　　a flock of sheep/bird/geese　一群羊/鳥/鵝

3. (**B**)　主要動詞是 have plagued，又兩動詞之間無連接詞，故第二
　　　　　　個動詞須改爲現在分詞，故選 (B) *stretching*。
　　　　　　stretch[2] 〔 strɛtʃ 〕 v. 延伸
　　　　　　而 (D) expanding「擴大」，則不合句意。

4. (**B**)　主要動詞是 have plagued，又兩動詞
　　　　　　之間無連接詞，故空格須用現在分詞，
　　　　　　依句意，選 (B) *leading to*「導致」。
　　　　　　而 (D) resulting from「起因於」，則
　　　　　　不合句意。

| contribute to　導致 |
| = lead to |
| = give rise to |
| = result in |
| = bring about |

The latest alert, *posted on the Interior Ministry's website*, was issued *after coastal guards said they had spotted new banks of jellyfish several kilometers off different areas along the coast in recent days.*

在最新的警報<u>發布</u>在內政部的網站之前，海岸警衛隊說，他們最近幾天，在離沿岸不同地區幾公里的外海處，發現新的水母群。

* alert⁴ 〔 əˋlɝt 〕 *n.* 警戒　　post² 〔 post 〕 *v.* 張貼
interior⁵ 〔 ɪnˋtɪrɪə 〕 *adj.* 內部的；國內的
ministry⁴ 〔ˋmɪnɪstrɪ 〕 *n.* 部　　***the Interior Ministry*** 內政部
website⁴ 〔ˋwɛb͵saɪt 〕 *n.* 網站　　guard² 〔 gɑrd 〕 *n.* 警衛；警備員
spot² 〔 spɑt 〕 *v.* 發現；看出　　bank¹ 〔 bæŋk 〕 *n.* 一堆；一團
off¹ 〔 ɔf 〕 *prep.* 在…之外　　recent² 〔ˋrisn̩t 〕 *adj.* 最近的

5. (**D**)　(A) entitle⁵ 〔 ɪnˋtaɪtl̩ 〕 *v.* 將…命名為；使有資格
　　　　　　(B) edit³ 〔ˋɛdɪt 〕 *v.* 編輯
　　　　　　(C) perform³ 〔 pɚˋfɔrm 〕 *v.* 表演；執行
　　　　　　(D) ***issue***⁵ 〔ˋɪʃju 〕 *v.* 發布

【補充資料】

被水母螫傷的急救和治療措施：

1. 使受傷者儘速離開水面移至岸邊，以浴巾、衣服等去除仍附於體表的刺絲胞，避免用手除去，以免二度螫傷。

2. 另外可以使用家庭用白醋或其他物質（如阿摩尼亞或硼酸等弱酸鹼類）清洗傷處，以去除刺絲胞的活性，再用清水沖洗；至於酒精或尿液則可能會促使刺絲胞釋放毒液，並不建議使用。

3. 可塗抹類固醇或抗組織胺藥膏，以減輕局部皮膚反應，必要時口服抗組織胺藥物，或施打止痛針止痛，皆有幫助。

4. 若有休克現象，應給予氧氣、靜脈輸液，及腎上腺素等急救藥物。

TEST 3

Read the following passage and choose the best answer for each blank from the choices below.

Onions make you cry, add flavor to food, and are promoted for their ___1___ benefits. Now the vegetable has another use—___2___ green energy.

A new system ___3___ onion juice into electricity at Gills Onions, the largest fresh onion processor in the United States. The Oxnard, California-based company expects its new ___4___ power to reduce its electric bill by US$700,000 a year and cut its ___5___ greenhouse gas emissions by as much as 30,000 tons.

1. (A) disability
   (C) medicinal
   (B) retirement
   (D) toxic

2. (A) powering up
   (C) hitting upon
   (B) interfering in
   (D) taking on

3. (A) transports
   (C) refines
   (B) converts
   (D) condenses

4. (A) fueling-onion
   (C) onion-fueling
   (B) fueled-onion
   (D) onion-fueled

5. (A) centennial
   (C) perennial
   (B) annual
   (D) biennial

TEST 3 詳解

Onions make you cry, add flavor *to food*, **and** are promoted

for their <u>medicinal</u> benefits. *Now* the vegetable has another use—
　　　　　　　　　　1

<u>powering up</u> green energy.
　　2

　　洋蔥讓你流淚、幫食物添加風味，它也因醫藥上的好處而被推廣。
現在這個蔬菜有了另一種用途——<u>提升</u>綠能。
　　　　　　　　　　　　　　　2

* onion² 〔ˋʌnjən 〕 *n.* 洋蔥　　add¹ 〔 æd 〕 *v.* 添加
  add A to B 加 A 到 B 上　　flavor³ 〔ˋflevə 〕 *n.* 風味
  promote³ 〔 prəˋmot 〕 *v.* 推銷　　benefit³ 〔ˋbɛnəfɪt 〕 *n.* 利益；好處
  use¹ 〔 jus 〕 *n.* 用途
  green energy 綠能【綠色能源，是指排放較少污染物，不使用耗竭燃料
  的能源，例如太陽能、水力、地熱發電以及生物產品所產生的能源】

1. (**C**)　(A) disability⁶ 〔ˌdɪsəˋbɪlətɪ 〕 *n.* 無能力；殘疾
　　　　　(B) retirement⁴ 〔 rɪˋtaɪrmənt 〕 *n.* 退休
　　　　　(C) ***medicinal*** 〔 məˋdɪsn̩l 〕 *adj.* 醫藥的；有藥效的
　　　　　　　【medicine⁴ 〔ˋmɛdəsn̩ 〕 *n.* 藥；醫學】
　　　　　(D) toxic⁵ 〔ˋtɑksɪk 〕 *adj.* 有毒的 (= *poisonous*⁴)

2. (**A**)　(A) ***power up*** 提升；增強　　(B) interfere in 介入；干涉
　　　　　(C) hit upon 偶然想到　　　　(D) take on 承擔；接受

A new system <u>converts</u> onion juice *into electricity at Gills Onions*,
　　　　　　　　　　　3

the largest fresh onion processor in the United States.

　　「吉爾斯洋蔥工廠」是美國最大的新鮮洋蔥加工業者，他們有一種
新的系統，能將洋蔥汁<u>轉變</u>成為電力。

* juice[1] 〔 dʒus 〕 *n.* 汁　　electricity[3] 〔 ɪ,lɛk'trɪsətɪ 〕 *n.* 電
fresh[1] 〔 frɛʃ 〕 *adj.* 新鮮的
processor 〔'prɑsɛsə 〕 *n.* 加工者；處理器

3. (**B**)　(A) transport[3] 〔 træns'port 〕 *v.* 運輸
　　　　(B) ***convert***[5] 〔 kən'vɜt 〕 *v.* 使轉變
　　　　convert A into B 把 A 轉變成 B (= *turn A into B*)
　　　　(C) refine[6] 〔 rɪ'faɪn 〕 *v.* 精煉；淨化
　　　　(D) condense[6] 〔 kən'dɛns 〕 *v.* 濃縮

The Oxnard, California-based company expects its new <u>onion-fueled</u>
　　　　　　　　　　　　　　　　　　　　　　　　　　4

<u>power to reduce its electric bill *by US$700,000 a year* **and** cut its</u>

<u>annual</u> greenhouse gas emissions *by as much as 30,000 tons.*
5
這家位於加州奧克斯納德的公司預計，他們<u>以洋蔥爲燃料的</u>新電力，能
　　　　　　　　　　　　　　　　　　　　　4
一年減少七十萬美元的電費，並減低<u>每年</u>的溫室氣體排放量達三萬噸。
　　　　　　　　　　　　　　　　　5

　　* Oxnard 〔'ɑksnɑrd 〕 *n.* 奧克斯納德【美國加州城市名】
　　　California-based 〔,kælə'fɔrnjə'bɛst 〕 *adj.* 以加州爲根據地的
　　　expect[2] 〔 ɪk'spɛkt 〕 *v.* 預期；期望
　　　power[1] 〔'pauə 〕 *n.* 電力　　electric[3] 〔 ɪ'lɛktrɪk 〕 *adj.* 電的
　　　bill[2] 〔 bɪl 〕 *n.* 帳單　　cut[1] 〔 kʌt 〕 *v.* 減少
　　　greenhouse gas 溫室氣體
　　　emission 〔 ɪ'mɪʃən 〕 *n.* 排放（量）
　　　ton[3] 〔 tʌn 〕 *n.* 公噸

e	+ miss	+ ion
out	+ send	+ n.

4. (**D**)　依句意，此種新能源是「以洋蔥爲燃料的」，a new power
　　　　which is fueled by onion，動詞與名詞是被動關係所組成
　　　　的複合形容詞，應選 (D) ***onion-fueled***。

5. (**B**)　(A) centennial 〔 sɛn'tɛnɪəl 〕 *adj.* 百年紀念的【cent = *hundred*】
　　　　(B) ***annual***[4] 〔'ænjuəl 〕 *adj.* 每年的；一年一次的【ann = *year*】
　　　　(C) perennial 〔 pə'rɛnɪəl 〕 *adj.* 終年的【per = *through*】
　　　　(D) biennial 〔 baɪ'ɛnɪəl 〕 *adj.* 兩年一次的【bi = *two*】

TEST 4

Read the following passage and choose the best answer for each blank from the choices below.

Looking for a quick way to feel lousy about yourself? Then forget the idea of a healthy diet and just eat what your body wants you to eat. Your body wants fat; your body wants sugar. Your body will ___1___ fruits and vegetables if it must, but only after all the fat and sugar are gone. And as for the question of where your food comes from—whether it's locally grown, ___2___ raised, or pesticide-free, your body doesn't notice.

But you and your body aren't the only ones with a(n) ___3___ in this game. Your doctor has opinions about what you should eat. The food purists, who lately seem to be everywhere, insist that everything that crosses your lips ___4___ in just the right way. If you find this tiresome, you're not alone. "We ___5___ people to eat sensibly and virtuously, and then we set this incredibly high bar for how they do it," says James McWilliams, a professor at Texas State University.

1. (A) put through (B) put up with (C) put out (D) put off
2. (A) objectively (B) miraculously
   (C) neutrally (D) organically
3. (A) stake (B) nightmare (C) organizer (D) personnel
4. (A) is harvested (B) harvests
   (C) be harvested (D) to harvest
5. (A) perish (B) encourage (C) reward (D) soak

TEST 4 詳解

Looking for a quick way *to feel lousy about yourself*? *Then*
forget the idea *of a healthy diet **and** just eat **what** your body wants
you to eat*. Your body wants fat; your body wants sugar. Your
body will <u>put up with</u> fruits **and** vegetables *if it must*, **but** *only **after***
all the fat **and** *sugar are gone*. **And** *as for the question of **where** your*
*food comes from—**whether** it's locally grown, <u>organically</u> raised, **or***
pesticide-free, your body doesn't notice.

　　正在找一個快速的方式,來讓你覺得自己很差勁嗎?那麼就忘記健
康飲食的概念,就吃你的身體要你吃的東西吧。你的身體想要脂肪;你
的身體想要糖分。如果有必要,你的身體會<u>忍受</u>水果和蔬菜,但這情況
只會在所有的脂肪和糖分都消失之後才會產生。而至於你的食物來自於
哪裡的這項問題——它是否是當地種植、<u>有機養殖</u>,或沒有殺蟲劑——
你的身體並不會注意到。

* **look for** 尋找　　lousy[4] 〔ˈlaʊzɪ〕 *adj.* 差勁的;討厭的
　fat[1] 〔fæt〕 *n.* 脂肪　　sugar[1] 〔ˈʃʊgɚ〕 *n.* 糖
　as for 至於　　**come from** 來自
　locally[2] 〔ˈlokəlɪ〕 *adv.* 在當地　　raise[1] 〔rez〕 *v.* 飼養;栽種
　pesticide[6]-free 〔ˈpɛstəˌsaɪdˈfri〕 *adj.* 無殺蟲劑的
　notice[1] 〔ˈnotɪs〕 *v.* 注意到

1. (**B**)　(A) put through　接通（電話）

(B) ***put up with*** 忍受

(C) put out　熄（燈）；滅（火）

(D) put off　拖延；延期（ = *postpone*[3] ）

> put up with 忍受
> = tolerate[4] 〔ˋtɑləˏret 〕
> = endure[4] 〔ɪnˋdjʊr 〕
> = bear[2] 〔bɛr 〕
> = stand[1] 〔stænd 〕

2. (**D**)　(A) objectively[4] 〔əbˋdʒɛktɪvlɪ 〕 *adv.* 客觀地

(B) miraculously[6] 〔məˋrækjələslɪ 〕 *adv.* 奇蹟般地

(C) neutrally[6] 〔ˋnjutrəlɪ 〕 *adv.* 中立地

(D) ***organically***[4] 〔ɔrˋgænɪklɪ 〕 *adv.* 有機地

But you and your body aren't the only ones *with a stake in this*
                                                            3
game. Your doctor has opinions *about **what** you should eat*. The

food purists, ***who** lately seem to be everywhere*, insist ***that** everything*

***that** crosses your lips be harvested in just the right way*. ***If** you find*
                                4
this tiresome, you're not alone. "We encourage people to eat *sensibly*
                                                                    5
***and** virtuously*, ***and** then* we set this *incredibly* high bar for ***how** they*

do it," says James McWilliams, *a professor at Texas State University.*

　　但你和你的身體，不是在這個遊戲中唯一有<u>利害</u>關係的。你的醫生
　　　　　　　　　　　　　　　　　　　　　　　　　3
對於你應該吃些什麼有意見。最近似乎無所不在的食物淨化主義者堅

稱，所有通過你嘴唇的食物，都應以正確的方式<u>被採收</u>。如果你覺得這
　　　　　　　　　　　　　　　　　　　　4
令人厭煩，你不是孤單的。「我們<u>鼓勵</u>人們明智且合乎道德地進食，然
　　　　　5
後我們爲他們如何做到，設定了驚人的高標準，」德州州立大學教授詹
姆斯・麥克威廉斯說。

* opinion² 〔əˈpɪnjən 〕 *n.* 意見

purist 〔ˈpjʊrɪst 〕 *n.* 純正主義者；淨化主義者

【 pure³ 〔 pjʊr 〕 *adj.* 純淨的 】

food purist 食物淨化主義者【堅持有機農業、有機畜牧業所生產之食物的人。他們聲稱，目前過於精緻的飲食習慣，不僅會傷害身體，還會讓整個地球的資源枯竭】

lately⁴ 〔ˈletlɪ 〕 *adv.* 最近 (= *recently²*)　　seem¹ 〔 sim 〕 *v.* 似乎

insist² 〔 ɪnˈsɪst 〕 *v.* 堅持　　cross² 〔 krɔs 〕 *v.* 橫過；越過

lip¹ 〔 lɪp 〕 *n.* 嘴唇　　find⁴ 〔 faɪnd 〕 *v.* 覺得

tiresome⁴ 〔ˈtaɪrsəm 〕 *adj.* 令人厭倦的

alone¹ 〔 əˈlon 〕 *adj.* 單獨的；孤獨的

sensibly³ 〔ˈsɛnsəblɪ 〕 *adv.* 明智地

virtuously 〔ˈvɜtʃʊəslɪ 〕 *adv.* 合乎道德地【 virtue⁴ 〔ˈvɜtʃʊ 〕 *n.* 美德 】

incredibly 〔 ɪnˈkrɛdəblɪ 〕 *adv.* 令人難以置信的；非常地；驚人地

bar¹ 〔 bɑr 〕 *n.* 限制；障礙　　professor⁴ 〔 prəˈfɛsə 〕 *n.* 教授

---

bar¹ 〔 bɑr 〕 *n.* 限制；障礙

raise the bar「設定高標準」(= *set a high standard*)，因為 raise 是「提高」，bar 是指「一根桿子」，字面的意思是「把桿子提高」，也就是「設定高標準」或「表現得很好」，源自「撐竿跳」。

Texas State University 德州州立大學

3. (**A**)　(A) *stake* 〔 stek 〕 *n.* 木樁；賭注；利害關係 < *in* >

　　　　　(B) nightmare⁴ 〔ˈnaɪtˌmɛr 〕 *n.* 惡夢

　　　　　(C) organizer⁵ 〔ˈɔrgənˌaɪzə 〕 *n.* 籌畫者；主辦人

　　　　　(D) personnel⁵ 〔ˌpɜsṇˈɛl 〕 *n.* 員工；人事部門

4. (**C**)　insist 是慾望動詞，其用法為：insist that + S. + (should) + V.，故選 (C) *be harvested*。harvest³ 〔ˈhɑrvɪst 〕 *v.* 收穫

5. (**B**)　(A) perish⁵ 〔ˈpɛrɪʃ 〕 *v.* 死亡

　　　　　(B) *encourage²* 〔 ɪnˈkɜɪdʒ 〕 *v.* 鼓勵

　　　　　(C) reward⁴ 〔 rɪˈwɔrd 〕 *v.* 獎勵　　(D) soak⁵ 〔 sok 〕 *v.* 浸泡

TEST 5

Read the following passage and choose the best answer for each blank from the choices below.

Earthquakes are one of the most powerful forces in nature. Even years after the Sichuan earthquake, a great number of people are ___1___ by the memories of the destruction and are still trying to rebuild their lives.

Earthquakes occur when the earth's crust ___2___ energy. This happens almost ___3___. Luckily, most earthquakes are small and cause little damage. However, at least one major earthquake ___4___ each year. This can happen anywhere on Earth, but earthquakes occur in some areas more often. For example, the area called the Pacific Ring of Fire has ___5___ earthquakes. This area includes countries such as Taiwan, Japan, the Philippines, and the United States.

1. (A) fascinated   (B) interrupted
   (C) reflected   (D) haunted
2. (A) respects   (B) releases   (C) relieves   (D) retrieves
3. (A) rarely   (B) eventually
   (C) constantly   (D) exclusively
4. (A) strikes   (B) sweeps   (C) erupts   (D) explodes
5. (A) at most   (B) at least   (C) the most   (D) the least

TEST 5 詳解

Earthquakes are one *of the most powerful forces in nature.*

Even years after the Sichuan earthquake, a great number of people

are <u>haunted</u> *by the memories of the destruction **and*** are *still* trying to
1

rebuild their lives.

地震是自然界中最強大的力量之一。即使是在四
川地震過後好幾年，毀滅的記憶仍縈繞許多人的腦海
1
中，他們仍然在試圖努力重建生活。

* earthquake² 〔'ɝθ,kwek 〕 *n.* 地震
powerful² 〔'pauəfəl 〕 *adj.* 強有力的
force¹ 〔 fors 〕 *n.* 力量　　nature¹ 〔'netʃɚ 〕 *n.* 大自然
a great number of 許多的　　memory² 〔'mɛmərɪ 〕 *n.* 記憶

a great number of + 可數名詞
a great amount/deal of + 不可數名詞
a great quantity of + 可數／不可數名詞
大量的…

destruction⁴ 〔 dɪ'strʌkʃən 〕 *n.* 破壞；毀滅
rebuild 〔 ri'bɪld 〕 *v.* 重建

1. (**D**)　(A) fascinate⁵ 〔'fæsə,net 〕 *v.* 使著迷
　　　　(B) interrupt³ 〔,ɪntə'rʌpt 〕 *v.* 打斷
　　　　(C) reflect⁴ 〔 rɪ'flɛkt 〕 *v.* 反射；反映
　　　　(D) ***haunt***⁵ 〔 hɔnt 〕 *v.* 縈繞（心中）；不斷地纏繞；
　　　　　　（鬼魂）出沒　　***be haunted by*** …縈繞於腦海中

Earthquakes occur ***when*** *the earth's crust <u>releases</u> energy*. This
₂

happens *almost <u>constantly</u>*. *Luckily*, most earthquakes are small ***and***
₃

cause little damage.

　　當地殼<u>釋放</u>能量時，就會發生地震。這種情況幾乎<u>不斷</u>在發生。幸
　　　　　₂　　　　　　　　　　　　　　　　　　　　　　　₃
運的是，大多數的地震都很小，而且造成的損害也很輕微。

　　* crust⁶ ﹝ krʌst ﹞ *n.* 地殼　　energy² ﹝'ɛnədʒɪ﹞ *n.* 能量
　　luckily¹ ﹝'lʌkɪlɪ﹞ *adv.* 幸運地
　　damage² ﹝'dæmɪdʒ﹞ *n.* 損害

2. (**B**)　(A) respect² ﹝ rɪ'spɛkt ﹞ *v.* 尊敬
　　　　　　(B) ***release***³ ﹝ rɪ'lis ﹞ *v.* 釋放
　　　　　　(C) relieve⁴ ﹝ rɪ'liv ﹞ *v.* 減輕
　　　　　　(D) retrieve⁶ ﹝ rɪ'triv ﹞ *v.* 尋回

> release³ *v.* 釋放
> relieve⁴ *v.* 減輕
> relax³ *v.* 放鬆

3. (**C**)　(A) rarely² ﹝'rɛrlɪ﹞ *adv.* 很少；罕見地
　　　　　　(B) eventually⁴ ﹝ ɪ'vɛntʃuəlɪ﹞ *adv.* 最後；終於 (= *finally*¹)
　　　　　　(C) ***constantly***³ ﹝'kɑnstəntlɪ﹞ *adv.* 不斷地 (= *continually*⁴) ；
　　　　　　　　 時常地 (= *frequently*³)
　　　　　　(D) exclusively⁶ ﹝ ɪks'klusɪvlɪ﹞ *adv.* 獨佔地；排外地

However, *at least* one major earthquake <u>strikes</u> *each year*. This can
₄

happen *anywhere on Earth*, ***but*** earthquakes occur *in some areas*

more often. *For example*, the area *called the Pacific Ring of Fire* has

the most earthquakes. This area includes countries *such as Taiwan,*
    5

Japan, the Philippines, and the United States.

然而，每年至少會有一次大地震侵襲。這可能會發生在地球上的任何地
                              4
方，但地震在某些地區發生的機會更頻繁。例如，被稱爲「太平洋火
環」的地區，地震是最多的。這個地區包括台灣、日本、菲律賓，以及
                        5
美國。

* *at least* 至少
  major³〔'medʒɚ〕*adj.*（程度）較大的
  （ ↔ minor³〔'maɪnɚ〕*adj.* 較小的)
  pacific〔pə'sɪfɪk〕*adj.* 太平洋的　　ring¹〔rɪŋ〕*n.* 圓環；圓圈
  Pacific Ring of Fire 太平洋火環帶

  【指北太平洋邊緣、亞洲東部邊緣和
  　美洲西海岸所組成的環形地帶，此
  　區地震頻繁，火山數目約佔全世界
  　的百分之七十五】
  the Philippines〔'fɪlə,pinz〕菲律賓共和國

4. (**A**)　(A) *strike*²〔straɪk〕*v.* 侵襲
　　　　　　(B) sweep²〔swip〕*v.* 橫掃
　　　　　　(C) erupt⁵〔ɪ'rʌpt〕*v.* 爆發
　　　　　　(D) explode³〔ɪk'splod〕*v.* 爆炸

5. (**C**)　依句意，選 (C) *the most*「最多的」。
　　　　　而 (A) at most「最多」，(B) at least「至少」，是副詞片語，
　　　　　用法不合；(D) the least「最少的」，則不合句意。

TEST 6

Read the following passage and choose the best answer for each blank from the choices below.

Now that people are getting interested in eco-friendly tours, glamping seems a great choice for those who are ___1___ to taking care of the environment but refuse to leave the comforts of home behind to go camping. Glamping, ___2___ glamorous camping, has all the benefits of camping—the proximity to nature ___3___—but with added luxuries such as antique furniture, personal service, exotic cuisine, etc. ___4___, if you want to experience glamping for yourself, you need to save up some money first as these unforgettable experiences will cost you an arm and a leg, sometimes upward of US $5,000. Be that as it may, glamping still ___5___ to more and more wealthy adventurers who would like to camp in style and conserve the planet at the same time.

1. (A) eager
   (C) concerning
   (B) willing
   (D) committed

2. (A) that is
   (C) or
   (B) and
   (D) the same as

3. (A) in particular
   (C) by any means
   (B) at any price
   (D) as a result

4. (A) However (B) To sum up (C) Instead (D) Moreover

5. (A) attracts (B) appeals (C) draws (D) impresses

TEST 6 詳解

Now that *people are getting interested in eco-friendly tours*, glamping seems a great choice for those who *are committed to taking care of the environment* but *refuse to leave the comforts of home behind to go camping*.

　　既然人們對環保旅遊越來越感興趣，對於那些<u>致力於</u>保護環境，卻不願離開家居舒適而去露營的人來說，豪華野營似乎是一個很好的選擇。

* **now that** 既然　　interested[1] 〔'ɪntrɪstɪd 〕 *adj.* 感興趣的
  be interested in 對～感興趣
  eco-friendly 〔'iko͵frɛndlɪ 〕 *adj.* 環保的；不損壞生態環境的
  tour[2] 〔 tʊr 〕 *n.* 旅行
  glamping 〔'glæmpɪŋ 〕 *n.* 豪華野營【由 glamorous 和 camping 組合而成】　　choice[2] 〔 tʃɔɪs 〕 *n.* 選擇　　**take care of** 照顧
  environment[2] 〔 ɪn'vaɪrənmənt 〕 *n.* 環境
  refuse[2] 〔 rɪ'fjuz 〕 *v.* 拒絕；不願
  leave…behind 忘了帶… ；留下…
  comforts[3] 〔'kʌmfɚts 〕 *n. pl.* 使生活舒服的東西
  camp[1] 〔 kæmp 〕 *v.* 露營

1. (**D**)　(A) eager[3] 〔'igɚ 〕 *adj.* 渴望的　　be eager to V. 渴望…
　　　　　(B) willing[2] 〔'wɪlɪŋ 〕 *adj.* 願意的　　be willing to V. 願意…
　　　　　(C) concerning[4] 〔 kən'sɝnɪŋ 〕 *prep.* 關於 (= *about*[1])
　　　　　(D) **commit**[4] 〔 kə'mɪtɪd 〕 *v.* 使投入；使專心致志
　　　　　　be committed to + V-ing 致力於…
　　　　　　(= *be dedicated to + V-ing* = *be devoted to + V-ing*)

Glamping, _**or**_ glamorous camping, has all the benefits ⌐of camping—
　　　　　　2

the proximity to nature in particular—_**but**_ with added luxuries such as
　　　　　　　　　　　3

antique furniture, personal service, exotic cuisine, etc.

豪華野營，也就是迷人的露營，有露營的所有好處——特別是接近大自
　　　　　2　　　　　　　　　　　　　　　　　　　　3

然——但附加了奢侈品，像是古董家具、個人服務、異國風味菜餚等。

* glamorous〔'glæmərəs〕adj. 富有魅力的；迷人的

【 glamour[6]〔'glæmə〕n. 魅力】

benefit[3]〔'bɛnəfɪt〕n. 利益；好處

proximity〔prɑk'sɪmətɪ〕n. 接近；親近 < to >

nature[1]〔'netʃə〕n. 大自然　　added[1]〔'ædɪd〕adj. 附加的；額外的

luxury[4]〔'lʌkʃərɪ〕n. 奢華；奢侈品；奢侈的事物　　_**such as**_　像是

antique[5]〔æn'tik〕adj. 古董的　　furniture[3]〔'fɝnɪtʃə〕n. 家具

exotic[6]〔ɪg'zɑtɪk〕adj. 有異國風味的

cuisine[5]〔kwɪ'zin〕n. 菜餚　　etc.〔ɛt'sɛtərə〕等等 (= et cetera)

2. (**C**)　依句意，選 (C) _or_「也就是」。而 (A) that is「也就是說」
　　　　　(= _that is to say_)，是副詞片語，通常後面會加逗點，
　　　　　(B) and「而且」，(D) the same as「和…一樣」，則不合句意。

3. (**A**)　(A) _**in particular**_ 特別是；尤其
　　　　　(B) at any price 不惜任何代價
　　　　　(C) by any means 無論如何　　(D) as a result 因此

However, _**if**_ you want to experience glamping _for yourself_, you need
　　4

to save up some money _first_ _**as**_ these unforgettable experiences will *cost you an arm **and** a leg, sometimes upward of US $5,000.　Be that **as***

it may, glamping still <u>appeals</u> to more **and** more wealthy adventurers
　　　　　　　　　　　5

who *would like to camp in style **and** conserve the planet at the same*

time.

<u>然而</u>，如果你想親自體驗豪華野營，你需要先存一些錢，因為這些難忘
　4
的經驗會讓你付出昂貴的代價，有時會超過 5,000 美元。即使如此，豪
華野營仍然<u>吸引</u>了越來越多的富有冒險家，他們想要時髦露營，同時也
　　　　　　5
想要保護地球。

* experience² 〔 ɪkˈspɪrɪəns 〕 v. 體驗　　n. 經驗
save up 存 (錢)　　　unforgettable¹ 〔 ˌʌnfəˈgɛtəbḷ 〕 adj. 難忘的
cost an arm and a leg 耗資不菲；付出昂貴的代價
upward⁵ 〔ˈʌpwɚd 〕 adv. 以上；超過
be that as it may 即使如此　　*more and more* 越來越多的
in style 時髦地；氣派地　　conserve⁵ 〔 kənˈsɝv 〕 v. 保護；節省
planet² 〔ˈplænɪt 〕 n. 行星【the planet 在此指「地球」】
at the same time 同時

4. (**A**)　依句意，選 (A) ***However*** 「然而」。
　　　　而 (B) To sum up 「總之」，(C) Instead 「作為代替」，
　　　　(D) Moreover 「此外」，則不合句意。

5. (**B**)　(A) attract³ 〔 əˈtrækt 〕 v. 吸引【為及物動詞，不加 to】
　　　　(B) ***appeal***³ 〔 əˈpil 〕 v. 吸引　　*appeal to* 吸引 (= *attract*)
　　　　(C) draw¹ 〔 drɔ 〕 v. 畫；拉；吸引【為及物動詞，不加 to】
　　　　(D) impress³ 〔 ɪmˈprɛs 〕 v. 使印象深刻
　　　　　　be impressed with/by 對⋯印象深刻

TEST 7

Read the following passage and choose the best answer for each blank from the choices below.

The bee hummingbird is the smallest bird in the world. Bee hummingbird males weigh approximately 1.7g and are only 5.5 centimeters long! The tail ___1___ up nearly one half of the total length. Often it is mistaken for a bee because it is so small, and that is ___2___ it got its name. Few people know that these small birds are actually very courageous. They even attack other birds that are ___3___ bigger. Many of these birds do not live longer than one or two years. Nevertheless, there are records of very old bee hummingbirds that lived for twelve years. Another interesting fact about bee hummingbirds is that they eat many times a day. ___4___ bee hummingbirds need a lot of sugar, they will find the flowers that have the most in their nectar. They ___5___ flowers that have less than a 10% sugar ratio. A female bee hummingbird never lays more than two eggs. The mother takes care of the young bee hummingbirds all by herself.

1. (A) makes   (B) composes   (C) produces   (D) does
2. (A) what   (B) when   (C) where   (D) how
3. (A) reversely   (B) compatibly
   (C) considerably   (D) barely
4. (A) Though   (B) Despite   (C) Thus   (D) Since
5. (A) pursue   (B) avoid   (C) consume   (D) destroy

TEST 7 詳解

The bee hummingbird is the smallest bird *in the world*. Bee

hummingbird males weigh *approximately* 1.7g *and* are only 5.5

centimeters long! The tail <u>makes</u> up *nearly* one half *of the total*
1

length. *Often* it is mistaken for a bee *because it is so small*, *and* that

is *how* it got its name.
2

　　蜜蜂蜂鳥是全世界最小的鳥。雄性蜜蜂蜂鳥重約 1.7 公克，而且只
有 5.5 公分長！尾巴幾乎佔總長的一半。通常蜜蜂蜂鳥都會被誤認成蜜
　　　　　　　　　　　1
蜂，因為體型很小，而牠的名字就是這樣得到的。
　　　　　　　　　　　　2

* *bee hummingbird* 蜜蜂蜂鳥【hum[2]〔hʌm〕v. 發出嗡嗡聲】
male[2]〔mel〕n. 男性；雄性動物　　weigh[1]〔we〕v. 重…
approximately[6]〔ə'prɑksəmɪtlɪ〕adv. 大約（= about[1]）
g（= gram[3]〔ɡæm〕）n. 公克
centimeter[3]〔'sɛntə,mitə〕n. 公分　　tail[1]〔tel〕n. 尾巴
nearly[2]〔'nɪrlɪ〕adv. 幾乎　　total[1]〔'totḷ〕adj. 全部的
length[2]〔lɛŋθ〕n. 長度　　mistake[1]〔mə'stek〕v. 誤解；弄錯
mistake A for B 把 A 誤認為 B

1. (**A**)　依句意，選 (A) *make up*「組成；構成」。
　　　而 (B) compose[4]〔kəm'poz〕n. 組成，不與 up 連用，
　　　(C) produce[2]〔prə'djus〕n. 生產；製造，
　　　(D) does「做」，則不合句意。

2. (**D**)　空格應填關係詞，引導名詞子句，依句意，選 (D) ***how*** 「（事情發生的）方式」。而 (A) what 爲複合關代，等於 the thing that，(B) when 表「時間」，(C) where 表「地點」，在此皆不合。

Few people know *that these small birds are actually very courageous.*

They *even* attack other birds *that* are <u>considerably</u> bigger.　Many *of*
　　　　　　　　　　　　　　　　　　3

these birds do not live longer *than one or two years.　Nevertheless,*

there are records *of very old bee hummingbirds that lived for twelve*

years.　Another interesting fact *about bee hummingbirds* is *that they*

eat many times a day.

很少人知道這些小型鳥其實相當勇敢。牠們甚至會攻擊比牠們還大<u>許多</u>
　　　　　　　　　　　　　　　　　　　　　　　　　　　　　　　　3
的鳥。這些鳥有很多都活不過一到兩年。然而，有紀錄顯示，很老的蜜蜂蜂鳥，活了有十二年之久。另一個關於蜜蜂蜂鳥有趣的事，就是牠們一天會進食很多次。

> * actually³〔ˋæktʃʊəlɪ〕*adv.* 實際上
> courageous⁴〔kəˋredʒəs〕*adj.* 勇敢的【courage²〔ˋkɝɪdʒ〕*n.* 勇氣】
> attack²〔əˋtæk〕*v.* 攻擊
> nevertheless⁴〔ˌnɛvəðəˋlɛs〕*adv.* 然而（= *however²*）
> record²〔ˋrɛkəd〕*n.* 紀錄　　interesting¹〔ˋɪntərɪstɪŋ〕*adj.* 有趣的
> fact¹〔fækt〕*n.* 事實　　time¹〔taɪm〕*n.* 次數

3. (**C**)　修飾比較級，可用 much, even, still, far 或 ***considerably***³
　　　　〔kənˋsɪdərəblɪ〕*adv.* 相當地；相當大地，故選 (C)。
　　　　(A) reversely〔rɪˋvɝslɪ〕*adv.* 相反地
　　　　　　reverse⁵ *adj.* 顚倒的；逆轉的

(B) compatibly〔kəm'pætəblɪ〕*adv.* 協調地

　　compatible[6]〔kəm'pætəbḷ〕*adj.* 相容的；合得來的

(D) barely[3]〔'bɛrlɪ〕*adv.* 幾乎不（= *hardly*[2]）

Since bee hummingbirds need a lot of sugar, they will find the flowers
　4

that have the most in their nectar. They <u>avoid</u> flowers *that* have
　　　　　　　　　　　　　　　　　　5

less than a 10% sugar ratio. A female bee hummingbird *never* lays

more than two eggs. The mother takes care of the young bee

hummingbirds *all by herself*.

因為蜜蜂蜂鳥需要很多糖份，所以牠們會找花蜜當中含有最多糖份的花
　　4

朵。牠們會<u>避開</u>含糖比例少於百分之十的花。雌性蜜蜂蜂鳥絕不會下超
　　　　　5

過兩顆蛋。蜜蜂蜂鳥媽媽會自己照顧年幼的蜜蜂蜂鳥。

* sugar[1]〔'ʃʊgɚ〕*n.* 糖　　　nectar〔'nɛktɚ〕*n.* 花蜜

　ratio[5]〔'reʃo〕*n.* 比例　　　female[2]〔'fimel〕*adj.* 女性的；雌性的

　lay[1]〔le〕*v.* 下（蛋）

　take care of 照顧

　all by oneself 獨自

| lie-lied-lied *v.* 說謊 |
| lie-lay-lain *v.* 躺；位於 |
| lay-laid-laid *v.* 下（蛋）；放置；奠定 |

4. (**D**) 空格應填從屬連接詞，依句意選 (D) *Since*「因為」。

而 (A) Though「雖然」，不合句意，(B) Despite「儘管」，

是介系詞，(C) Thus「因此」，是副詞，文法與句意皆不合。

5. (**B**) (A) pursue[3]〔pɚ'su〕*v.* 追求

　　　　　(B) *avoid*[2]〔ə'vɔɪd〕*v.* 避開；避免

　　　　　(C) consume[4]〔kən'sum〕*v.* 消耗；吃（喝）

　　　　　(D) destroy[3]〔dɪ'strɔɪ〕*v.* 破壞

TEST 8

Read the following passage and choose the best answer for each blank from the choices below.

Have you ever worked in a factory? If you have, you know how __1__ work on a conveyor belt is. At first, when you are not familiar with it, it is difficult to __2__. When you are tired, it is quite merciless. After a while, when you have got used to it, the fact that you cannot work faster irritates you. From time to time, when things are going well, you feel that you can go fast for a while so you can slow up later when you are tired. But no, you must work at exactly the __3__ speed, making exactly the same movements. You have to __4__ your energy as much as you can and learn how to properly use your arms and wrists so that the muscles are strengthened and do not ache. It looks easy and it __5__, but the most important thing is to make the movements as easy as possible. One false move repeated three thousand times is a painful mistake.

1. (A) reckless   (B) uncomfortable
   (C) entertaining   (D) indifferent
2. (A) stay up   (B) sit up   (C) keep up   (D) lay up
3. (A) extended (B) expanded (C) inscribed (D) prescribed
4. (A) preserve (B) conserve (C) utilize   (D) suspend
5. (A) does   (B) is   (C) may   (D) has

TEST 8 詳解

Have you *ever* worked *in a factory*?　*If you have*, you know *how*

<u>uncomfortable</u> work on a conveyor belt is.　At first, *when* you are not
　　1

familiar with it, it is difficult to <u>keep up</u>.　*When* you are tired, it is
　　　　　　　　　　　　　　　　　　　　2

quite merciless.

你曾在工廠工作過嗎？如果你有，你就知道在輸送帶上工作有多麼
<u>不舒服</u>。起初，當你不熟悉它時，會很難<u>跟上</u>。當你累了時，它是相
　1　　　　　　　　　　　　　　　　　　　　2
當無情的。

conveyor belt

*　factory[1] 〔'fæktrɪ〕*n.* 工廠
　conveyor belt〔kən've&æ 'bɛlt〕*n.* 輸送帶
　merciless〔'mɝsɪlɪs〕*adj.* 無情的；冷酷的
　【mercy[4] 〔'mɝsɪ〕*n.* 慈悲】

1. (**B**)　(A) reckless[5] 〔'rɛklɪs〕*adj.* 魯莽的
　　　　　(B) ***uncomfortable*[2]** 〔ʌn'kʌmfɚtəbl̩〕*adj.* 不舒服的
　　　　　(C) entertaining[4] 〔͵ɛntɚ'tenɪŋ〕*adj.* 令人愉快的；有趣的
　　　　　(D) indifferent[5] 〔ɪn'dɪfrənt〕*adj.* 漠不關心的

2. (**C**)　(A) stay up 熬夜
　　　　　(B) sit up 坐直；端坐
　　　　　(C) ***keep up*** 跟上
　　　　　(D) lay up 儲存

After a while, *when you have got used to it*, the fact *that you cannot work faster* irritates you. *From time to time*, *when things are going well*, you feel *that you can go fast for a while* *so you can slow down later when you are tired*. *But* no, you must work *at exactly the prescribed speed*, *making exactly the same movements*. You have to conserve your energy *as much as you can* *and* learn *how* to properly use your arms *and* wrists *so that the muscles are strengthened* *and* do not ache.

過了一段時間，當你已漸漸習慣它時，你無法工作得更快的現實，會使你惱怒。有時候，當事情進展順利，你會覺得你可以快一點，所以稍後當你累時，你可以減慢速度。但是不行，你必須完全按照規定的速度工作，做出完全相同的動作。你必須儘可能多保存你的精力，並且學習如何正確使用你的手臂和手腕，這樣肌肉才會強壯，並且不會酸痛。

* *get used to* 漸漸習慣於　　irritate[6] ('ɪrə,tet) *v.* 激怒
  from time to time 有時；偶爾
  things[1] (θɪŋz) *n. pl.* 事情；情況
  go[1] (go) *v.* 進行工作　　*slow down* 減慢
  exactly[2] (ɪg'zæktlɪ) *adv.* 確切地；完全地
  speed[2] (spid) *n.* 速度　　movement[1] ('muvmənt) *n.* 動作
  energy[2] ('ɛnɚdʒɪ) *n.* 活力；精力
  properly[3] ('prɑpɚlɪ) *adv.* 適當地；正確地

wrist[3] 〔 rɪst 〕 *n.* 手腕　　***so that*** 以便於
muscle[3] 〔'mʌsḷ 〕 *n.* 肌肉　　strengthen[4] 〔'strɛŋθən 〕 *v.* 加強；增強
ache[3] 〔 ek 〕 *v.* 痛

3. (**D**)　(A) extended[4] 〔 ɪk'stɛndɪd 〕 *adj.* 延長的
　　　　　(B) expanded[4] 〔 ɪk'spændɪd 〕 *adj.* 擴大的
　　　　　(C) inscribed[1] 〔 ɪn'skraɪbd 〕 *adj.* 銘刻的
　　　　　(D) ***prescribed***[6] 〔 prɪ'skraɪbd 〕 *adj.* 規定的

> pre ＋ scribe
> ｜　　　｜
> *before* ＋ *write*
> 之前先寫好，就是
> 「規定」或「開藥
> 方」。

4. (**B**)　(A) preserve[4] 〔 prɪ'zɝv 〕 *v.* 保存
　　　　　(B) ***conserve***[5] 〔 kən'zɝv 〕 *v.* 節省
　　　　　(C) utilize[6] 〔'jutḷ,aɪz 〕 *v.* 利用
　　　　　(D) suspend[5] 〔 sə'spɛnd 〕 *v.* 暫停；使停職

> con ＋ serve
> ｜　　　｜
> *all* ＋ *keep*
> 全部都留下來，
> 就是「節省」。

It looks easy ***and*** it <u>is</u>, ***but*** the *most* important thing is to make the
movements *as easy as possible.* One false move *repeated three*

thousand times is a painful mistake.

它看起來容易，而它確實是容易，但最重要的是，要使動作儘可能容

易。一個錯誤的動作重複三千次，是個令人痛苦的錯誤。

　　* false[1] 〔 fɔls 〕 *adj.* 錯誤的　　move[1] 〔 muv 〕 *n.* 動作
　　repeat[2] 〔 rɪ'pit 〕 *v.* 重複　　time[1] 〔 taɪm 〕 *n.* 次數
　　painful[2] 〔'penfəl 〕 *adj.* 使人痛苦的

5. (**B**)　依句意，It looks easy ***and*** it ＿＿＿＿ (easy)，省略了前面
　　　　　提到過的形容詞，故空格應填 (B) ***is***，才能和主詞及形容詞
　　　　　搭配。

TEST 9

Read the following passage and choose the best answer for each blank from the choices below.

Like many other youth subcultures, like graffiti, tattooing, and cosplay, street dance is an imported ___1___. It originated in American hip-hop culture.

Hip-hop culture began in 1970s America, growing out of the cultures of African-American, Hispanic, and Caribbean youth, and ___2___ four major elements—rap, DJing, graffiti, and street dance. Hip hop emphasizes the expression of self and spirit, as well as the courage to try new things. Its perspective on life is ___3___ of being true to oneself and doing everything with dedication and spirit.

To many people, hip hop and street dance are essentially interchangeable. ___4___, hip hop is a much broader concept, while street dance is only a part of the culture. As American popular culture has swept the globe in the past three decades, hip-hop culture has come along with it, and street dance has become one of the most ___5___ dance forms in the world today.

1. (A) exercise   (B) incident
   (C) entertainment   (D) phenomenon
2. (A) consisted in   (B) made up
   (C) was made of   (D) was composed of
3. (A) one   (B) it   (C) which   (D) what
4. (A) What's more   (B) In fact   (C) At last   (D) That is
5. (A) aboriginal   (B) imaginary
   (C) recognizable   (D) fascinated

TEST 9 詳解

*Like many other youth subcultures, like graffiti, tattooing, **and***

cosplay, street dance is an imported <u>phenomenon</u>. It originated
1

in American hip-hop culture.

　　像是許多其他的青年次文化，如塗鴉、刺青，以及角色扮演，街舞
是一種被引進的<u>現象</u>。它起源於美國嘻哈文化。
1

* youth[2] 〔 juθ 〕 *n.* 年輕；年輕人
  subculture 〔 sʌb'kʌltʃə 〕 *n.* 次文化
  graffiti 〔 grə'fitɪ 〕 *n. pl.* 塗鴉　　tattoo 〔 tæ'tu 〕 *v. n.* 刺青
  cosplay 〔 kɔz'ple 〕 *n.* 角色扮演【由 costume[4] 〔'kɑstjum 〕 *n.* 服裝和
　　play 縮合而成，只利用服裝、飾品、道具及化妝來完成角色扮演】
  import[3] 〔 ɪm'port 〕 *v.* 進口　　originate[6] 〔 ə'rɪdʒə,net 〕 *v.* 起源
  hip-hop 〔'hɪp,hɑp 〕 *adj.* 嘻哈的　　culture[2] 〔'kʌltʃə 〕 *n.* 文化

1. (**D**)　(A) exercise[2] 〔'ɛksə,saɪz 〕 *n.* 運動
　　　　　(B) incident[4] 〔'ɪnsədənt 〕 *n.* 事件
　　　　　(C) entertainment[4] 〔,ɛntə'tenmənt 〕 *n.* 娛樂
　　　　　(D) **phenomenon**[4] 〔 fə'namə,nan 〕 *n.* 現象
　　　　　* 因為 graffiti, tattooing 和 cosplay 都不是「運動」或「娛
　　　　　　樂」，故 (A) (C) 不可選。

Hip-hop culture began in 1970s America, growing out of the

*cultures of African-American, Hispanic, **and** Caribbean youth, **and***

<u>*was composed of*</u> *four major elements—rap, DJing, graffiti, **and** street*
2

dance. Hip hop emphasizes the expression *of self **and** spirit*, ***as well***
***as** the courage to try new things*. Its perspective *on life* is <u>one</u> *of*
3
*being true to oneself **and** doing everything with dedication **and** spirit*.

　　嘻哈文化開始於 1970 年代的美國，是源自非裔美籍的、拉丁美洲裔的和加勒比海的年輕人的文化，是由四個主要元素所<u>組成</u>——饒舌、
2
DJ、塗鴉和街舞。嘻哈強調自我和心靈的表達，以及敢於嘗試新事物的勇氣。嘻哈對生活的看法，是<u>人</u>要忠於自我，而且做任何事都要投入而且用心。
3

> * ***grow out of*** 產生於
> African-American〔ˈæfrɪkənəˈmɛrɪkən〕*adj.* 非裔美國籍的
> Hispanic〔hɪsˈpænɪk〕*adj.* 拉丁美洲裔的
> Caribbean〔kəˈrɪbɪən〕*adj.* 加勒比海的
> major³〔ˈmedʒɚ〕*adj.* 主要的　　element²〔ˈɛləmənt〕*n.* 元素
> rap〔ræp〕*n.* 饒舌音樂；饒舌歌曲
> ***DJ*** 唱片播放員；音樂節目主持人
> ***hip hop*** 嘻哈樂；嘻哈文化　　emphasize³〔ˈɛmfəˌsaɪz〕*v.* 強調
> expression³〔ɪkˈsprɛʃən〕*n.* 表達　　self¹〔sɛlf〕*n.* 自己
> spirit²〔ˈspɪrɪt〕*n.* 精神；靈魂　　***as well as*** 以及
> perspective⁶〔pɚˈspɛktɪv〕*n.* 看法；正確的眼光
> ***be true to*** 忠於　　dedication⁶〔ˌdɛdəˈkeʃən〕*n.* 專心致力；奉獻

2. (**D**)　(A) consist in　在於（= *lie in*）
　　　　　　(B) make up　組成
　　　　　　(C) be make of　由…製造
　　　　　　(D) ***be composed of***　由…組成（= *be made up of* = *consist of*）

3. (**A**)　依句意，空格應填入 a perspective（一種看法），為了避免重複，故用不定代名詞 ***one*** 代替，選 (A)。

To many people, hip hop **and** street dance are *essentially*
interchangeable.　*In fact*, hip hop is a *much* broader concept, **while**
street dance is only a part *of the culture.*　*As American popular*
culture has swept the globe in the past three decades, hip-hop culture
has come along with it, **and** street dance has become one *of the most*
recognizable dance forms in the world today.

對許多人來說，嘻哈和街舞本質上是可以互換的。事實上，嘻哈是
一個更廣泛的概念，而街舞只是嘻哈文化的一部分。隨著美國流行文化
在過去三十年來席捲全球，嘻哈文化也隨之而來，而且街舞也已成為現
今全世界最易辨識的舞蹈形式之一。

* essentially[4] 〔 ə'sɛnʃəlɪ 〕 *adv.* 本質上
  interchangeable 〔 ͵ɪntɚ'tʃendʒəbļ 〕 *adj.* 可互換的
  broad[2] 〔 brɔd 〕 *adj.* 廣大的　　concept[4] 〔'kɑnsɛpt 〕 *n.* 概念
  popular culture 流行文化　　sweep[2] 〔 swip 〕 *v.* 掃橫
  globe[4] 〔 glob 〕 *n.* 地球　　past[1] 〔 pæst 〕 *adj.* 過去的
  decade[3] 〔'dɛked 〕 *n.* 十年　　form[2] 〔 fɔrm 〕 *n.* 形式

4. (**B**)　(A) What's more 此外（ = *Moreover*[4]）
　　　　　(B) ***In fact*** 事實上　　　　(C) At last 最後；終於
　　　　　(D) That is 也就是（ = *That is to say*）

5. (**C**)　(A) aboriginal[6] 〔 ͵æbə'rɪdʒənļ 〕 *adj.* 原始的　*n.* 原住民
　　　　　(B) imaginary[4] 〔 ɪ'mædʒə͵nɛrɪ 〕 *adj.* 虛構的
　　　　　(C) ***recognizable***[5] 〔'rɛkəg͵naɪzəbļ 〕 *adj.* 可辨識的
　　　　　　　【recognize[3] 〔'rɛkəg͵naɪz 〕 *v.* 認得】
　　　　　(D) fascinated[5] 〔'fæsņ͵etɪd 〕 *adj.* 著迷的

TEST 10

Read the following passage and choose the best answer for each blank from the choices below.

Banks nowadays give their customers ATM cards with PIN numbers to enable them to access their money easily.   1   , in the future, banks may start using iris scanners. These are machines that can distinguish one person's eyes from another's. They may have advantages   2   the current system. For example, while ATM cards can be lost or stolen, one's irises are   3   attached to one's eyes. Furthermore, it would be unnecessary to remember PIN numbers,   4   is often difficult for people with multiple bank accounts.

Unlike old biometric scanning systems that scanned hand or face geometry, iris scanners are almost impossible to fool. They have been   5   for some time by government offices and military facilities, so they are not an untested technology, but one that has been shown to be reliable and effective.

1. (A) Therefore   (B) As a result
   (C) However   (D) On the other hand
2. (A) in   (B) on   (C) by   (D) over
3. (A) sufficiently   (B) permanently
   (C) currently   (D) voluntarily
4. (A) which   (B) it   (C) that   (D) what
5. (A) symbolized   (B) admonished
   (C) utilized   (D) regulated

TEST 10 詳解

Banks *nowadays* give their customers ATM cards *with PIN*
numbers to enable them to access their money easily. *However*, *in*
the future, banks may start using iris scanners. These are machines
that can distinguish one person's eyes from another's. They may
have advantages *over the current system*.

銀行現在會給他們的顧客有密碼的提款卡，使他們能夠輕易地取得
自己的錢。然而，未來銀行可能會開始使用虹膜掃描機。這種機器能分
辨人的眼睛。它們可能會優於目前的系統。

* nowadays⁴ 〔'nauə‚dez 〕 *adv.* 現今   customer² 〔'kʌstəmə 〕 *n.* 顧客
  ***ATM*⁴** *n.* 自動提款機 (= *automated-teller machine*)
  PIN *n.* 個人密碼 (= *personal identification number*)
  enable³ 〔 ɪn'ebl̩ 〕 *v.* 使能夠   access⁴ 〔'æksɛs 〕 *v.* 存取；取得
  iris 〔'aɪrɪs 〕 *n.* (眼球的) 虹膜
  scanner 〔'skænə 〕 *n.* 掃描器【scan⁵ 〔 skæn 〕 *v.* 掃描】
  distinguish⁴ 〔 dɪs'tɪŋgwɪʃ 〕 *v.* 分辨
  distinguish A from B 分辨 A 與 B
  advantage² 〔 əd'væntɪdʒ 〕 *n.* 優點；好處
  current³ 〔'kɝənt 〕 *adj.* 現在的；目前的

1. (**C**) 依句意，選 (C) ***However*** 「然而」。
    而 (A) therefore 「因此」，(B) as a result 「結果」，
    (D) on the other hand 「另一方面」，則不合句意。

2. (**D**) *have advantages over* 比～有優勢

*For example, **while** ATM cards can be lost **or** stolen*, one's irises

are *permanently* attached to one's eyes. *Furthermore*, it would be
　　　　3

unnecessary to remember PIN numbers, *__which__ is often difficult for*
　　　　　　　　　　　　　　　　　　　　　　4

people with multiple bank accounts.

例如，提款卡可能會遺失或被偷，但一個人的虹膜卻是永遠附著在眼睛
　　　　　　　　　　　　　　　　　　　　　　　　　　3
上。此外，這樣就不需要記住密碼，而記密碼對擁有多個銀行帳戶的人
　　　　　　　　　　　　　　　　4
來說，往往很困難。

　　* while[1] 〔 hwaɪl 〕*conj.* 雖然；儘管　　 attach[4] 〔 ə'tætʃ 〕*v.* 附上
　　 be attached to 附著在
　　 furthermore[4] 〔'fɝðə,mor 〕*adv.* 此外 (= *moreover*[4])
　　 unnecessary[2] 〔 ʌn'nɛsə,sɛrɪ 〕*adj.* 不需要的；不必要的
　　 multiple[4] 〔'mʌtəpḷ 〕*adj.* 多數的　　 account[3] 〔 ə'kaʊnt 〕*n.* 帳戶

3. (**B**)　(A) sufficiently[3] 〔 sə'fɪʃəntlɪ 〕*adv.* 足夠地
　　　　　　(B) ***permanently***[4] 〔'pɝmənəntlɪ 〕*adv.* 永久地
　　　　　　(C) currently[3] 〔'kɝəntlɪ 〕*adv.* 目前；現在
　　　　　　(D) voluntarily[4] 〔'vɑlən,tɛrəlɪ 〕*adv.* 自願地

4. (**A**)　要代替前面一整句話，關代用 ***which***，選 (A)。而 (B) it 爲代名
　　　　　詞，不具連接詞作用，在此不合；(C) 關代 that 前面不可有逗
　　　　　點，故不選；(D) what 爲複合關代，等於 the thing that，在此
　　　　　用法不合。

*Unlike old biometric scanning systems **that** scanned hand **or** face*

geometry, iris scanners are *almost* impossible to fool. They have

been <u>utilized</u> *for some time by government offices **and** military*
    5

facilities, ***so*** they are not an untested technology, ***but*** one ***that has***

*been shown to be reliable **and** effective.*

　　和掃描手部及臉部形狀的老舊生物掃描系統不同的是，虹膜掃描器
幾乎不可能被騙。因爲它們已經在政府部門和軍事場所<u>使用</u>了一段時
                                                5
間，所以並非是未經測試的科技，而已是經過證實，是可靠且有效的系
統。

* unlike〔ʌn'laɪk〕*prep.* 不像
biometric〔͵baɪə'mɛtrɪk〕*adj.* 生物測定的
scanning〔'skænɪŋ〕*adj.* 掃描的
geometry[5]〔dʒɪ'amətrɪ〕*n.* 幾何學；形狀；外形；構造
fool[2]〔ful〕*v.* 欺騙　　facilities[4]〔fə'sɪlətɪz〕*n. pl.* 設施；設備
untested〔ʌn'tɛstɪd〕*adj.* 未經測試的
technology[3]〔tɛk'nɑlədʒɪ〕*n.* 科技
not A but B 不是 A，而是 B　　show[1]〔ʃo〕*v.* 顯示；證明
reliable[3]〔rɪ'laɪəbḷ〕*adj.* 可靠的
effective[2]〔ə'fɛktɪv〕*adj.* 有效的

like	*v.* 喜歡	*prep.* 像
dislike	*v.* 不喜歡	
unlike	*prep.* 不像	

5.(**C**)　(A) symbolize[6]〔'sɪmbḷ͵aɪz〕*v.* 象徵
　　　　　　【symbol[2]〔'sɪmbḷ〕*n.* 象徵】
　　　　(B) admonish〔əd'mɑnɪʃ〕*v.* 告誡
　　　　(C) ***utilize***[6]〔'jutḷ͵aɪz〕*v.* 利用
　　　　　　【utilities[6]〔ju'tɪlətɪz〕*n. pl.* 公共事業（鐵路、公共汽車、
　　　　　　　瓦斯、電力、自來水事業等）】
　　　　(D) regulate[4]〔'rɛgjə͵let〕*v.* 規定；管制；調整
　　　　　　【regulation[4]〔͵rɛgjə'leʃən〕*n.* 規定】

TEST 11

Read the following passage and choose the best answer for each blank from the choices below.

Green sea turtles live most of their lives in the ocean. __1__, adult females must return to land so as to lay their eggs. Biologists believe that nesting female turtles often travel long distances from their feeding grounds to the same beach __2__ they were born. Hawaii's green sea turtles may migrate as far as 800 miles to their nesting beaches in the Hawaiian islands. Green sea turtle eggs usually __3__ about two months to incubate. Studies show that the temperature of the eggs during incubation affects the sex of baby sea turtles. Lower temperatures __4__ produce males, while higher temperatures are likely to produce females. Once out of the nest, the tiny baby turtles find their way to the ocean by heading towards the brightest horizon and swim __5__ for days. The young turtles remain at sea and do not come ashore until at least one year later.

1. (A) Besides　(B) However　(C) Therefore　(D) Despite
2. (A) where　(B) which　(C) that　(D) when
3. (A) spend　(B) consume　(C) take　(D) manage
4. (A) are supposed to　(B) likely to
　(C) mean to　(D) tend to
5. (A) continuously　(B) politely
　(C) accidentally　(D) miraculously

TEST 11 詳解

Green sea turtles live most *of their lives in the ocean.* *However*,
1

adult females must return *to land so as to lay their eggs.*

綠蠵龜一生大部分的時間都在海洋中渡過。然而,成年雌龜必須返
1
回陸地以便產卵。

green sea turtle

* turtle² ('tɜtḷ) *n.* 烏龜
  green sea turtle 綠蠵龜
  ocean¹ ('oʃən) *n.* 海洋
  adult¹ (ə'dʌlt) *adj.* 成年的
  female² ('fimel) *n.* 女性;雌性動物
  so as to 為了　　lay¹ (le) *v.* 下 (蛋);產 (卵)

1. (**B**)　依句意,選 (B) ***However*** 「然而」。而 (A) Besides 「此外」,
   (C) Therefore 「因此」, (D) Despite 「儘管」,皆不合句意。

Biologists believe ***that*** *nesting female turtles often travel long*

distances *from their feeding grounds to the same beach **where** they*
2

were born. Hawaii's green sea turtles may migrate *as far as 800*

miles to their nesting beaches in the Hawaiian islands.

生物學家認為,築巢的雌龜經常會從牠們的覓食場,長途跋涉回到牠們
出生時的同一個海灘。夏威夷的綠蠵龜可能會遷徙長達 800 哩,到牠們
在夏威夷群島築巢的海灘。

* biologist⁴ (baɪ'alədʒɪst) *n.* 生物學家
  【 biology⁴ (baɪ'alədʒɪ) *n.* 生物學 】

nest² 〔 nɛst 〕 v. 築巢　 n. 巢　　 travel² 〔'trævl 〕 v. 行進
feed¹ 〔 fid 〕 v. 餵食；覓食；進食
feeding ground （動物、鳥類或魚的）覓食場；聚食場
Hawaii 〔 hə'waɪji 〕 n. 夏威夷　　 migrate⁶ 〔'maɪgret 〕 v. 遷移
as far as 和…一樣遠　　 island² 〔'aɪlənd 〕 n. 島
the Hawaiian Islands 夏威夷群島

2. (**A**)　表「地點」，關係副詞用 ***where***，故選 (A)。

Green sea turtle eggs *usually* take about two months *to incubate*.
　　　　　　　　　　　　　 3

Studies show ***that*** *the temperature of the eggs during incubation*

affects the sex of baby sea turtles.　Lower temperatures tend to
　　　　　　　　　　　　　　　　　　　　　　　　　　　　 4

produce males, ***while*** higher temperatures are likely to produce

females.

綠蠵龜的蛋通常要花大約兩個月的時間孵化。研究顯示，蛋孵化期間的
　　　　　　　　　　 3
溫度，會影響綠蠵龜寶寶的性別。較低的溫度容易生出雄性，而較高的
溫度，則可能生出雌性。
　　　　　　　 4

　　* incubate 〔'ɪnkjə‚bet 〕 v. 孵化　　 study¹ 〔'stʌdɪ 〕 n. 研究
　　 temperature² 〔'tɛmpərətʃ∂ 〕 n. 溫度
　　 incubation 〔‚ɪnkjə'beʃən 〕 n. 孵化　　 affect³ 〔 ə'fɛkt 〕 v. 影響
　　 produce² 〔 prə'djus 〕 n. 產生；生
　　 male² 〔 mel 〕 n. 男性；雄性動物

3. (**C**)　 (A) spend¹ 〔 spɛnd 〕 v. （人）花費（時間、金錢）
　　　　　　 (B) consume⁴ 〔 kən'sum 〕 v. 消耗；吃（喝）
　　　　　　 (C) ***take***¹ 〔 tek 〕 v. （事情）花費（時間）
　　　　　　 (D) manage³ 〔'mænɪdʒ 〕 v. 設法；管理

4. (**D**)　(A) are supposed to「應該」，不合句意，因爲有可能是另
　　　　　　　一種情況。

　　　　　(B) 須改爲 are likely to「可能」，才能選。

　　　　　(C) mean to　有意…

　　　　　(D) ***tend to***；易於；傾向於（ = *be inclined to* ）

Once out of the nest, the tiny baby turtles find their way *to the ocean*

*by heading towards the brightest horizon **and** swim <u>continuously</u> for*
　　　　　　　　　　　　　　　　　　　　　　　　　5

days. The young turtles remain *at sea **and** do not come ashore until*

at least one year later.

一旦出了巢穴，小綠蠵龜寶寶就會設法前往大海，朝最明亮的地平線前
進，持續地游泳好幾天。年幼的綠蠵龜會待在海中，至少直到一年後才
　　　5
會上岸。

　　* once[1]〔 wʌns 〕*conj.* 一旦　　tiny〔 'taɪnɪ 〕*adj.* 微小的
　　　find** one's **way to 設法到達（某處）　　head[1]〔 hɛd 〕*v.* 前進
　　　towards[1]〔 tordz 〕*prep.* 朝著　　horizon[4]〔 hə'raɪzn̩ 〕*n.* 地平線
　　　young[1]〔 jʌŋ 〕*adj.* 年幼的　　remain[3]〔 rɪ'men 〕*v.* 留下
　　　ashore〔 ə'ʃor 〕*adv.* 向岸地　　***come ashore*** 上岸

5. (**A**)　(A) ***continuously***[4]〔 kən'tɪnjʊəslɪ 〕*adv.* 不停地；不斷地

　　　　　(B) politely[2]〔 pə'laɪtlɪ 〕*adv.* 有禮貌地

　　　　　(C) accidentally[4]〔 ͵æksə'dɛntl̩ɪ 〕*adv.* 偶然地；意外地

　　　　　(D) miraculously[6]〔 mə'rækjələslɪ 〕*adv.* 奇蹟般地；
　　　　　　　不可思議地

TEST 12

Read the following passage and choose the best answer for each blank from the choices below.

If you want to be happy, then the best country to move to is Denmark. Named the happiest country in the world in a published survey, the home of Lego beats the United States, despite the ___1___ being the most prosperous nation. As for the unhappiest nation, it is, unsurprisingly, Zimbabwe, which has been ___2___ by violence. Based on the result, the director of the survey, Ronald Inglehart, believes that there may be a strong correlation between peace and happiness.

The survey is basically conducted by asking two easy questions: "___3___ all things together, would you say you are very happy, pretty happy, not very happy, or not at all happy?" as well as "All things considered, how satisfied are you with your life ___4___ these days?" Inglehart and his team questioned 350,000 people, and then concluded that the most important determinant of happiness is the extent ___5___ people have free choice in how to live their lives.

1. (A) letter   (B) later   (C) late   (D) latter
2. (A) ravaged   (B) registered   (C) radiated   (D) resumed
3. (A) Taking   (B) Take   (C) Taken   (D) Took
4. (A) at random   (B) by degrees
   (C) as a whole   (D) in a sense
5. (A) in which   (B) to which   (C) what   (D) why

TEST 12 詳解

If you want to be happy, *then* the best country *to move to* is

Denmark. *Named the happiest country in the world in a*

published survey, the home *of Lego* beats the United States, *despite*

the latter being the most prosperous nation.
1

　　如果你想幸福快樂，那麼最棒的移居國是丹麥。在一份已發表的調查中，這個樂高玩具的發源地被稱爲世界上最幸福的國家，打敗美國，儘管後者是最富裕的國家。
　　　1

　*　move¹〔muv〕v. 移居；搬家　　Denmark〔'dɛnmɑrk〕n. 丹麥
　　name¹〔nem〕v. 把…叫作；指名
　　publish⁴〔'pʌblɪʃ〕v. 發表；出版　　survey³〔'sɝve〕n. 調查
　　home¹〔hom〕n. 發源地　　Lego〔'lɛgo〕n. 樂高
　　beat¹〔bit〕v. 擊敗　　despite⁴〔dɪ'spaɪt〕prep. 儘管
　　prosperous⁴〔'prɑspərəs〕adj. 繁榮的；富裕的

1.(**D**)　(A) letter¹〔'lɛtɚ〕n. 信；字母　　(B) later⁵〔'letɚ〕adj. 較晚的
　　　　(C) late¹〔let〕adj. 遲的；晚的　　(D) **latter**³〔'læLtɚ〕pron. 後者

As for the unhappiest nation, it is, *unsurprisingly,* Zimbabwe, ***which***

have been ravaged by violence.　Based on the result, the director *of*
　　　　　　　　　　2

the survey, Ronald Inglehart, believes ***that*** *there may be a strong*

*correlation between peace **and** happiness.*

至於最不快樂的國家，不意外地，就是一直<u>被</u>暴<u>力</u><u>蹂躪</u>的辛巴威了。根
據這項結果，這個調查的主導者羅南・英格勒哈特相信，和平與快樂之
間，可能密切相關。

* ***as for*** 至於
  unsurprisingly[1] 〔ˌʌnsəˈpraɪzɪŋlɪ〕 *adv.* 不出意料地
  Zimbabwe 〔 zɪmˈbɑbwe 〕 *n.* 辛巴威
  violence[3] 〔ˈvaɪələns 〕 *n.* 暴力
  based on 根據 (= *according to*)
  director[2] 〔 dəˈrɛktɚ 〕 *n.* 主任；主導者
  correlation 〔ˌkɔrəˈleʃən 〕 *n.* 相互關係
  【relation[2] 〔 rɪˈleʃən 〕 *n.* 關係 】
  peace[2] 〔 pis 〕 *n.* 和平

as for 至於
= as regards
= regarding
= concerning
= about

2. (**A**)   (A) ***ravage***[6] 〔ˈrævɪdʒ 〕 *v.* 蹂躪；毀壞
          (B) register[4] 〔ˈrɛdʒɪstɚ 〕 *v.* 登記；註冊
          (C) radiate[6] 〔ˈredɪˌet 〕 *v.* 散發
          (D) resume[5] 〔 rɪˈzum 〕 *v.* 恢復；再繼續

The survey is *basically* conducted *by asking two easy questions*:

"*Taking* all things together, *would you say you are very happy, pretty*
3

happy, not very happy, ***or*** *not at all happy?*" ***as well as*** "*All things*

considered, ***how*** *satisfied are you with your life* <u>*as a whole*</u> *these days?*"
4

　　進行這項調查，基本上是藉由詢問兩個簡單的問題：「總括來說，
你會說你是非常快樂、相當快樂、不太快樂，或完全不快樂？」以及
「把所有的事情綜合起來看，最近你對你<u>整體的</u>生活有多滿意？」

* basically[1] 〔'bɛsɪkḷɪ〕 *adv.* 基本上
conduct[5] 〔kən'dʌkt〕*v.* 進行；做
pretty[1] 〔'prɪtɪ〕*adv.* 相當　　*not at all* 一點也不
as well as 以及　　consider[2] 〔kən'sɪdɚ〕*v.* 認為；考慮
all things considered 考量一切情形後
satisfied[2] 〔'sætɪs,faɪd〕*adj.* 滿意的　　*these days* 最近

3. (**A**)　依句意可知，空格的原句應為 If you take all things together
的副詞子句，可簡化成分詞構句，故選 (A) *Taking*。

4. (**C**)　(A) at random 隨意地　　(B) by degrees 逐漸地
(C) *as a whole* 整體而言　　(D) in a sense 從某種意義上來看

Inglehart *and* his team questioned 350,000 people, *and then*
concluded *that the most important determinant of happiness is the*
extent *to which people have free choice in how to live their lives.*
5

英格勒哈特和他的團隊詢問了三十五萬人，然後做出的結論是，決定快
樂最重要的因素，在於人們對於要怎麼過生活，能自由選擇的程度。

* team[2] 〔tim〕*n.* 團隊　　question[1] 〔'kwɛstʃən〕*v.* 詢問
conclude[3] 〔kən'klud〕*v.* 下結論；斷定
determinant 〔dɪ'tɝmənənt〕*n.*
決定因素【determine[3] *v.* 決定】

| -clude 表示 close 之意，如： |
| conclude *v.* 下結論 |
| include *v.* 包括 |
| exclude *v.* 將…排除在外 |

extent[4] 〔ɪk'stɛnt〕*n.* 程度
choice[2] 〔tʃɔɪs〕*n.* 選擇

5. (**B**)　依句意，空格之後是形容詞子句，修飾先行詞 the extent，而
與 extent 搭配之介系詞是 to，如：to some extent「到某種程
度」，故選 (B) *to which*。

TEST 13

Read the following passage and choose the best answer for each blank from the choices below.

The French go to restaurants more often than their northern European neighbors. Almost every restaurant has at least one fixed-price menu (a selection of two or three dishes for each course at a __1__ price), as well as a menu offering individual selections. In most of France it is usual to choose from the fixed-price menu unless it is a special occasion.

Fast food has been resisted by the French, although this resistance has not been __2__ successful, and many hamburger restaurants operate across the country. However, in France the traditional fast food is cream __3__ croissants and sandwiches, which can be purchased in shops and cafés.

Modern French people generally eat a light breakfast, which may __4__ croissants or bread and coffee or hot chocolate. Lunch was once the main meal of the day, but now many people have a lighter lunch and eat their main meal in the evening. In Paris, lunch is usually eaten at around 1 p.m. and dinner at 9 p.m. or later, though people tend to eat __5__ in other areas.

1. (A) wholesale   (B) retail   (C) set   (D) steep
2. (A) impartially   (B) entirely   (C) equally   (D) partly
3. (A) fetched   (B) fastened   (C) filled   (D) filtered
4. (A) consist of   (B) call for   (C) serve as   (D) stand for
5. (A) latter   (B) later   (C) sooner   (D) earlier

TEST 13 詳解

The French go to restaurants *more often **than** their northern European neighbors*. *Almost every* restaurant has *at least* one fixed-price menu (a selection of *two **or** three dishes for each course* at a <u>set</u> price), ***as well as*** a menu *offering individual selections*.
 1
In most of France it is usual to choose *from the fixed-price menu* ***unless*** *it is a special occasion*.

　　法國人比他們歐洲北部的鄰居更常上餐館。幾乎每間餐廳都至少有一份定價套餐的菜單(選兩三道菜做組合，而每道菜都是<u>固定的</u>價格)，
 1
以及提供個別選擇的菜單。在法國大部分的地區，除了特殊場合外，選擇定價套餐組合的餐點是很常見的。

　　　　* northern[2] 〔'nɔrðən 〕 *adj.* 北方的　　neighbor[2] 〔'nebɚ 〕 *n.* 鄰國的人
　　　　at least 至少　　fixed[2] 〔 fɪkst 〕 *adj.* 固定的
　　　　fixed-price menu 定價套餐的菜單【固定菜色的組合，價格是固定的】
　　　　course[1] 〔 kors 〕 *n.* 一道（菜）　　***as well as*** 以及
　　　　offer[2] 〔'ɔfɚ 〕 *v.* 提供　　individual[3] 〔ˌɪndə'vɪdʒʊəl 〕 *adj.* 個別的
　　　　selection[2] 〔 sə'lɛkʃən 〕 *n.* 選擇　　unless[3] 〔 ən'lɛs 〕 *conj.* 除非
　　　　occasion[3] 〔 ə'keʒən 〕 *n.* 場合

1. (**C**)　(A) wholesale[5] 〔'holˌsel 〕 *adj.* 批發的
　　　　　　　wholesale price 批發價

> <u>retail</u>[6] *adj., n.* 零售（的）
> <u>detail</u>[3] *n.* 詳細；細節

　　　　　　(B) retail[6] 〔'ritel 〕 *adj.* 零售的　　retail price 零售價
　　　　　　(C) ***set***[1] 〔 sɛt 〕 *adj.* （價格）固定的
　　　　　　(D) steep[3] 〔 stip 〕 *adj.* 陡峭的；（價格）過高的

Fast food has been resisted *by the French,* ***although*** *this*

resistance has not been <u>entirely</u> successful, ***and*** *many hamburger*
　　　　　　　　　　　　　　2

restaurants operate <u>across the country</u>.

　　法國人一直都抗拒速食，即使這樣的抵抗並非<u>完全</u>成功，而且全國
　　　　　　　　　　　　　　　　　　　　　　　2
各地有很多漢堡餐廳在營業。

　　＊ resist³〔rɪ'zɪst〕*v.* 抵抗；抗拒　　resistance⁴〔rɪ'zɪstəns〕*n.* 抵抗
　　operate²〔'ɑpə,ret〕*v.* 經營；運轉　　***across the country*** 在全國

2.(**B**)　(A) impartially〔ɪm'parʃəlɪ〕*adv.* 公正地
　　　　　【partial⁴ *adj.* 偏袒的】
　　　　　(B) ***entirely²***〔ɪn'taɪrlɪ〕*adv.* 完全地（＝*completely²* ＝*fully¹*
　　　　　　　＝*wholly¹* ＝*totally¹*）
　　　　　(C) equally¹〔'ikwəlɪ〕*adv.* 平等地
　　　　　(D) partly⁵〔'partlɪ〕*adv.* 部分地

im + part + ial + ly
not + part + adj. + adv.

However, *in France* the traditional fast food is cream <u>filled</u> croissants
　　　　　　　　　　　　　　　　　　　　　　　　　　　　3

and sandwiches, ***which*** *can be purchased in shops* ***and*** *cafés.*

然而，在法國最傳統的速食是<u>包有奶油餡料的</u>可頌和三明治，這些在商
　　　　　　　　　　　　　3　　　3

店及咖啡廳裡都可以買到。

　　＊ croissant〔krwɑ'zɑn〕*n.* 法式新月形麵包；可頌
　　purchase⁵〔'pɝtʃəs〕*v.* 購買　　café²〔kə'fe〕*n.* 咖啡廳

3.(**C**)　(A) fetch⁴〔fɛtʃ〕*v.* 拿來　　　　(B) fasten¹〔'fæsn̩〕*v.* 繫上
　　　　　(C) ***fill¹***〔fɪl〕*v.* 填滿　　***cream filled*** 填滿奶油的
　　　　　(D) filter¹〔'fɪltɚ〕*v.* 過濾

Modern French people *generally* eat a light breakfast, ***which***

may <u>consist of</u> croissants ***or*** bread ***and*** coffee ***or*** hot chocolate.　Lunch
　　4

was *once* the main meal *of the day*, ***but*** *now* many people have a

lighter lunch ***and*** eat their main meal *in the evening.*　*In Paris*, lunch

is *usually* eaten *at around 1 p.m.* ***and*** dinner *at 9 p.m.* ***or later***, ***though***

people tend to eat <u>earlier</u> in other areas.
　　　　　5

　　現在的法國人通常早餐吃得很簡單，可能<u>包括</u>可頌或麵包，咖啡或
　　　　　　　　　　　　　　　　　　　4
熱巧克力。以前午餐曾是一天中最主要的一餐，但現在很多人午餐吃得
較簡單，並且把主餐挪到晚上。在巴黎，午餐通常在下午一點左右吃，
而晚餐在晚上九點，甚至更晚才吃，雖然其他地區的人，都傾向於<u>早點</u>
　　　　　　　　　　　　　　　　　　　　　　　　　　　　　　5
吃晚餐。

　　* modern[2] 〔ˋmɑdɚn〕 *adj.* 現代的
　　　 light[1] 〔laɪt〕 *adj.* 清淡的；簡單的　　　 main[2] 〔men〕 *adj.* 主要的
　　　 meal[2] 〔mil〕 *n.* 一餐　　　 have[1] 〔hæv〕 *v.* 吃
　　　 tend to V. 易於…；傾向於…

4.(**A**)　(A) ***consist of*** 由…組成；包含
　　　　　(B) call for 需要
　　　　　(C) serve as 充當；當作　　　(D) stand for 代表

```
con    +  sist
 |         |
together + stand
```

5.(**D**)　(A) latter[3] 〔ˋlætɚ〕 *adj.* (兩者中) 後者的　　　 the latter 後者
　　　　　(B) later[1] 〔ˋletɚ〕 *adj.* 較晚的；更晚的
　　　　　(C) sooner 〔ˋsunɚ〕 *adv.* 較快地
　　　　　(D) ***earlier***[1] 〔ˋɝlɪr〕 *adv.* 較早地

TEST 14

Read the following passage and choose the best answer for each blank from the choices below.

A new review of research suggests that fish oil supplements, originally taken to reduce the risk of heart disease, might protect against another deadly cancer in women, breast cancer.   1   , a high intake of fatty acids in fish oil is connected with a 14 percent reduced risk of breast cancer in postmenopausal women.   2   these findings seem to have health implications with regard to prevention of breast cancer through diet, some doctors point out that past studies actually drew different conclusions regarding the consumption of fish oil and breast cancer risk and that the connection is still   3   .

For one thing, such an association was not found in a number of studies and only two large studies and several case-control studies have indicated a protective effect of fish oil. For another, the relation between fish oil consumption and breast cancer prevention was not highly significant,   4   only modest. Therefore, it's still difficult to say that fish oil deserves all the   5   . Nevertheless, little research suggests increasing the intake of fish oil is harmful to one's health. Including oily fish in your diet may be a good choice.

1. (A) Roughly (B) Generally (C) Specifically (D) Literally
2. (A) While (B) Because (C) Since (D) As
3. (A) strong (B) unproven (C) substantial (D) ironic
4. (A) and (B) otherwise (C) or (D) but
5. (A) blame (B) credit (C) review (D) usage

TEST 14 詳解

A new review *of research* suggests *that fish oil supplements,*

originally taken to reduce the risk of heart disease, might protect

against another deadly cancer in women, breast cancer. <u>Specifically</u>,
1

a high intake *of fatty acids in fish oil* is connected with a 14 percent

reduced risk *of breast cancer in postmenopausal women.*

　　新的研究報告指出，魚油補給品原本是爲了降低罹患心臟病的風險
而服用，但也許也有助於保護女性，免於受到另一種致命癌症──乳癌
的侵襲。<u>更確切地說</u>，大量攝取魚油中的脂肪酸，與停經後的婦女罹患
　　　　　1
乳癌的機率降低百分之十四有所關連。

* review[2] (rɪ'vju) *n.* 評論；報告 (= *report*[1])
  suggest[3] (sə'dʒɛst) *v.* 指出
  supplement[6] ('sʌpləmənt) *n.* 營養補給品
  originally[3] (ə'rɪdʒənḷɪ) *adv.* 原本
  take[1] (tek) *v.* 服用　　risk[3] (rɪsk) *n.* 風險
  disease[3] (dɪ'ziz) *n.* 疾病　　deadly[6] ('dɛdlɪ) *adj.* 致命的
  cancer[2] ('kɛnsɚ) *n.* 癌症　　breast[3] (brɛst) *n.* 胸部；乳房
  breast cancer 乳癌　　intake ('ɪn,tek) *n.* 攝取量
  acid[4] ('æsɪd) *n.* 酸　　*fatty acid* 脂肪酸
  be connected with 和⋯有關
  reduced[3] (rɪ'djust) *adj.* 降低的
  postmenopausal (post,mɛno'pɔzḷ) *adj.* 停經後的

1. (**C**) (A) Roughly[4] 〔'rʌflɪ 〕*adv.* 粗略地；大約
      (B) Generally[2] 〔'dʒɛnərəlɪ 〕*adv.* 一般地；普遍地；通常
      (C) ***Specifically***[3] 〔 spɪ'sɪfɪklɪ 〕*adv.* 明確地；具體地說
      (D) Literally[6] 〔'lɪtərəlɪ 〕*adv.* 照字面意義地；實在地；完全地

___

While these findings seem to have health implications with regard
___2

to prevention of breast cancer through diet, some doctors point out

that past studies actually drew different conclusions regarding the

consumption of fish oil **and** breast cancer risk **and that** the connection

is still unproven.
3

雖然這些研究發現，似乎暗示著可以透過飲食來預防乳癌，然而有些醫
2
生卻指出，過去的研究對於魚油的攝取和罹患乳癌的風險，其實有著不
同的結論，所以這兩者的關連仍未經證實。
3

* implication[6] 〔ˌɪmplɪ'keʃən 〕*n.* 暗示；關連
  with regard to 關於（ = *with respect to* ）
  diet[3] 〔'daɪət 〕*n.* 飲食   ***point out*** 指出
  past[1] 〔 pæst 〕*adj.* 過去的
  study[1] 〔'stʌdɪ 〕*n.* 研究
  draw[1] 〔 drɔ 〕*v.* 獲得
  conclusion[3] 〔 kən'kluʒən 〕*n.* 結論
  regarding[4] 〔 rɪ'gɑrdɪŋ 〕*prep.* 關於
  consumption[6] 〔 kən'sʌmpʃən 〕*n.* 食用；攝取
  connection[3] 〔 kən'nɛkʃən 〕*n.* 關連

  | regarding[4] *prep.* 關於 |
  | = respecting |
  | = concerning[4] |
  | = about[1] |

2. (**A**)　依句意，選 (A) *While*「雖然」（= *Although*）。
而 (B) Because「因為」，(C) Since「既然」，(D) As「因為；
當…時候」，則不合句意。

3. (**B**)　(A) strong[1]〔strɔŋ〕*adj.* 強的；穩固的
(B) ***unproven***[1]〔ʌn'pruvən〕*adj.* 未經證實的
(C) substantial[5]〔səb'stænʃəl〕*adj.* 實質的；相當多的
(D) ironic[6]〔aɪ'rɑnɪk〕*adj.* 諷刺的

For one thing, such an association was not found *in a number of*

studies and only two large studies *and* several case-control studies

have indicated a protective effect *of fish oil*. *For another*, the

relation *between fish oil consumption and breast cancer prevention*

was not *highly* significant, ***but*** only modest.
　　　　　　　　　　　　　　　4

　　首先，這樣的關連並不是在多數研究中都能找到，只有兩個大型研
究，和幾個病例對照研究，曾指出魚油有防護效果。其次，攝取魚油和
預防乳癌之間的關連也不是非常顯著，只能說有些微的關連。
　　　　　　　　　　　　　　　4

　　*　for one thing…for another* 首先…其次
　　association[4]〔ə,soʃɪ'eʃən〕*n.* 關連　　*a number of* 幾個；很多
　　case-control study 病例對照研究【即針對特定疾病，比較族群中有
　　　該疾病（試驗組）與無該疾病（對照組）的二群人，找出疾病與其先
　　　前暴露的危險因子之關連性。對少數或罕見可被準確量測的疾病，有
　　　助於確定病因】
　　indicate[2]〔'ɪndə,ket〕*v.* 指出
　　protective[3]〔prə'tɛktɪv〕*adj.* 防護的
　　effect[2]〔ɪ'fɛkt〕*n.* 效果

association[4] *n.* 關連
= connection[3]
= relation[2]

relation[2] 〔rɪ'leʃən 〕 n. 關係；關連
highly[4] 〔'haɪlɪ 〕 adv. 高度地；非常
significant[3] 〔 sɪg'nɪfəkənt 〕 adj. 顯著的
modest[4] 〔'mɑdɪst 〕 adj. (程度) 不太大的

4. (**D**)　　*not A but B*　不是 A，而是 B
　　　　而 (A) and「以及」，(B) otherwise「否則」，(C) or「或者」，
　　　　則不合句意。

Therefore, it's *still* difficult to say ***that*** *fish oil deserves all the* <u>credit</u>.
5

Nevertheless, little research suggests *increasing the intake of fish oil*

is harmful to one's health.　Including oily fish *in your diet* may be a

good choice.

因此，要將一切歸功於魚油，還是有困難。儘管如此，幾乎沒有任何研
　　　　　　5
究顯示，增加魚油攝取量有害健康。把富含油脂的魚類納入飲食當中，
也許是個不錯的選擇。

　　* deserve[4] 〔 dɪ'zɝv 〕 v. 值得；應得
　　　nevertheless[4] 〔,nɛvəðə'lɛs 〕 adv. 儘管如此 (= however[1])
　　　little[1] 〔'lɪtl̩ 〕 adj. 幾乎沒有的
　　　suggest[3] 〔 səg'dʒɛst 〕 v. 指出；顯示
　　　include[2] 〔 ɪn'klud 〕 v. 包括；包含　　　oily[1] 〔'ɔɪlɪ 〕 adj. 富含油脂的

5. (**B**)　(A) blame[3] 〔 blem 〕 n. 責備
　　　　　(B) ***credit***[3] 〔'krɛdɪt 〕 n. 功勞；榮譽；信用
　　　　　　　例如：The ***credit*** goes to him. (那是他的功勞。)
　　　　　(C) review[2] 〔 rɪ'vju 〕 n. 評論
　　　　　(D) usage[4] 〔'jusɪdʒ 〕 n. 用法

TEST 15

Read the following passage and choose the best answer for each blank from the choices below.

You are a professional who is accustomed to stress, but all the uncertainty and anxiety in the workplace these days is putting you under more pressure than usual. You feel burned out. What steps can you take to prevent burnout? According to a psychologist, you should start by recognizing that this is a difficult time for business and ___1___ anxiety and uncertainty are now facts of life. Next, change your expectations from idealistic to ___2___. Expect life to be tough sometimes but also expect that you are resilient and will ___3___. Focus on the positives in your life—like family or hobbies—because it's rare that everything ___4___ at once. Last but not least, make time for exercise and be conscious of your diet. Good nutrition and exercise help fight depression and lethargy. Set aside time for things you enjoy outside of work, like painting, music or time with family. By taking these steps, you can move forward ___5___ there are negative things happening.

1. (A) which   (B) what   (C) while   (D) that
2. (A) imaginary   (B) creative   (C) courageous (D) realistic
3. (A) talk over   (B) bounce back
   (C) lie low   (D) give up
4. (A) falls apart   (B) pops up
   (C) breaks out   (D) gets together
5. (A) if only   (B) even so   (C) if not   (D) even if

TEST 15 詳解

You are a professional *who is accustomed to stress*, *but* all the uncertainty *and* anxiety *in the workplace these days* is putting you under more pressure *than* usual. You feel burned out. What steps can you take *to prevent burnout*? *According to a psychologist, you should start by recognizing that this is a difficult time for business and that anxiety and uncertainty are now facts of life.* Next, change
1
your expectations *from idealistic to realistic*.
2

你是個習慣壓力的專業人士，但現今職場中的不確定性和焦慮感，讓你承受比平常還大的壓力。你感覺筋疲力盡。能採取什麼方法來預防精力耗盡呢？根據心理學家的說法，你應該要認清，現在不是做生意的好時機，還要認清，現在的焦慮和不確定性，是生活中的現實。其次，改變自己的期望，別太理想化，要實際一點。
2

* professional[4] (prə'fɛʃənḷ) n. 專家；職業選手
  accustom[5] (ə'kʌstəm) v. 使習慣於
  be accustomed to 習慣於　　stress[2] (strɛs) n. 壓力
  uncertainty[6] (ʌn'sɝtṇtɪ) n. 不確定性
  anxiety[2] (æŋ'zaɪətɪ) n. 焦慮
  workplace ('wɝk,ples) n. 職場　　*these days* 最近
  put sb. under pressure 使某人承受壓力
  burn out 燒盡；使筋疲力盡
  take steps 採取行動　　prevent[3] (prɪ'vɛnt) v. 預防

burnout〔'bɝn͵aʊt〕*n.* 耗竭
psychologist⁴〔saɪ'kɑlədʒɪst〕*n.* 心理學家
recognize³〔'rɛkəg͵naɪz〕*v.* 認清
fact of life 生活中的（不快）現實
（= *something unpleasant that cannot be avoided*）
expectation³〔͵ɛkspɛk'teʃən〕*n.* 期望
idealistic〔͵aɪdɪəl'ɪstɪk〕*adj.* 理想主義的
【ideal³〔aɪ'dɪəl〕*adj.* 理想的】

1.（**D**）　對等連接詞 and，連接兩個由 that 引導的名詞子句，在
　　　　　that…and that 的句型中，第二個 that 不可省略，故選
　　　　　(D) *that*。

> that 引導名詞子句可做：
> ①主詞：<u>That he lied</u> is true.
> ②受詞：They say <u>(that) he lied</u>.
> ③補語：The problem is <u>that he lied</u>.
> ④同位語：The fact <u>that he lied</u> is true.

2.（**D**）　(A) imaginary⁴〔ɪ'mædʒə͵nɛrɪ〕*adj.* 想像的；虛構的
　　　　　(B) creative³〔krɪ'etɪv〕*adj.* 有創意的；獨創性的
　　　　　(C) courageous⁴〔kə'redʒəs〕*adj.* 勇敢的
　　　　　(D) *realistic⁴*〔͵rɪə'lɪstɪk〕*adj.* 現實的；實際的

> istic 為 ism（學說；特性）和 ist（人）的形容詞字尾，例如：
> ⎰ real<u>ism</u>⁶ *n.* 現實主義　　　⎰ ego<u>ism</u> *n.* 自我中心主義
> ⎱ real<u>istic</u>⁴ *adj.* 現實的　　　⎱ ego<u>istic</u> *adj.* 自我中心的
> ⎰ enthusi<u>asm</u>⁴ *n.* 熱忱　　　⎰ art<u>ist</u>² *n.* 藝術家
> ⎱ enthusi<u>astic</u>⁵ *adj.* 熱中的　⎱ art<u>istic</u>⁴ *adj.* 藝術的

Expect life to be tough *sometimes **but** also* expect ***that** you are resilient **and** will <u>bounce back</u>*. Focus on the positives *in your life—like family*

3

*or hobbies—**because** it's rare **that** everything <u>falls apart</u> at once*. Last

4

but not least, make time *for exercise **and*** be conscious of your diet.

Good nutrition ***and*** exercise help fight depression ***and*** lethargy.

有時要預期生活有辛苦的一面，但也要期待，自己適應力很強，而且精神會再度<u>恢復</u>。把焦點放在生活中的正面事物——像是家人或嗜好——

3

因爲不太可能所有事情都同時<u>崩毀</u>。最後一項重點是，找時間運動，並

4

注意自己的飲食。良好的營養和運動，有助於對抗憂鬱以及無精打采。

* expect[2] (ɪkˋspɛkt) v. 期待；預期　　　tough[4] (tʌf) adj. 困難的
  resilient (rɪˋzɪlɪənt) adj. 適應力強的；有彈性的
  (= *able to become healthy, happy, or strong again after an*
  　 illness, disappointment or other problem)

  focus on 專注於

  positive[2] (ˋpɑzətɪv) n. 正面事物

  hobby[2] (ˋhɑbɪ) n. 嗜好

  rare[2] (rɛr) adj. 罕見的　　　*at once* 立刻；同時

  last but not least 最後但並非最不重要的是

  make time 騰出時間　　　*be conscious of* 知道；察覺到；注意

  diet[3] (ˋdaɪət) n. 飲食　　　nutrition[6] (nuˋtrɪʃən) n. 營養

  depression[4] (dɪˋprɛʃən) n. 沮喪；憂鬱

  lethargy (ˋlɛθədʒɪ) n. 無精打采

resilient *adj.* 有彈性的 = flexible[4]

lethargy *n.* 無精打采 lethargic (ləˋθɑrdʒɪk) *adj.* 無精打采的

3. (**B**) (A) talk over 邊喝…邊談
　　　　(B) **bounce back** 反彈；恢復（健康、信心）
　　　　(C) lie low 避風頭；躲起來
　　　　(D) give up 放棄；戒除（習慣）

4. (**A**) (A) **fall apart** 破碎；瓦解；崩潰
　　　　(B) pop up 突然出現
　　　　(C) break out （戰爭、疾病等）突然爆發
　　　　(D) get together 聚集；團結

Set aside time *for things you enjoy outside of work*, *like painting, music*

or time with family. *By taking these steps*, you can move *forward*

even if there are negative things happening.
　　5

撥出時間給工作以外你喜歡的事情，像是畫畫、聽音樂，或是花時間跟
家人相處。藉由這些步驟，<u>即使</u>有不開心的事，你也能繼續走下去。
　　　　　　　　　　　　　　5

　　* **set aside** 撥出；留出　　**outside of** 在…之外；除…外
　　　move forward 往前進　　negative[2] (ˈnɛɡətɪv) *adj.* 負面的

5. (**D**) 依句意，故選 (D) **even if**「即使」。
　　　　而 (A) if only「要是；只要」，(B) even so「儘管如此」，
　　　　(C) if not「要不；不然」，皆不合句意。

TEST 16

Read the following passage and choose the best answer for each blank from the choices below.

In 1988 artist Friedensreich Hundertwasser declared himself willing to ___1___ the exterior redesign of the Spittelau refuse incineration plant in Austria, which had been extensively damaged by fire. As part of the same renovation process, the plant—which provides Vienna with long-distance heating—was re-equipped with the latest and most environmentally acceptable technology. While Hundertwasser was an enthusiastic supporter of the avoidance of waste, he also knew that the consequences for the environment would actually be worse if the heating station were not ___2___.

In his artistic scheme for Spittelau, Hundertwasser ___3___ the conventional materials of industrial buildings, such as concrete, steel, glass, ceramic and enamel, but employed them in a fashion which robbed the plant of its aggressive and threatening character. He turned the exterior walls into a mosaic of shimmering tiles, planted trees on the roofs and terraces, clothed the chimney stack in blue enamel panels and encircled it with a ___4___ sphere which sparkles like a second sun in the sky.

This spectacular industrial building is an example of a harmonious symbiosis of technology, ecology and art, and acts as a symbol of inspiration for a __5__ society.

1. (A) undergo　　　　　　　(B) undertake
　　(C) underestimate　　　　(D) undermine
2. (A) gone to pieces　　　　(B) put back into operation
　　(C) come into being　　　(D) got into debt
3. (A) refrained from　　　　(B) interfered in
　　(C) left off　　　　　　　(D) drew upon
4. (A) light-reflected　　　　(B) light-reflecting
　　(C) light-reflection　　　(D) light-reflect
5. (A) toll-free　　　　　　　(B) waste-free
　　(C) duty-free　　　　　　(D) pain-free

做題目一定要做7000字範圍內
的，否則就偏離方向了。因為英文
單字無限多，你永遠背不完。做題
目等於複習7000字，愉快無比。

TEST 16 詳解

In 1988 artist Friedensreich Hundertwasser declared himself

willing to <u>undertake</u> the exterior redesign *of the Spittelau refuse*
　　　　　　　　1

incineration plant in Austria, **which** *had been extensively damaged*

by fire.

　　1988 年，藝術家弗登萊斯・漢德瓦薩宣布，他將<u>負責</u>重新設計之
　　　　　　　　　　　　　　　　　　　　　　　　　1
前在奧地利，被大火嚴重損毀的許皮特勞垃圾焚化廠的外觀。

* Hundertwasser〔ˈhʌndɚtˌvɑsɑr〕*n.* 漢德瓦薩
　【1928-2000，全名弗登萊斯・漢德瓦薩
　（Friedensreich Hundertwasser），20 世紀末
　奧地利最有名，也是最具爭議的藝術家。作品外
　型特殊奇異，屬後現代解構主義】

declare[4]〔dɪˈklɛr〕*v.* 宣布　　willing[2]〔ˈwɪlɪŋ〕*adj.* 願意的
exterior[5]〔ɪkˈstɪrɪɚ〕*adj.* 外部的
redesign[2]〔ˌridɪˈzaɪn〕*n.* 重新設計
Spittelau〔ˈʃpɪtˈlaʊ〕*n.* 許皮特勞【維也納市區地名，也是焚化爐
　名稱】

refuse[2]〔ˈrɛfjus〕*n.* 垃圾；廢物；廢料
incineration〔ɪnˌsɪnəˈreʃən〕*n.* 焚燒
plant[1]〔plænt〕*n.* 工廠

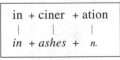

in + ciner + ation
 |　　　|　　　|
in + ashes + *n.*

Spittelau refuse incineration plant 許皮特勞垃圾焚化廠【位於
　維也納市中心，1988 年動工，直到 1992 年竣工。原址被大火焚毀，
　後來由漢德瓦薩重新設計，廠區內利用垃圾焚化所產生的熱能，提
　供暖氣給維也納地區多達 23 萬戶住家，及學校或工業用暖氣】

extensively[5] 〔ɪkˋstɛnsɪvlɪ〕 *adv.* 廣泛地；大規模地
damage[2] 〔ˋdæmɪdʒ〕 *v.* 損害

1. (**B**)　(A) undergo[6] 〔͵ʌndəˋgo〕 *v.* 經歷
　　　　(B) ***undertake***[6] 〔͵ʌndəˋtek〕 *v.* 承擔；負責
　　　　(C) underestimate[6] 〔ˋʌndəˋɛstə͵met〕 *v.* 低估
　　　　(D) undermine[6] 〔͵ʌndəˋmaɪn〕 *v.* 損害

As part of the same renovation process, the plant—***which** provides*

Vienna with long-distance heating—was re-equipped *with the latest*

***and** most environmentally acceptable technology.* **While**

Hundertwasser was an enthusiastic supporter of the avoidance of

waste, he *also* knew ***that** the consequences for the environment would*

*actually be worse **if** the heating station were not* <u>put back into operation</u>.
　　　　　　　　　　　　　　　　　　　　　　　　　　　2

這座提供維也納廣大地區暖氣的焚化廠，重新裝設了最新，而且在環境
方面也最被接受的科技設備，這是修繕過程的一部份。雖然漢德瓦薩是
熱衷於支持避免垃圾，但他也知道，如果焚化暖氣廠沒有<u>恢復運作</u>的
話，對環境造成的結果其實會更糟。
　　　　　　　　　　　　　　　　　　　　　　2

* renovation 〔͵rɛnəˋveʃən〕 *n.* 修繕；翻新
　process[3] 〔ˋprɑsɛs〕 *n.* 過程
　provide[2] 〔prəˋvaɪd〕 *v.* 提供；供應
　Vienna 〔vɪˋɛnə〕 *n.* 維也納【奧地利首都】
　long-distance[2] 〔ˋlɔŋˋdɪstəns〕 *adj.* 遠距離的；長途的
　heating[1] 〔ˋhitɪŋ〕 *n.* 暖氣　　re-equip[4] 〔͵riiˋkwɪp〕 *v.* 重新裝設

re	+ nov	+ ation
again	+ *new*	+ *n.*

latest[2] 〔'letɪst 〕 *adj.* 最新的
environmentally[3] 〔 ɪn,vaɪrən'mɛntl̩ɪ 〕 *adv.* 在環境方面
acceptable[3] 〔 ək'sɛptəbl̩ 〕 *adj.* 可接受的；可容忍的
technology[3] 〔 tɛk'nɑlədʒɪ 〕 *n.* 科技
enthusiastic[4] 〔 ɪn,θuzɪ'æstɪk 〕 *adj.* 狂熱的
supporter[2] 〔 sə'portɚ 〕 *n.* 擁護者；支持者
avoidance[2] 〔 ə'vɔɪdn̩s 〕 *n.* 避免
waste[1] 〔 west 〕 *n.* 廢棄物
consequence[4] 〔'kɑnsə,kwɛns 〕 *n.* 後果

2. (**B**) (A) go to pieces 粉碎；崩潰
   (B) ***be put back into operation*** 再次開始運轉
   (C) come into being 產生；存在
   (D) get into debt 負債 debt[2] 〔 dɛt 〕 *n.* 債務

In his artistic scheme for Spittelau, Hundertwasser <u>drew upon</u>
                     3

the conventional materials *of industrial buildings, such as concrete,*

*steel, glass, ceramic **and** enamel, **but** employed them | in a fashion*

***which** robbed the plant of its aggressive **and** threatening character.*

  在漢德瓦薩對許皮特勞焚化廠的藝術方案中，他利用工業建築的傳
                  3
統材料，像是混凝土、鋼鐵、玻璃、陶土，以及琺瑯，運用它們來去除
焚化廠具侵略性和威脅性的特質。

  * artistic[4] 〔 ɑr'tɪstɪk 〕 *adj.* 藝術的
   scheme[5] 〔 skim 〕 *n.* 方案
   conventional[4] 〔 kən'vɛnʃənl̩ 〕 *adj.* 傳統的
   material[2] 〔 mə'tɪrɪəl 〕 *n.* 材料
   concrete[4] 〔'kɑnkrit 〕 *n.* 混凝土 steel[2] 〔 stil 〕 *n.* 鋼鐵

ceramic³ ﹝ sə'ræmɪk ﹞ *n.* 陶瓷

enamel ﹝ ɪ'næml̩ ﹞ *n.* 琺瑯；搪瓷   employ³ ﹝ ɪm'plɔɪ ﹞ *v.* 運用

fashion³ ﹝'fæʃən ﹞ *n.* 方式

rob³ ﹝ rɑb ﹞ *v.* 去除

aggressive⁴ ﹝ ə'grɛsɪv ﹞ *adj.* 有攻擊性的

threatening³ ﹝'θrɛtn̩ɪŋ ﹞ *adj.* 威脅的

character² ﹝'kærɪktɚ ﹞ *n.* 特質

> employ³ *v.* 運用
> = apply²
> = use¹

3. (**D**)   (A) refrain from 克制自己不要   (B) interfere in 干涉

          (C) leave off 停止   (D) ***draw upon*** 利用

He turned the exterior walls *into a mosaic of shimmering tiles*,

planted trees *on the roofs **and** terraces*, clothed the chimney stack

*in blue enamel panels **and*** encircled it *with a light-reflecting sphere*
4

***which** sparkles like a second sun in the sky.*

他將外牆變成閃亮的馬賽克拼貼瓷磚，並在屋頂跟平台上種植樹木，
又在煙囪外部披上藍色釉片的外衣，再用<u>反射光線的</u>巨大球面圍繞著
4
煙囪，這個球體就像空中的第二顆太陽一樣閃閃發亮。

   * ***turn A into B*** 使 A 變成 B

      mosaic ﹝ mo'zeɪk ﹞ *n.* 馬賽克；鑲嵌工藝

      shimmering ﹝'ʃɪmərɪŋ ﹞ *adj.* 閃閃發光的

      tile⁵ ﹝ taɪl ﹞ *n.* 瓷磚   roof¹ ﹝ ruf ﹞ *n.* 屋頂

      terrace⁵ ﹝'tɛrɪs ﹞ *n.* 陽台；高台

      clothe² ﹝ kloð ﹞ *v.* 使穿上衣服

      chimney³ ﹝'tʃɪmnɪ ﹞ *n.* 煙囪

      stack⁵ ﹝ stæk ﹞ *n.* 大煙筒；煙囪   ***chimney stack*** 煙囪

panel[4] 〔 'pæn! 〕 *n.* 金屬板;嵌板　　encircle 〔 ɪn'sɝk! 〕 *v.* 圍繞
sphere[6] 〔 sfɪr 〕 *n.* 球面;球體
sparkle[4] 〔 'spɑrk! 〕 *v.* 閃耀;發亮

4.(**B**)　空格應選形容詞修飾 sphere,依句意,球面(sphere)會自
　　　　行反射(reflect)光(light),應選形態為 N–V-ing 的複
　　　　合形容詞(動詞與所修飾的名詞為主動關係),故選 (B)
　　　　light-reflecting「 反射光線的 」。reflect[4] 〔 rɪ'flɛkt 〕 *v.* 反射

This *spectacular industrial* building is an example *of a*

*harmonious symbiosis of technology, ecology **and** art,* **and** acts as a

symbol *of inspiration for a <u>waste-free</u> society.*
　　　　　　　　　　　　　　　　5

　　這個壯觀的工業建築,是科技、生態,與藝術三者和諧共生的範
例,並且可以作為<u>無垃圾</u>社會的啓發象徵。
　　　　　5

　　* spectacular[6] 〔 spɛk'tækjələ 〕 *adj.* 壯觀的
　　industrial[3] 〔 ɪn'dʌstrɪəl 〕 *adj.* 工業的
　　harmonious[4] 〔 hɑr'monɪəs 〕 *adj.* 和諧的
　　symbiosis 〔ˏsɪmbaɪ'osɪs 〕 *n.* 共生關係
　　ecology[6] 〔 ɪ'kɑlədʒɪ 〕 *n.* 生態(學)
　　act as 當作　　symbol[2] 〔 'sɪmb! 〕 *n.* 象徵
　　inspiration[4] 〔ˏɪnspə'reʃən 〕 *n.* 靈感;啓發

sym	+ bio + sis
together	+ *life* + *n.*

act as 充當;當作
= serve as
= function as

5.(**B**)　(A) toll-free 〔ˏtol'fri 〕 *adj.* 不必付電話費的
　　　　　　toll[6] 〔 tol 〕 *n.* 通行費;長途電話費
　　　　　　free[1] 〔 fri 〕 *adj.* 免於⋯的;沒有⋯的
　　　　(B) ***waste-free*** 〔 'west'fri 〕 *adj.* 無垃圾的
　　　　(C) duty-free 〔 'djutɪ'fri 〕 *adj.* 免稅的　　duty[2] 〔 'djutɪ 〕 *n.* 關稅
　　　　(D) pain-free 〔 'pen'fri 〕 *adj.* 無痛的

TEST 17

Read the following passage and choose the best answer for each blank from the choices below.

Universally recognized as a symbol of good luck, the four-leaf clover is a frequent image on good luck coins, and good luck postcards. It ___1___ a lot of effort to find four-leaf clovers.

___2___ you have sharp eyesight can you find them among the other leaves. The origins of this belief are lost in time, but it's likely to come from the fact that the nutritional value of clover is high and domesticated animals ___3___ on a diet rich in clover grow fat and produce good milk. From this perhaps, the plant ___4___ the idea that it had the power to do good things. Throughout history four-leaf clovers have been thought to bring luck, ___5___ because they are uncommon. There are no clover plants that naturally produce four leaves. The mystique of the four-leaf clover continues today since finding a real four-leaf clover is still a rare occurrence and an omen of good luck.

1. (A) takes   (B) costs   (C) spends   (D) makes
2. (A) As if   (B) If only
   (C) Only when   (D) Even though
3. (A) which fed   (B) fed   (C) feed   (D) to feed
4. (A) added to   (B) gave in   (C) made for   (D) took on
5. (A) tentatively   (B) mostly   (C) lately   (D) scarcely

TEST 17 詳解

Universally recognized as a symbol of good luck, the four-leaf clover is a frequent image [*on good luck coins*, **and** good luck postcards.] It takes a lot of effort *to find four-leaf clovers*.
1

四葉幸運草普遍被認為是好運的象徵，是幸運幣、幸運明信片上經常用的圖像。要找到四葉幸運草，要花不少工夫。
1

* universally[4] 〔ˌjunəˈvɚslɪ〕 *adv.* 普遍地
  recognize[3] 〔ˈrɛkəgˌnaɪz〕 *v.* 承認　　symbol[2] 〔ˈsɪmbḷ〕 *n.* 象徵
  clover[5] 〔ˈklovɚ〕 *n.* 三葉草　　***four-leaf clover*** 四葉幸運草
  frequent[3] 〔ˈfrikwənt〕 *adj.* 經常的　　image[3] 〔ˈɪmɪdʒ〕 *n.* 形象；圖像
  postcard[2] 〔ˈpostˌkɑrd〕 *n.* 明信片　　effort[2] 〔ˈɛfɚt〕 *n.* 努力

1. (**A**)　依句意，表「花（工夫）；費（心血/努力）」，須用 take，
　　　　it ***take***(*s*) + effort + to V. 「做…花費努力」，故選 (A)。
　　　　而 (B) cost「花費（金錢）」，it cost(s) + 人 + 錢 + to V.，
　　　　(C) spend「（人）花（時間/金錢）」，(D) make「做」，
　　　　皆不合句意。

*Only **when** you have sharp eyesight* can you find them *among the*
2
other leaves. The origins *of this belief* are lost *in time*, **but** it's likely to come from the fact ***that** the nutritional value of clover is high **and** domesticated animals fed on a diet rich in clover* grow fat **and** produce
3
good milk.

只有當你眼光夠銳利的時候，才可能在其他葉草中找到它們。四葉
草的起源已不可考，但可能是因為這種植物的營養價值相當高，而且以
它為食的家畜不僅長得很好，也能產出很棒的乳汁。

* sharp¹〔 ʃɑrp 〕 *adj.* 銳利的   eyesight⁶〔 'aɪ,saɪt 〕 *n.* 視力
  origin³〔 'ɔrədʒɪn 〕 *n.* 起源   belief²〔 bɪ'lif 〕 *n.* 信念；看法
  be lost in time 不可考   ***be likely to V.*** 可能…
  come from 來自   nutritional⁶〔 nju'trɪʃən! 〕 *adj.* 營養的
  domesticated〔 də'mɛstə,ketɪd 〕 *adj.*（動物）被馴養的
  rich¹〔 rɪtʃ 〕 *adj.* 豐富的   ***be rich in*** 有豐富的…

2. (**C**) 由主要子句 can you find 可知，本句為倒裝，「Only + 副詞/
   副詞片語/副詞子句 + 助動詞/be + 主詞」，故選 (C) *Only when*
   「只有在…的時候」。而 (A) as if「就好像」，(B) if only「要
   是；只要」，(D) even though「即使」，用法與句意皆不合。

3. (**B**) 空格應填關代引導形容詞子句，修飾先行詞 animals，又「以
   …為食」是 feed on 或 be fed on，而 *which feed* on…或
   which are fed on…也可簡化為 feeding on 或 being fed on，
   又 being 可省略，故選 (B) *fed*。

From this perhaps, the plant <u>took on</u> the idea *that it had the power*
                                              4
to do good things. Throughout history four-leaf clovers have been

thought to bring luck, <u>*mostly* **because** *they are uncommon*</u>. There are
                              5
no clover plants ***that** naturally produce four leaves*. The mystique *of*

the four-leaf clover continues *today* **since** *finding a real four-leaf*

clover is still a rare occurrence **and** *an omen of good luck.*

也許就是因爲這樣，這種植物<u>讓</u>大家認爲它具有帶來好事的力量。自古
　　　　　　　　　　　　　 4
以來，四葉幸運草一直被認爲能帶來好運，<u>主要是因爲它們很罕見</u>。沒
　　　　　　　　　　　　　　　　　　　　5
有任何的三葉草會自然生長出四瓣葉子。直到今天，四葉草依舊很神
祕，因爲找到它仍然是很罕見的事，也是個好預兆。

> * ***throughout history*** 歷史上；自古以來
> uncommon[1] 〔 ʌn'kɑmən 〕 *adj.* 不常見的
> mystique 〔 mɪs'tik 〕 *n.* 神祕性　　　rare[2] 〔 rɛr 〕 *adj.* 罕見的
> occurrence[5] 〔 ə'kʒəns 〕 *n.* 事件　　omen 〔'omən 〕 *n.* 預兆

4. (**D**)　(A) add to 增加　　　　　　(B) give in 讓步
　　　　　　(C) make for 導致　　　　　(D) ***take on*** 呈現；獲得
　　　　　　From this perhaps, this plant took on the idea that it had
　　　　　　the power to do good things.
　　　　　　= Perhaps this is why people began to believe that a
　　　　　　four-leaf clover had the power to do good things.

5. (**B**)　(A) tentatively[5] 〔'tɛntətɪvlɪ 〕 *adv.* 試驗性地；暫時地
　　　　　　(B) ***mostly***[4] 〔'mostlɪ 〕 *adv.* 大多；主要地
　　　　　　(C) lately[4] 〔'letlɪ 〕 *adv.* 最近 (= *recently*[2])
　　　　　　(D) scarcely[4] 〔'skɛrslɪ 〕 *adv.* 幾乎不 (= *hardly*[2])

【補充資料】
　　四葉草是車軸草屬植物的稀有變種，在西方認爲能找到四葉
草是幸運的象徵，在日本則認爲會得到幸福，所以又稱幸運草，
大概十萬株三葉草中只會有一株是四葉的。傳說中幸運草的四片
葉子所代表的意思，有以下兩種說法：
1. 第一片葉子代表希望，第二片表示信心，第三片是愛情，而多出來的第
　　四片葉子則是幸運的象徵。這種說法與基督教的信、望、愛相符。
2. 第一片葉子代表真愛，第二片代表健康，第三片代表名譽，第四片代表
　　財富。
　　在臺灣，因爲其葉子形狀與酢漿草相似，所以「四葉草」普遍所指的
是四葉的酢漿草，而不是四葉的三葉草。

TEST 18

Read the following passage and choose the best answer for each blank from the choices below.

TED (Technology, Entertainment and Design) is a worldwide set of conferences owned by the private non-profit Sapling Foundation, formed to __1__ ideas __2__.

TED was founded in 1984 as a one-off event. The annual conference began in 1990, in Monterey, California. TED's early emphasis was technology and design, __3__ its origins in the Silicon Valley. The events are now held in Long Beach and Palm Springs in the U.S. and in Europe and Asia and offer __4__ streaming of the talks. They address a wide range of topics within the research and practice of science and culture, often through storytelling. The speakers are given a maximum of 18 minutes to present their ideas in the most innovative and engaging ways they can. Past presenters include Bill Clinton, Bill Gates, Larry Page, and many Nobel Prize winners, __5__ many others.

1. (A) paralyze   (B) publicize   (C) bet   (D) dig
2. (A) worth to be spread   (B) worthy being spreading
   (C) worth spreading   (D) to be worthy to spread
3. (A) familiar with   (B) accompanied by
   (C) abiding by   (D) consistent with
4. (A) liberal   (B) main   (C) off-record   (D) live
5. (A) among   (B) not to mention
   (C) so are   (D) let alone

TEST 18 詳解

TED (Technology, Entertainment and Design) is a worldwide

set of conferences *owned by the private non-profit Sapling*

Foundation, formed to publicize ideas worth spreading.
　　　　　　　　　1　　　　　2

　　　TED（科技、娛樂和設計）是一組由私人非營利的沙普林基金會所擁有的全球性會談，旨在宣傳，值得傳播的想法。
　　　　　　　　　　　　　　　　1　　　2

* technology[3] 〔tɛk'nɑlədʒɪ〕 *n.* 科技
  entertainment[4] 〔͵ɛntɚ'tenmənt〕 *n.* 娛樂
  design[2] 〔dɪ'zaɪn〕 *n.* 設計
  worldwide 〔'wɜld'waɪd〕 *adj.* 世界性的；遍及全球的
  set[1] 〔sɛt〕 *n.* 一套；一組
  conference[4] 〔'kɑnfərəns〕 *n.* 會議；會談
  private[2] 〔'praɪvɪt〕 *adj.* 私人的
  non-profit 〔͵nɑn'prɑfɪt〕 *adj.* 非營利的
  sapling 〔'sæplɪŋ〕 *n.* 樹苗；年輕人
  foundation[4] 〔faʊn'deʃən〕 *n.* 基金會
  form[2] 〔fɔrm〕 *v.* 形成；建立　　idea[1] 〔aɪ'diə〕 *n.* 想法

1. (**B**)　(A) paralyze[6] 〔'pærə͵laɪz〕 *v.* 使麻痺；使癱瘓
   　　　　　(B) ***publicize***[5] 〔'pʌblɪs͵aɪz〕 *v.* 公布；發表；宣傳
   　　　　　(C) bet[2] 〔bɛt〕 *v.* 打賭
   　　　　　(D) dig[1] 〔dɪg〕 *v.* 挖

2. (**C**)　「值得傳播的想法」ideas which are worth spreading，可省略關代和 be 動詞，故選 (C) *worth spreading*。
   　　　　　worth[2] 〔wɝθ〕 *adj.* 值得…的　　*be worth + V-ing* 值得…
   　　　　　spread[2] 〔dprɛd〕 *v.* 散播；傳播

TED was founded *in 1984 as a one-off event*. The annual

conference began *in 1990*, *in Monterey, California*. TED's early

emphasis was technology **and** design, <u>*consistent with* its origins in</u>
3

the Silicon Valley. The events are *now* held *in Long Beach **and** Palm*

Springs in the U.S. **and** *in Europe and Asia* **and** offer <u>live</u> streaming
4

of the talks.

　　TED 成立於 1984 年，就像是僅只一次的大型活動。年度會談開始
於 1990 年，在加州的蒙特雷舉辦。TED 早期的重點是科技和設計，<u>與</u>
　　　　　　　　　　　　　　　　　　　　　　　　　　　　　　3
<u>其在矽谷的起源</u><u>一致</u>。現在會談活動在美國的長堤和棕櫚泉舉行，在歐
　　　　　　3
洲和亞洲舉行的會談，則是提供<u>現場</u><u>直播</u>串流。
　　　　　　　　　　　　　　4

* found³ 〔 faʊnd 〕 v. 創立　　one-off adj. 僅一次的
  event² 〔 ɪˈvɛnt 〕 n. 事件；大事；大型活動
  annual⁴ 〔ˈænjʊəl 〕 adj. 每年的；一年一度的
  Monterey 〔ˌmɑntəˈre 〕 n. 蒙特雷
  emphasis⁴ 〔ˈɛmfəsɪs 〕 n. 強調；重視；重點

$$\begin{array}{ccc} \text{ann} & + & \text{ual} \\ | & & | \\ \textit{year} & + & \textit{adj.} \end{array}$$

  origins³ 〔ˈɔrədʒɪnz 〕 n. pl. 起源；出身；來歷
  silicon⁶ 〔ˈsɪlɪkən 〕 n. 矽　　valley² 〔ˈvælɪ 〕 n. 山谷
Silicon Valley 矽谷【在美國加州舊金山市郊，為精密電子工業集中地】
Long Beach 長堤【美國加州洛杉磯南方的一個城市】
Palm Springs 棕櫚泉【位於洛杉磯東邊的沙漠綠洲】
streaming² 〔ˈstrimɪŋ 〕 n. 串流【將一連串的影音壓縮後，經網際網路
　　分段傳送資料，在網路上及時傳輸影音的一種技術】

3. (**D**)　(A) familiar with　對…熟悉
　　　　　(B) accompanied by　由…陪伴；和…同時發生
　　　　　(C) abiding by　遵守
　　　　　(D) ***consistent with***　和…一致

4. (**D**)　(A) liberal³ (ˈlɪbərəl) *adj.* 開明的
　　　　　(B) main² (men) *adj.* 主要的
　　　　　(C) off-record (ˌɔfˈrɛkəd) *adj.* 非正式的；不得發表的
　　　　　(D) ***live***¹ (laɪv) *adj.* 現場的

They address a wide range of topics *within the research **and** practice of science **and** culture, often through storytelling.* The speakers are given a maximum *of 18 minutes* to present their ideas *in the most innovative **and** engaging ways they can.* Past presenters include Bill Clinton, Bill Gates, Larry Page, ***and*** many Nobel Prize winners, *among many others.*
　5

他們通常透過講故事，來演說各式各樣的主題，都和研究、科學的應用，以及文化有關。演講者最多有18分鐘，以最創新，和最有吸引力的方式，來呈現他們的想法。過去的演講者包括比爾‧克林頓、比爾‧蓋茲、賴瑞‧佩吉，以及許多諾貝爾獎得主也在其中。
　　　　　　　　　　　　　　　　5

* address¹ (əˈdrɛs) *v.* 演說
range² (rendʒ) *n.* 範圍；（變化的）幅度
a wide range of 各式各樣的
within² (wɪðˈɪn) *prep.* 在…之內

Bill Clinton

practice[1] 〔'præktɪs 〕 *n.* 實行；實踐；（知識的）應用

maximum[4] 〔'mæksəməm 〕 *n.* 最大量

present[2] 〔 prɪ'zɛnt 〕 *v.* 呈現

innovative[6] 〔'ɪnə,vetɪv 〕 *adj.* 創新的

engaging[3] 〔 ɪn'gedʒɪŋ 〕 *adj.* 吸引人的

Larry Page *n.* 賴瑞・佩吉【全球知名的搜尋引擎 Google 創辦人
之一】

Nobel Prize 諾貝爾獎　　winner[2] 〔'wɪnɚ 〕 *n.* 得獎者

5. (**A**)　(A) ***among***[1] 〔 ə'mʌŋ 〕 *prep.* 在…當中

　　　　(B) not to mention　更不用說

　　　　(C) so are　…也是

　　　　(D) let alone　更不用說（ = *not to mention* = *not to speak of*
　　　　　 = *to say nothing of* ）

---

among 的用法：

作「在…當中；被…所圍繞」解

(= *in the middle of* ; *surrounded by*) 。

He built a house ***among*** the trees.

（他在樹林中蓋了一棟房子。）

The town lies ***among*** the mountains.

（這個城鎮被群山圍繞。）

【詳見「文法寶典」p.552】

TEST 19

Read the following passage and choose the best answer for each blank from the choices below.

Modern people often feel pressure to meet our society's preferences in looks. It can become hard for one to achieve success in life and love ___1___ he or she fits a certain image. For the last few decades, the desired look has been to be extremely thin. It is important, therefore, to be aware that habits you develop in order to achieve or maintain a low weight can become excessive and make you ___2___ potentially serious illnesses, one of which is an eating disorder.

The difference between trying to lose weight and having an eating disorder is not easy to detect. Serious eating problems may ___3___ as a simple wish, such as the desire to fit into a favorite swimsuit, but eventually become a preoccupation in the person's life. When a person's diet and fitness routine becomes extremely strict and inflexible and interferes with his or her ability to enjoy life and stay in good health, ___4___ when his or her self worth is determined by his or her size, that is a sign of an eating disorder.

If you have an eating disorder, don't ___5___. Talk to someone you trust, and ask for support. Usually the best way of dealing with an eating disorder is just a change of attitude and behavior.

1. (A) while   (B) despite
   (C) unless   (D) as

2. (A) familiar with   (B) vulnerable to
   (C) similar to   (D) popular with

3. (A) end up   (B) drop in
   (C) start out   (D) stand by

4. (A) so   (B) but
   (C) or   (D) for

5. (A) show it off   (B) speed it up
   (C) give it a try   (D) keep it a secret

要養成做題目的習慣，越做越喜歡做，這本「7000字克漏字測驗詳解」完全不需要查字典，你會越做越快。可自己給自己計時。

TEST 19 詳解

Modern people often feel pressure *to meet our society's preferences in looks.* It can become hard *for one* to achieve success in life **and** love **unless** he **or** she fits a certain image. *For the last few decades*, the desired look has been to be *extremely* thin. It is important, *therefore*, to be aware **that** habits you develop in order to achieve **or** maintain a low weight can become excessive **and** make you vulnerable to *potentially* serious illnesses, *one of **which** is an eating disorder.*

現代人為了要符合社會所偏好的外表，經常會覺得有壓力。除非他或她符合某種形象，否則要在生活和愛情裡取得成功，可能會變得困難。最近幾十年來，社會所期望的外表，一直是極度苗條的。因此，很重要的一點是，要察覺你自己為了達到或維持很輕的體重而養成的習慣，可能是過度的，而且會讓你容易得到可能會很嚴重的疾病，其中之一就是飲食失調。

* modern[2] (ˈmɑdən) *adj.* 現代的　　pressure[3] (ˈprɛʃə) *n.* 壓力
  meet[1] (mit) *v.* 符合；達到　　preference[5] (ˈprɛfərəns) *n.* 偏好
  looks[1] (lʊks) *n. pl.* 外表　　achieve[3] (əˈtʃiv) *v.* 達到；獲得
  fit[2] (fɪt) *v.* 符合；適合　　certain[1] (ˈsɝtn̩) *adj.* 某種

image[3] 〔'ɪmɪdʒ 〕 *n.* 形象　　decade[3] 〔'dɛked 〕 *n.* 十年
desired[2] 〔 dɪ'zaɪrd 〕 *adj.* 所期望的；所想要的
extremely[3] 〔 ɪk'strimlɪ 〕 *adv.* 極度地；非常
aware[3] 〔 ə'wɛr 〕 *adj.* 知道的；察覺到的　　habit[2] 〔'hæbɪt 〕 *n.* 習慣
develop[2] 〔 dɪ'vɛləp 〕 *v.* 培養　　*in order to V.* 為了…
maintain[3] 〔 men'ten 〕 *v.* 維持　　weight[1] 〔 wet 〕 *n.* 體重
excessive[6] 〔 ɪk'sɛsɪv 〕 *adj.* 過度的
potentially[5] 〔 pə'tɛnʃəlɪ 〕 *adv.* 潛在地；可能地
illness[2] 〔'ɪlnɪs 〕 *n.* 疾病

ex	+	cess	+	ive
out	+	go	+	adj.

disorder[4] 〔 dɪs'ɔrdɚ 〕 *n.* 失調；疾病　　*eating disorder* 飲食失調

1. (**C**)　依句意，選 (C) *unless*「除非」。
　　　　而 (A) while「當…的時候；雖然」，(B) despite「儘管」，
　　　　(D) as「當…的時候」，皆不合句意。

2. (**B**)　(A) familiar with　對…熟悉
　　　　(B) *vulnerable to*　易受…傷害；易受…影響
　　　　(C) similar to　和…類似
　　　　(D) popular with　受…歡迎

The difference *between trying to lose weight **and** having an*

eating disorder is not easy to detect.　Serious eating problems may

start out *as a simple wish, such as the desire to fit into a favorite*
　3

swimsuit, ***but** eventually* become a preoccupation *in the person's life.*

　　想要減重和患有飲食失調之間的差別，是不容易發現的。嚴重的飲
食問題，可能是從一個簡單的願望開始，像是想穿進一件最喜愛的泳裝
　　　　　　　　　　　　　　　3
的願望，但是到最後卻變成了在生活中全神貫注的事。

```
* detect² 〔 dɪˈtɛkt 〕v. 發現　　　wish¹ 〔 wɪʃ 〕n. 願望
  such as 像是　　　desire² 〔 dɪˈzaɪr 〕v. 渴望
  fit into 穿進　　　swimsuit 〔ˈswɪmˌsut 〕n. 泳裝
  eventually⁴ 〔 ɪˈvɛntʃʊəlɪ 〕adv. 最後
  preoccupation 〔 priˌɑkjəˈpeʃən 〕n. 熱中的事物；全神貫注之事
```

3. (**C**)　(A) end up 結果（成為）　　　(B) drop in 順道拜訪
　　　　　　(C) **start out** 開始　　　　　　(D) stand by 待命

When a person's diet **and** fitness routine becomes extremely strict **and** inflexible **and** interferes with his **or** her ability to enjoy life **and** stay in good health, **or when** his or her self worth is determined by his or her
　　　　　　　　　　　4
size, that is a sign of an eating disorder.

當一個人的飲食控制和健身規劃，變得過於嚴格死板，而且妨礙到自己享受人生和維持健康的能力時，或是當他或她的自身價值，是由身材來
　　　　　　　　　　　　　　　4
決定時，那就是飲食失調的徵兆。

```
* diet³ 〔ˈdaɪət 〕n. 飲食控制
  fitness 〔ˈfɪtnɪs 〕n. 健康
  routine⁴ 〔 ruˈtin 〕n. 例行公事；
    慣常的程序
  fitness routine 健身規劃　　strict² 〔 strɪkt 〕adj. 嚴格的
  inflexible⁴ 〔 ɪnˈflɛksəbl̩ 〕adj. 無彈性的；不可改變的
  interfere⁴ 〔ˌɪntəˈfɪr 〕v. 妨礙 < with >
  self worth 自我價值
  determine³ 〔 dɪˈtɜmɪn 〕v. 決定（ = decide¹ ）
  size¹ 〔 saɪz 〕n. 尺寸；身材
  sign² 〔 saɪn 〕n. 跡象；徵兆
```

balanced diet 均衡的飲食
low-calorie diet 低卡路里飲食
proper diet 適當的飲食
vegetarian diet 素食

self worth 自我價值
self-esteem n. 自尊
self-reliance n. 自立
self-defense n. 自衛

4. (**C**)　依句意，選 (C) *or*「或；或者」。
　　　　　而 (A) so「所以」，(B) but「但是」，(D) for「因爲」，
　　　　　皆不合句意。

If you have an eating disorder, don't <u>keep it a secret</u>.　Talk to
　　　　　　　　　　　　　　　　　　　　5

someone *you trust*, **and** ask for support.　*Usually* the best way *of*

dealing with an eating disorder is *just* a change *of attitude* **and**

behavior.

　　如果你飲食失調，不要<u>隱瞞</u>這件事。告訴你信任的人，並請求幫
　　　　　　　　　　　5
助。通常處理飲食失調的最佳辦法，就只是改變態度和行爲而已。

　　* *ask for* 請求　　　support[2]〔sə'port〕*n.* 支持；援助
　　　deal with 應付；處理 (= *cope with* = *handle*[2])
　　　attitude[3]〔'ætə,tjud〕*n.* 態度
　　　behavior[4]〔bɪ'hevjɚ〕*n.* 行爲

5. (**D**)　(A) show it off 炫耀
　　　　　(B) speed it up 加速
　　　　　(C) give it a try 試試看
　　　　　(D) *keep it a secret* 保密；隱瞞

TEST 20

Read the following passage and choose the best answer for each blank from the choices below.

A great number of people travel on wheels to and from work. For commuters in major cities all over the world, nothing is ___1___ than being stuck in a traffic jam at the end of a long day. In some of the worst affected cities, commuters spend two to three hours ___2___ per day traveling to and from work. It goes without saying that officials in those cities ___3___ to come up with methods aimed at preventing traffic jams.

In 2003, a congestion charge was introduced in London for vehicles entering the city center between 7:00 AM and 6:00 PM on weekdays. The London government hopes that people will switch to public transportation due to the charge, ___4___ substantially reducing the traffic.

The Netherlands, with one of the most congested traffic zones in Europe, is planning to implement a pay-per-kilometer scheme, where motorists will be monitored by GPS and charged ___5___ the distance they drive.

Whatever the scheme is, traffic jams are here to stay. As long as the number of cars keeps rising, cities will never cease to work on ways to reduce the mess caused by traffic jams.

1. (A) better   (B) more
   (C) less   (D) worse

2. (A) in person   (B) on average
   (C) with time   (D) at ease

3. (A) spare no effort (B) make ends meet
   (C) strike a balance (D) break the ice

4. (A) so that   (B) however
   (C) thus   (D) though

5. (A) regardless of   (B) in case of
   (C) on account of   (D) according to

每做一回新試題前，立刻把
前面的試題唸一遍，再做下一回
試題，就變簡單了！試試看，會
有想不到的效果。

TEST 20 詳解

A great number of people travel *on wheels to and from work.*

For commuters in major cities all over the world, nothing is <u>worse</u>
1

than being stuck in a traffic jam at the end of a long day. *In some of*

the worst affected cities, commuters spend two to three hours <u>*on*</u>

<u>*average*</u> *per day* traveling *to and from work.* It goes without saying
2

that officials in those cities <u>spare no effort</u> to come up with methods
3

aimed at preventing traffic jams.

　　許多人上下班以車代步。對全球大都市的通勤者來說，沒有什麼比
忙完了一天，卻被困在交通阻塞之中<u>更糟</u>的事了。在一些交通最糟糕的
　　　　　　　　　　　　　　　　　1
都市中，通勤者<u>平均</u>每天花費兩到三小時通勤上下班。當然，那些市府
　　　　　　2
官員都<u>不遺餘力</u>地試圖想出防止交通阻塞的方法。
　　　3

*　＊ a great number of* 很多的 (*= many*[1])
　　travel[2] (ˋtrævḷ) *v.* 行進
　　wheel[2] (hwil) *n.* 輪子；(*pl.*) 汽車 (*= a car*)
　　commuter[5] (kəˋmjutɚ) *n.* 通勤者【commute[5] *v.* 通勤】
　　major[3] (ˋmedʒɚ) *adj.* 主要的；較大的　　*major city* 大都市
　　be stuck in 被困在…當中 (*= be trapped in*)

a traffic jam 塞車 (= *traffic congestion*)
affect[3] ﹝ əˈfɛkt ﹞ *v.* 影響
it goes without saying that 不用說 (= *needless to say*)
official[2] ﹝ əˈfɪʃəl ﹞ *n.* 官員　　*come up with* 提出；想出
method[2] ﹝ˈmɛθəd ﹞ *n.* 方法　　*be aimed at* 針對
prevent[3] ﹝ prɪˈvɛnt ﹞ *v.* 防止

1. (**D**)　依句意，選 (D) *worse*「更糟的；更差的」。
　　　　　而 (A) better「更好的」，(B) more「更多的」，
　　　　　(C) less「更少的」，則不合句意。

2. (**B**)　(A) in person 親自
　　　　　(B) *on average* 平均而言
　　　　　(C) with time 隨著時間
　　　　　(D) at ease 自在的

3. (**A**)　(A) *spare no effort* 不遺餘力
　　　　　　　spare[4] ﹝ spɛr ﹞ *v.* 吝惜；節省使用
　　　　　(B) make ends meet 使收支平衡
　　　　　(C) strike a balance 達到平衡
　　　　　(D) break the ice 打破僵局

In 2003, a congestion charge was introduced *in London for*

*vehicles entering the city center between 7:00 AM **and** 6:00 PM on*

weekdays. The London government hopes ***that** people will switch to*

public transportation due to the charge, <u>thus</u> substantially reducing

the traffic.

　　2003 年，倫敦推行了一項交通阻塞稅，於平日早上七點至晚上六點之間進入市中心的車輛必須繳交。倫敦市政府希望這項費用能讓人們轉而搭乘大眾運輸工具，<u>因而</u>大幅減低交通流量。
4

* congestion〔kənˈdʒɛstʃən〕*n.* 阻塞
　charge[2]〔tʃɑrdʒ〕*n.* 費用　*v.* 收費
　introduce[2]〔ˌɪntrəˈdjus〕*v.* 引進；推行
　vehicle[3]〔ˈviɪkl̩〕*n.* 車輛　　weekday[2]〔ˈwikˌde〕*n.* 平日
　switch[3]〔swɪtʃ〕*v.* 轉換　　*public transportation*　大眾運輸工具
　due to　由於（＝*owing to*）
　substantially[5]〔səbˈstænʃəlɪ〕*adv.* 實質上；大大地
　reduce[3]〔rɪˈdjus〕*v.* 減少　　traffic[2]〔ˈtræfɪk〕*n.* 交通流量

4.(**C**)　依句意，應選 (C) *thus*「因此」。
　　　而 (A) so that「以便於；所以」，(B) however「然而」，
　　　(D) though「雖然」，則不合句意。

　　The Netherlands, *with one of the most congested traffic zones in Europe*, is planning to implement a pay-per-kilometer scheme, *where motorists will be monitored by GPS and charged <u>according to</u> the distance they drive.*
5

　　全歐洲交通最擁塞區域之一的荷蘭，正打算實施一個依公里數付費的計畫，汽車駕駛人將被全球定位系統監控，<u>並且依據</u>他們所行駛的距離收費。
5

* *the Netherlands*　荷蘭
　congested〔kənˈdʒɛstɪd〕*adj.* 阻塞的
　implement[6]〔ˈɪmpləˌmɛnt〕*v.* 實施　　per[2]〔pɝ〕*prep.* 每…

kilometer[3] (ˈkɪləˌmitɚ) *n.* 公里　　scheme[5] (skim) *n.* 計畫
motorist (ˈmotərɪst) *n.* 汽車駕駛人
monitor[4] (ˈmɑnətɚ) *v.* 監控
GPS 全球定位系統 (= *Global Positioning System*)
distance[2] (ˈdɪstəns) *n.* 距離

5. (**D**)　(A) regardless of　不管；不論；不分
　　　　　(B) in case of　如果有
　　　　　(C) on account of　因為 (= *because of*)
　　　　　(D) *according to*　依據

Whatever the scheme is, traffic jams are here to stay. *As long as*

the number of cars keeps rising, cities will *never* cease to work on

ways *to reduce the mess caused by traffic jams.*

　　無論計畫是什麼，交通阻塞是不會消失的。只要車輛的數量持續攀
升，城市就必須不停地想辦法，減少交通阻塞帶來的混亂。

*　* be here to stay　會持續存在
　as long as　只要 (= *so long as*)
　rise[1] (raɪz) *v.* 上升；增加
　cease[4] (sis) *v.* 停止
　work on　致力於
　mess[3] (mɛs) *n.* 混亂
　cause[1] (kɔz) *v.* 造成

| rise *v.* 上升；升起 |
| raise *v.* 提高；舉起；養育 |
| arise *v.* 發生 |
| arouse *v.* 喚起 |

TEST 21

Read the following passage and choose the best answer for each blank from the choices below.

Fish and chips is a popular <u>take-away</u> food in the United Kingdom. It __1__ fish which is <u>battered</u> and then <u>deep-fried</u> served with <u>chips</u>. It is sometimes accompanied by other items such as mushy peas or tartar sauce. Fish and chips became a stock meal among the <u>working classes</u> in Great Britain __2__ the rapid development of <u>trawl fishing</u> in the <u>North Sea</u>, and the development of railways which connected the ports to major industrial cities during the second half of the 19th century, which meant that fresh fish could be rapidly transported to the heavily __3__ areas. Fish-and-chip shops traditionally wrapped their product in newspaper, or with an inner layer of white paper and an outer layer of newspaper or blank <u>newsprint</u> for __4__ and to absorb grease, though the use of newspaper for wrapping has almost ceased by virtue of hygiene. Nowadays establishments usually use food-quality wrapping paper, occasionally __5__ on the outside to emulate newspaper.

1. (A) lies in   (B) applies for (C) consists of (D) relies on
2. (A) as a result of   (B) in accordance with
   (C) with a view to   (D) in search of
3. (A) populated   (B) popular
   (C) productive(D) prospective
4. (A) consolation   (B) insulation
   (C) resolution   (D) revolution
5. (A) printing   (B) printed   (C) print   (D) to print

TEST 21 詳解

Fish **and** chips is a popular <u>take-away</u> food *in the United Kingdom*. It <u>consists of</u> fish **which** *is <u>battered</u>* **and** *then <u>deep-fried</u> served with <u>chips</u>*. It is *sometimes* accompanied *by other items such as mushy peas* **or** *tartar sauce*. Fish **and** chips became a stock meal *among the <u>working classes</u> in Great Britain* <u>*as a result of*</u> *the rapid development of <u>trawl fishing</u> in the <u>North Sea</u>,* **and** *the development of railways* **which** *connected the ports to major industrial cities during the second half of the 19th century,* **which** *meant* **that** *fresh fish could be rapidly transported to the heavily <u>populated</u> areas.*

在英國，炸魚薯條是很受歡迎的外帶食物。它是由裹著麵粉的魚下去油炸，佐以薯條而<u>組成</u>。它有時會搭配其他品項，像是豌豆泥或塔塔醬。炸魚薯條成為英國勞動階級間的慣用飲食，這是<u>因為</u>北海拖網捕魚的快速發展，以及十九世紀後半期間，連接港口和主要工業城市的鐵路的發展，這意味著鮮魚可以迅速運送到<u>人口居住</u>稠密的地區。

* chips³〔tʃɪps〕*n. pl.* 炸薯條；洋芋片　　***fish and chips*** 炸魚薯條
take-away〔'tekə'we〕*adj.* 外帶的 (= *take-out*)
the United Kingdom 英國 (= *the U.K.*)
batter⁵〔'bætɚ〕*v.* 裹麵糊；重擊　　deep-fry〔'dip'fraɪ〕*v.* 油炸
serve¹〔sɝv〕*v.* 供應；上（菜）

accompany[4]〔ə'kʌmpənɪ〕v. 伴隨
item[2]〔'aɪtəm〕n. 物品；項目　　mushy〔'mʌʃɪ〕adj. 糊狀的
pea[3]〔pi〕n. 豌豆　　***tartar sauce*** 塔塔醬
stock[6]〔stɑk〕adj. 慣用的；常備的　　***working class*** 勞動階級
Great Britain 大不列顛；英國　　rapid[2]〔'ræpɪd〕adj. 快速的
development[2]〔dɪ'vɛləpmənt〕n. 發展　　trawl〔trɔl〕n. 拖網
fishing〔'fɪʃɪŋ〕n. 捕魚　　***the North Sea*** 北海
railway[1]〔'rel‚we〕n. 鐵路
connect A to B 連接 A 與 B (= *connect A with B* = *connect A and B*)
port[2]〔pɔrt〕n. 港口　　industrial[3]〔ɪn'dʌstrɪəl〕adj. 工業的
transport[3]〔træns'port〕v. 運送　　heavily[1]〔'hɛvɪlɪ〕adj. 大量地

1. (**C**)　(A) lie in　在於；位於
　　　　　(B) apply for　申請；應徵
　　　　　(C) ***consist of***　由⋯組成；包含
　　　　　(D) rely on　依賴

> consist of　由⋯組成
> = comprise
> = be $\begin{cases} \text{composed} \\ \text{made up} \\ \text{comprised} \end{cases}$ of

2. (**A**)　(A) ***as a result of***　因為；由於
　　　　　(B) in accordance with　依照；與⋯一致
　　　　　(C) with a view to　為了
　　　　　(D) in search of　尋找

3. (**A**)　(A) ***populate***[6]〔'pɑpjə‚let〕v. 居住於
　　　　　heavily populated 人口稠密的
　　　　　(B) popular[3]〔'pɑpjələ〕adj. 受歡迎的
　　　　　(C) productive[4]〔prə'dʌktɪv〕adj. 有生產力的
　　　　　(D) prospective[6]〔prə'spɛktɪv〕adj. 有希望的；有未來的

Fish-and-chip shops *traditionally* wrapped their product *in*

newspaper, ***or*** *with an inner layer of white paper* ***and*** *an outer layer*

of newspaper ***or*** *blank* <u>*newsprint*</u> *for* <u>*insulation*</u> ***and*** *to absorb grease,* *though* the use of newspaper for wrapping has almost ceased by

virtue of hygiene. *Nowadays* establishments *usually* use food-quality

wrapping paper, *occasionally printed on the outside to emulate*
5

newspaper.

傳統上，炸魚薯條店會將他們的商品包在報紙裡，也就是內層白紙和外層報紙或空白新聞紙，為了<u>隔絕</u>和吸附油脂，雖然由於衛生的關係，幾
4
乎已經停止使用報紙來包裝了。如今，企業通常使用食品級包裝紙，偶爾會仿照報紙，在包裝紙外面<u>印東西</u>。
5

* traditionally² 〔 trə'dıʃənəḷı 〕 *adv.* 傳統上　　wrap³ 〔 ræp 〕 *v.* 包裹
product³ 〔'prɑdəkt 〕 *n.* 產品　　inner³ 〔'ınɚ 〕 *adj.* 內部的
layer⁵ 〔'leɚ 〕 *n.* 層　　outer³ 〔'aʊtɚ 〕 *adj.* 外部的
blank² 〔 blæŋk 〕 *adj.* 空白的　　newsprint 〔'njuz,prınt 〕 *n.* 新聞用紙
absorb⁴ 〔 əb'sɔrb 〕 *v.* 吸收　　grease⁵ 〔 gris 〕 *n.* 油脂
cease⁴ 〔 sis 〕 *v.* 停止　　*by virtue of* 由於
hygiene⁶ 〔'haɪdʒin 〕 *n.* 衛生　　nowadays⁴ 〔'naʊə,dez 〕 *adv.* 現在
establishment⁴ 〔 ə'stæblıʃmənt 〕 *n.* 建立的機構；企業
food-quality 〔'fud'kwɑlətı 〕 *adj.* 食品等級的
occasionally⁴ 〔 ə'keʒəṇḷı 〕 *adv.* 偶爾　　emulate 〔'ɛmjə,let 〕 *v.* 模仿

4. (**B**)　(A) consolation⁶ 〔,kɑnsə'leʃən 〕 *n.* 安慰
　　　　(B) *insulation* 〔,ınsə'leʃən 〕 *n.* 隔絕
　　　　(C) resolution⁴ 〔,rɛzə'luʃən 〕 *n.* 決心
　　　　(D) revolution⁴ 〔,rɛvə'luʃən 〕 *n.* 革命

5. (**B**)　此句主詞為 establishments，主要動詞為 use，由此可知，空格應填分詞來修飾 wrapping paper，原句是由 ..., *which is* occasionally *printed* on the outside.... 省略關代 which 和 be 動詞 is 簡化而來，且依句意為被動，故選 (B) *printed*「印刷」。

TEST 22

Read the following passage and choose the best answer for each blank from the choices below.

Natural history contains many astonishing examples of the ability of animals to find their way home after making distant journeys. Salmon, __1__, are born in freshwater streams and soon afterward journey down to the sea. Several years later, after they have attained __2__, they swim back upstream to spawn. In many cases, they swim back to die. The particular stream that serves as the journey's end is almost invariably the same one __3__ they were born. It is chosen out of dozens or hundreds of equally suitable streams. What underwater guideposts can these fish possibly follow? It was discovered that salmon, like many other fish, have an acute sense of smell. They are able to remember slight differences in the chemical __4__ of water. The most reasonable theory to explain salmon homing is that each individual remembers the distinctive "fragrance" of its native stream. As it moves upstream, it makes the correct choice each time a new stream is encountered __5__ finally it arrives home.

1. (A) as a result   (B) on the other hand
   (C) for instance   (D) that is
2. (A) position   (B) maturity   (C) goal   (D) level
3. (A) that   (B) what   (C) where   (D) for which
4. (A) ingredient   (B) composition
   (C) hazard   (D) reaction
5. (A) until   (B) once   (C) as though   (D) even if

TEST 22 詳解

Natural history contains many astonishing examples *of the ability of animals to find their way home after making distant journeys.* Salmon, *for instance*, are born *in freshwater streams **and** soon afterward* journey *down to the sea. Several years later, **after** they have attained* maturity, they swim *back upstream to spawn.*

關於動物在長途旅行之後找到回家的路，在自然史上有許多驚人的例子。以鮭魚為例，牠們出生在淡水的溪流中，之後馬上展開游向大海的旅程。過了幾年，牠們變成成魚後，就會逆流而上，游回出生地產卵。

* ***natural history*** 自然史；博物學　　contain² (kən'ten) v. 包含
astonishing⁵ (ə'stɑnɪʃɪŋ) adj. 驚人的
example¹ (ɪg'zæmpl) n. 例子　　distant² ('dɪstənt) adj. 長途的
journey³ ('dʒɝnɪ) n. v. 旅行　　salmon⁵ ('sæmən) n. 鮭魚
freshwater ('frɛʃ,wɔtɚ) adj. 淡水的
stream² (strim) n. 溪流　　afterward³ ('æftɚwəd) adv. 之後
attain⁶ (ə'ten) v. 達到；獲得
upstream (,ʌp'strim) adv. 逆流地
spawn (spɔn) v. (魚、蛙等) 產卵

1. (**C**)　(A) as a result　因此
　　　　　　(B) on the other hand　另一方面
　　　　　　(C) ***for instance***　例如
　　　　　　(D) that is　也就是說 (= *that is to say*)

> for instance　例如
> = for example
> = let's say
> = say

2.(**B**)　(A) position[1] 〔 pəˋzɪʃən 〕 n. 位置；（社會上的）地位；身分
　　　　　(B) ***maturity***[4] 〔 məˋtʃʊrətɪ 〕 n. 成熟
　　　　　　　　【mature[3] 〔 məˋtʃʊr 〕 adj. 成熟的 】
　　　　　(C) goal[2] 〔 gol 〕 n. 目標
　　　　　(D) level[1] 〔 ˋlɛvḷ 〕 n. 程度；等級

In many cases, they swim *back to die*. The particular stream *that*

serves as the journey's end is *almost invariably* the same one **_where_**
　　　　　　　　　　　　　　　　　　　　　　　　　　　　　　3

they were born. It is chosen *out of dozens **or** hundreds of equally*

suitable streams. What underwater guideposts can these fish

possibly follow? It was discovered ***that*** *salmon, like many other fish,*

have an acute sense of smell.

在大多數的情況下，鮭魚會游回去牠們的出生地結束生命。作為旅程終
點的特定河流，大多就是牠們出生的那條河。牠們從數十或數百條同樣
適合的溪流中選出那條河。這些魚究竟是循著河裡的什麼路標呢？據發
現，鮭魚就像許多其他的魚一樣，擁有敏銳的嗅覺。

　　　* case[1] 〔 kes 〕 n. 情況；例子
　　　in many cases 在大多數的情況下
　　　particular[2] 〔 pəˋtɪkjələ 〕 adj. 特定的　　　***serve as*** 充當；當作
　　　end[1] 〔 ɛnd 〕 n. 終點；結束
　　　invariably 〔 ɪnˋvɛrɪəblɪ 〕 adv. 不變地；必定
　　　dozen[1] 〔 ˋdʌzṇ 〕 n. 一打；十二個
　　　dozens of 幾十個；許多
　　　equally[1] 〔 ˋikwəlɪ 〕 adv. 同樣地
　　　suitable[3] 〔 ˋsutəbḷ 〕 adj. 適合的

> vary[3] v. 改變；不同
> variable adj. 易變的
> invariably adv. 不變地；必定

guidepost〔'gaɪd,post〕 *n.* 路標【post[2] *n.* 柱子；標桿】
follow[1]〔'falo〕*v.* 遵循　　acute[6]〔ə'kjut〕*adj.* 敏銳的
sense[1]〔sɛns〕*n.* 感覺　　smell[1]〔smɛl〕*n.* 嗅覺

3. (**C**)　依句意，「牠們出生的那條河」，應選表地點的關係副詞，
　　　故選 (C) *where*。

They are able to remember slight differences *in the chemical*

composition of water.　The *most* reasonable theory *to explain salmon*
　　　　4

homing is **that** *each individual remembers the distinctive "fragrance"*

of its native stream.　**As it moves upstream**, it makes the correct choice

each time *a new stream is encountered* **until** *finally it arrives home.*
　　　　　　　　　　　　　　　　　　　5

　　牠們能夠記住水中化學成分組成的細微差異。解釋鮭魚返鄉最合理
　　　　　　　　　　　　4
的說法就是，每條鮭魚都記得出生那條河的獨特「氣味」。當牠逆流迴
游時，能在每次遇上新河流時做出正確的選擇，直到最後回到家鄉。
　　　　　　　　　　　　　　　　　　　　　　5

*　* ***be able to V***. 能夠…　　slight[4]〔slaɪt〕*adj.* 細微的
chemical[2]〔'kɛmɪkl̩〕*adj.* 化學的
reasonable[3]〔'riznəbl̩〕*adj.* 合理的
theory[3]〔'θiərɪ〕*n.* 理論；說法
homing〔'homɪŋ〕*n.* (某些動物的) 返回原地的能力
individual[3]〔,ɪndə'vɪdʒuəl〕*n.* 個體
distinctive[5]〔dɪ'stɪŋktɪv〕*adj.* 獨特的
fragrance[4]〔'fregrəns〕*n.* 香味；氣味
native[3]〔'netɪv〕*adj.* 出生地的
encounter[4]〔ɪn'kauntɚ〕*v.* 遭遇

4. (**B**)　(A) ingredient^4〔ɪnˈɡridɪənt〕*n.* 原料；成分

　　　　(B) ***composition***^{4}〔ˌkɑmpəˈzɪʃən〕*n.* 組成；構成

　　　　(C) hazard^6〔ˈhæzəd〕*n.* 危險（= *danger* ）

　　　　(D) reaction^3〔rɪˈækʃən〕*n.* 反應

5. (**A**)　依句意，選 (A) ***until***「直到」。而 (B) once「一旦」，(C) as though「就好像」，(D) even if「即使」，皆不合句意。

【補充資料】

　　鮭魚通常出生於離海 10 到 700 哩的淡水河床上，經過三到四個月後，長成約一吋的魚苗，然後根據不同品種的鮭魚習性，在河流或湖裡生活一年，等到隔年春天，才隨著融化的冰雪一路游入海洋。

　　鮭魚在擁有豐富食物的海洋中大肆進食並快速成長，約二到五年後成為肥碩的銀白色成魚。等到初夏，鮭魚開始展開產卵迴游 (spawning migration) 之旅。根據解剖學的研究，鮭魚的嗅覺能力已經高度進化到人類的 500 倍以上，所以牠們記得淡水家鄉的味道，再加上星光的指引，找出回到淡水河域的方向。在這趟旅程中，牠們會停止覓食，只靠體內所儲存的豐厚脂肪和蛋白質維持生命，中途必須躍過瀑布和急流，穿越重重困難，平均每天要游 29 公里，此時牠們的外觀會轉變成為準備產卵的深紅色。

　　到了終點，鮭魚的身體會產生化學變化，牠們的頭變成深綠色，公鮭會長出隆起的背和鉤狀的鼻子，母鮭膨大的腹中則藏了大約 4,000 顆卵。一旦到達了出生的淺河床，牠們會開始配對，並為了搶奪最佳產卵地點而彼此爭鬥，母鮭喜歡選擇在流通的水域，用尾巴奮力拍打河床，並於沙礫中挖一個約十八吋的深坑洞產卵，公鮭一面在卵上射精，一面趕走其他來犯的鮭魚，最後公鮭跟母鮭會一同將卵覆蓋起來，接著繼續往上游，重複爭鬥與產卵的過程，直到筋疲力盡死亡為止。

　　鮭魚卵通常產在好幾呎的冰雪之下，經過一個寒冬，才孵化成透明的孵化卵。在良好的產卵環境下，大約有百分之二十的卵會孵化成為魚苗，其中又有百分之七十五能夠安然游回到大海中繼續成長。而未受精的卵和鮭魚的屍骸，則成為了鳥類及食腐肉動物在冬季來臨前的大餐。

TEST 23

Read the following passage and choose the best answer for each blank from the choices below.

Water is essential for life and good health. Yet a lack of water to __1__ daily needs is a reality today for one in three people around the world. __2__, the problem is getting worse as cities and populations grow and the need for water increases in agriculture, industry and households.

Water scarcity forces people to rely on unsafe sources of drinking water. It also means they cannot bathe or clean their clothes or homes properly. __3__, water scarcity encourages people to store water in their homes. __4__ increases the risk of household water contamination and provides breeding grounds for mosquitoes, carriers of diseases like dengue fever and malaria.

Water __5__ life. As governments make it a priority to deliver adequate supplies of quality water to people, individuals can help by learning how to conserve and protect the resource in their daily lives.

1. (A) meet　　(B) live on　(C) require　　(D) cut back
2. (A) Contrarily (B) Globally (C) Accordingly (D) Virtually
3. (A) To name but a few　　(B) To cut the long story short
   (C) To make matters worse　(D) To say the least
4. (A) And　　(B) Which　(C) This　　(D) What
5. (A) contains　　(B) sustains
   (C) suspects　　(D) suspends

TEST 23 詳解

Water is essential *for life **and** good health.* **Yet** a lack *of water*

to <u>meet</u> daily needs is a reality *today for one in three people around*
  1

the world. <u>Globally</u>, the problem is getting worse *as cities and*
  2

*populations grow **and** the need for water increases in agriculture,*

*industry **and** households.*

水對於生活以及良好的健康是不可或缺的。但現在全世界每三人就
有一人，缺乏滿足日常需求的水，這是事實。以全球來說，隨著城市發
  1   2
展和人口的成長，以及農業、工業和家庭對水的需求增加，缺水的問題
變得越來越嚴重。

* essential⁴〔ə'sɛnʃəl〕*adj.* 必要的；不可或缺的
  yet¹〔jɛt〕*conj.* 但是　　lack¹〔læk〕*n.* 缺乏
  daily³〔'delɪ〕*adj.* 每天的；日常的
  reality²〔rɪ'ælətɪ〕*n.* 現實；事實
  population²〔,pɑpjə'leʃən〕*n.* 人口
  grow¹〔gro〕*v.* 成長；發展
  agriculture³〔'ægrɪ,kʌltʃɚ〕*n.* 農業
  industry²〔'ɪndəstrɪ〕*n.* 工業　　household⁴〔'haʊs,hold〕*n.* 家庭

1. (**A**)　(A) *meet*¹〔mit〕*v.* 滿足；符合
　　　　　(B) live on 以…為食
　　　　　(C) require²〔rɪ'kwɛr〕*v.* 需要
　　　　　(D) cut back 削減；減少

2. (**B**)　(A) Contrarily[4] 〔ˋkɑn͵trɛrəlɪ〕 *adv.* 相反地

　　　　(B) ***Globally***[3] 〔ˋglɑblɪ〕 *adv.* 全球地

　　　　(C) Accordingly[6] 〔əˋkɔrdɪŋlɪ〕 *adv.* 因此 (= *Therefore*[2])

　　　　(D) Virtually[6] 〔ˋvɝtʃʊəlɪ〕 *adv.* 實際上；幾乎 (= *Almost*[1])

Water scarcity forces people to rely on unsafe sources *of drinking water.* It *also* means *they cannot bathe **or** clean their clothes **or** homes properly.* <u>*To make matters worse*</u>, water scarcity encourages people *to store water in their homes.* <u>This</u> increases the risk *of household water contamination **and*** provides breeding grounds *for mosquitoes, carriers of diseases like dengue fever and malaria.*

　　水資源的缺乏，迫使人們依賴不安全的飲用水源。這也意味著，他們不能適當地洗澡、清洗衣服或打掃家裡。<u>更糟的是</u>，缺水會促使人們在家中儲水。<u>這</u>會增加家用水污染的風險，並且為登革熱和瘧疾等疾病的帶原者蚊子，提供了繁殖地。

> * scarcity[3] 〔ˋskɛrsətɪ〕 *n.* 不足；缺乏【scarce[3] 〔skɛrs〕 *adj.* 稀少的】
> force[1] 〔fors〕 *v.* 強迫；迫使　　***rely on*** 依賴
> source[2] 〔sors〕 *n.* 來源　　***drinking water*** 飲用水
> bathe[1] 〔beð〕 *v.* 洗澡　　properly[3] 〔ˋprɑpɚlɪ〕 *adv.* 適當地
> encourage[2] 〔ɪnˋkɝɪdʒ〕 *v.* 鼓勵；促進　　store[1] 〔stor〕 *v.* 儲存
> contamination[5] 〔kən͵tæməˋneʃən〕 *n.* 污染
> ***breeding ground*** 繁殖地　　carrier[4] 〔ˋkærɪɚ〕 *n.* 帶菌者
> dengue fever 〔ˋdɛŋgɪ͵fivɚ〕 *n.* 登革熱
> malaria[6] 〔məˋlɛrɪə〕 *n.* 瘧疾

3. (**C**)   (A) To name but a few 僅列舉幾項 (= *To name just a few*)

       (B) To cut the long story short 長話短說;簡言之

          (= *To make a long story short*)

       (C) ***To make matters worse*** 更糟的是 (= *What's worse*)

       (D) To say the least 最保守地說

4. (**C**) 空格應選可做此句的主詞,依句意「人們在家中儲水」的「這件事」,應用有避免重複功能的指示代名詞,故選 (C) ***This***。

Water <u>sustains</u> life. *As governments make it a priority to deliver*
           5

adequate supplies of quality water to people, individuals can help *by*

*learning **how** to conserve **and** protect the resource in their daily lives.*

水<u>使</u>生命能<u>維持</u>下去。因為政府把能提供人們足夠且品質優良的水
     5   5
擺在第一順位,所以每個人都可藉由學習如何在日常生活中省水,以及
保護水資源盡一份心力。

* priority[5] (praɪˈɔrətɪ) *n.* 優先的事物   deliver[2] (dɪˈlɪvɚ) *v.* 遞送
adequate[4] (ˈædəkwɪt) *adj.* 足夠的
supplies[2] (səˈplaɪz) *n. pl.* 供應量
quality[2] (ˈkwɑlətɪ) *adj.* 品質好的
individual[3] (ˌɪndəˈvɪdʒuəl) *n.* 個人
conserve[5] (kənˈsɝv) *v.* 節省   protect[2] (prəˈtɛkt) *v.* 保護
resource[3] (rɪˈsors) *n.* 資源

5. (**B**)   (A) contain[2] (kənˈten) *v.* 包含

       (B) ***sustain***[5] (səˈsten) *v.* 支撐;維持

       (C) suspect[3] (səˈspɛkt) *v.* 懷疑

       (D) suspend[5] (səˈspɛnd) *v.* 暫停;使停職

TEST 24

Read the following passage and choose the best answer for each blank from the choices below.

Oktoberfest, the world's largest beer festival, is held annually in Munich, Germany. The 16-day party attracts over 6 million people every year who __1__ 1.5 million gallons of beer, 200,000 pounds of pork sausage, and 480,000 roasted chickens during the two-week extravaganza. __2__ advertisements for the event feature scores of beer-loving, meat-loving Germans, visitors to the festival actually come from all over the world.

Oktoberfest is in fact one of Munich's largest and most __3__ tourist attractions. It brings over 450 million euros to the city each year. The folk festival has given its name to similar festivals worldwide that are at least in part __4__ the original Bavarian Oktoberfest. The largest Oktoberfest outside of Germany takes place each year in the twin cities of Kitchener-Waterloo in Canada, __5__ a large German population resides. The largest such event in the United States is Oktoberfest-Zinzinnati in Ohio, which boasts half a million visitors each year.

1. (A) consume   (B) resume   (C) presume (D) assume
2. (A) Because   (B) Since   (C) While   (D) So
3. (A) disposable (B) profitable (C) suitable   (D) probable
4. (A) derived from   (B) turned into
   (C) made up   (D) made from
5. (A) which   (B) where   (C) when   (D) that

TEST 24 詳解

Oktoberfest, *the world's largest beer festival*, is held *annually in*

Munich, Germany. The 16-day party attracts over 6 million people

every year **who** <u>consume</u> *1.5 million gallons of beer, 200,000 pounds*
 　　　　　　　　　　　1

of pork sausage, **and** *480,000 roasted chickens during the two-week*

extravaganza. <u>**While**</u> *advertisements for the event feature scores of*
 　　　　　　　　2

beer-loving, meat-loving Germans, visitors *to the festival actually*

come *from all over the world.*

　　全世界最大的啤酒節，慕尼黑啤酒節，每年在德國的慕尼黑舉行。
這個爲期十六天的派對，每年吸引超過六百萬人，在這兩星期的盛會期
間，<u>喝掉</u>一百五十萬加侖的啤酒、二十萬磅的豬肉香腸，以及四十八萬
　　　1
隻烤雞。<u>雖然</u>這個活動廣告的主角，是許多愛喝啤酒、愛吃肉類的德國
　　　2
人，但來參加慶典的，事實上是來自世界各地的遊客。

* Oktoberfest〔ɑk'tobɚ,fɛst〕*n.* 德國慕尼黑的啤酒節【又稱「十月節」】
beer[2]〔bɪr〕*n.* 啤酒　　festival[2]〔'fɛstəvḷ〕*n.* 慶典
hold[1]〔hold〕*v.* 舉行　　annually[4]〔'ænjuəlɪ〕*adv.* 一年一度地
Munich〔'mjunɪk〕*n.* 慕尼黑【德國第三大城】
attract[3]〔ə'trækt〕*v.* 吸引　　gallon[3]〔'gælən〕*n.* 加侖
pound[2]〔paund〕*n.* 磅　　pork[3]〔pɔrk〕*n.* 豬肉

sausage[3] (ˈsɔsɪdʒ) *n.* 香腸　　roast[3] (rost) *v.* 烤
extravaganza (ɪkˌstrævəˈgænzə) *n.* 盛大慶典；盛事
advertisement[3] (ˌædvəˈtaɪzmənt) *n.* 廣告
event[2] (ɪˈvɛnt) *n.* 事件；大型活動
feature[3] (ˈfitʃə) *v.* 以…為特色；以…為主角
score[2] (skor) *n.* 二十個　　***scores of*** 許多的
meat[1] (mit) *n.* 肉　　German (ˈdʒɜmən) *n.* 德國
actually[3] (ˈæktʃuəlɪ) *adv.* 事實上

1. (**A**)　(A) ***consume***[4] (kənˈsum, kənˈsjum) *v.* 消耗；吃；喝
　　　　(B) resume[5] (rɪˈsum, rɪˈsjum) *v.* 恢復；再繼續
　　　　(C) presume[6] (prɪˈsum, prɪˈsjum) *v.* 假定；
　　　　(D) assume[4] (əˈsum, əˈsjum) *v.* 假定；認為

2. (**C**)　依句意，選 (C) ***While*** 「雖然」 (= *Though*)。
　　　　而 (A) Because 「因為」，(B) Since 「自從」，
　　　　(D) So 「所以」，皆不合句意。

Oktoberfest is *in fact* one *of Munich's largest **and** most _profitable_*
 _3_

tourist attractions. It brings over 450 million euros *to the city each*

year. The folk festival has given its name *to similar festivals*

*worldwide **that** are at least in part _derived from_ the original Bavarian*
 _4_

Oktoberfest. The largest Oktoberfest *outside of Germany* takes place

*each year in the twin cities of Kitchener-Waterloo in Canada, **_where_***
 _5_

a large German population resides. The largest such event *in the United States* is Oktoberfest-Zinzinnati *in Ohio,* **which** boasts half a million visitors each year.

　　事實上，啤酒節是慕尼黑最大和最能獲利的觀光景點之一。它每年
　　　　　　　　　　　　　　　　3
為這個城市帶來超過四億五千萬歐元。世界各地有著相似名稱的民俗節
慶，其名稱至少部分是起源於原本的巴伐利亞慕尼黑啤酒節。在德國之
　　　　　　　　　　　　4
外的最大啤酒節，每年在加拿大的雙子城基奇納–滑鐵盧舉行，那裡有
　　　　　　　　　　　　　　　　　　　　　　　　　　　5
大批德國人口居住。在美國，如此大型的活動，是在俄亥俄州的辛辛那
提啤酒節，這個啤酒節每年有五十萬名觀光客。

　　* *in fact* 事實上　　tourist[3] 〔'turɪst 〕 *adj.* 適合觀光客的
　　attraction[4] 〔 ə'trækʃən 〕 *n.* 吸引人的事物
　　tourist attraction 旅遊勝地；觀光景點
　　euro 〔'juro 〕 *n.* 歐元　　folk[3] 〔 fok 〕 *adj.* 民間的
　　give *one's* ***name to*** 以…的名字為名
　　similar[2] 〔'sɪmələ 〕 *adj.* 類似的
　　worldwide 〔'wɜld'waɪd 〕 *adv.* 在全世界
　　at least 至少（ ↔ ***at most*** 最多 ）　　***in part*** 部份地
　　original[3] 〔 ə'rɪdʒənḷ 〕 *adj.* 最初的；原本的
　　Bavarian 〔 bə'vɛrɪən 〕 *adj.* 巴伐利亞的
　　take place 舉行　　***twin cities*** 雙子城；姊妹市
　　population[2] 〔,pɑpjə'leʃən 〕 *n.* 人口
　　reside[5] 〔 rɪ'zaɪd 〕 *v.* 居住（ = *live* = *dwell* ）
　　Ohio 〔 o'haɪo 〕 *n.* 俄亥俄州
　　boast[4] 〔 bost 〕 *v.* 以有…而自豪（ = *brag* ）；吹噓

3. (**B**)　(A) disposable[6] 〔dɪ'spozəbḷ〕 *adj.* 用完即丟的
　　　　(B) ***profitable***[4] 〔'prɑfɪtəbḷ〕 *adj.* 有利可圖的；能獲利的
　　　　(C) suitable[3] 〔'sutəbḷ〕 *adj.* 適合的
　　　　(D) probable[3] 〔'prɑbəbḷ〕 *adj.* 可能的

4. (**A**)　(A) ***derive from*** 起源於
　　　　(B) turn into 變成
　　　　(C) make up 組成；編造；和好
　　　　(D) make from 用⋯製成

$$\left\{\begin{array}{l} \text{derive from} \quad \text{起源於} \\ = \text{be derived from} \end{array}\right.$$
$$\left\{\begin{array}{l} = \text{stem from} \\ = \text{spring from} \end{array}\right.$$
$$\left\{\begin{array}{l} = \text{originate from} \\ = \text{come from} \end{array}\right.$$

5. (**B**)　表地點，關係副詞用 ***where***，選 (B)。
　　　　【比較】

This is the house *where I live.*

= This is the house *which I live in.*

關係副詞和關係代名詞都可引導形容詞子句，關係代名詞
which 有代名詞作用，關係副詞 where 無代名詞作用。
　　【詳見「文法寶典」p.243 關係副詞與關係代名詞的比較】

【補充資料】
　　「慕尼黑啤酒節」於每年九月下旬到十月初在慕尼黑
舉行，為期 16 天。啤酒節源自 1810 年，是為了慶祝皇儲

路德威一世與特瑞莎公主結婚而舉辦，時值啤酒花收成的十月，於是人民穿
著巴伐利亞傳統服飾飲酒狂歡作樂數日。當年辦婚宴的那片草地，即今日啤
酒節的活動場地，故當地人也稱啤酒節為 Wiesn（德語「草地」）。啤酒節
的啤酒是酒商特製，濃度最低6%。在慶典中除了啤酒棚和遊樂設施，還供
應許多巴伐利亞傳統美食，像是德國烤豬腳、扭結麵包，和白香腸。依循傳
統，節慶在正午時分，人們高呼「敲開啤酒桶蓋吧！」（O'zapft is）後正式
揭幕。

TEST 25

Read the following passage and choose the best answer for each blank from the choices below.

Awarded many awards for its excellence and cultural values, Doraemon, ____1____ a futuristic robotic cat named Doraemon and a teenage boy, Nobita Nobi, is a precious ____2____ of Japanese animation. In this anime, Doraemon has a magical pocket containing numerous high-tech gadgets, which help Nobita Nobi ____3____ the problems he encounters in life and thus give him a carefree childhood.

Although most of the episodes are comedies and the plots seem ordinary and commonplace, critics unanimously ____4____ the series for its contribution to the introduction of Japanese culture to the world. For example, most of the devices from the magical pocket are fancifully created based on real Japanese household devices. In addition, the moral lessons conveyed in the series are values like honesty, courage, family and perseverance, ____5____ are highly regarded in Japanese culture. Some informative topics regarding the history of Japan are also covered. No wonder Doraemon has become an essential icon of Japanese culture.

1. (A) to feature   (B) featuring   (C) featured by (D) features
2. (A) possession (B) belongings (C) property   (D) asset
3. (A) cope with   (B) run into
   (C) correspond to   (D) take in
4. (A) applaud   (B) condemn   (C) charge   (D) prepare
5. (A) all of them   (B) X
   (C) all of which   (D) they alone

TEST 25 詳解

*Awarded many awards for its excellence **and** cultural values,*

Doraemon, *featuring a futuristic robotic cat named Doraemon **and** a*
　　　　　　1

teenage boy, Nobita Nobi, is a precious <u>asset</u> *of Japanese animation.*
　　　　　　　　　　　　　　　　　2

In this anime, Doraemon has a magical pocket *containing numerous*

*high-tech gadgets, **which** help Nobita Nobi <u>cope with</u> the problems he*
　　　　　　　　　　　　　　　　　3

*encounters in life **and** thus give him a carefree childhood.*

　　哆啦 A 夢因為它的卓越和文化價值,獲頒了許多獎項,是日本動畫
的珍貴<u>資產</u>。在這部動畫中,是以一隻名為哆啦 A 夢的未來機器貓和一
　　　　2
個叫野比大雄的十幾歲男孩<u>為主角</u>,哆啦 A 夢有個神奇的口袋,裡面有
　　　　　　　　　　　　　1
許多高科技的小玩意,能幫助野比大雄<u>應付</u>他在生活中遇到的問題,因
而給了他一個無憂無慮的童年。　　　　　　3

　　* award³〔əˋwɔrd〕v. 頒發　　n. 獎
　　excellence³〔ˋɛksḷəns〕n. 優秀　　value²〔ˋvæljʊ〕n. 價值
　　futuristic〔ˌfjutʃəˋrɪstɪk〕adj. 未來的【future² n. 未來】
　　robotic〔roˋbɑtɪk〕adj. 機器人的【robot¹〔ˋrobət〕n. 機器人】
　　Doraemon 哆啦 A 夢【為日本漫畫家藤子・F・不二雄筆下最受歡迎
　　　的漫畫作品,故事主角哆啦 A 夢是一隻來自 22 世紀的機器貓】
　　teenage²〔ˋtinˌedʒ〕adj. 十幾歲的
　　Nobita Nobi 野比大雄【哆啦 A 夢的主人】
　　precious³〔ˋprɛʃəs〕adj. 珍貴的

animation〔͵ænə'meʃən〕*n.* 動畫；卡通電影
anime〔'ænɪme〕*n.* 日本動畫片
magical³〔'mædʒɪkḷ〕*adj.* 神奇的　　pocket¹〔'pɑkɪt〕*n.* 口袋
contain²〔kən'ten〕*v.* 包含　　numerous⁴〔'njumərəs〕*adj.* 許多的
high-tech〔'haɪ'tɛk〕*adj.* 高科技的
gadget〔'gædʒɪt〕*n.* 裝置；小玩意；小器具
encounter⁴〔ɪn'kaʊntɚ〕*v.* 遭遇　　thus¹〔ðʌs〕*adv.* 因此
carefree⁵〔'kɛr͵fri〕*adj.* 無憂無慮的

1. (**B**)　本句的主詞是 Doraemon，動詞是 is，故空格應填分詞，
　　　　　　依句意爲主動，故選 (B) *featuring*。
　　　　　feature³〔'fitʃɚ〕*v.* 以⋯爲特色；使⋯主演

2. (**D**)　(A) possession⁴〔pə'zɛʃən〕*n.* 擁有；所有物
　　　　　(B) belongings⁵〔bə'lɔŋɪŋz〕*n. pl.* 個人隨身物品
　　　　　(C) property³〔'prɑpɚtɪ〕*n.* 財產
　　　　　(D) *asset*⁵〔'æsɛt〕*n.* 資產

3. (**A**)　(A) *cope with* 應付 (= *deal with*)
　　　　　(B) run into 偶然遇到 (= *bump into* = *come across*)
　　　　　(C) correspond to 和⋯一致
　　　　　　　【比較】correspond with 和⋯通信
　　　　　(D) take in 留宿；接受；欺騙

*Although most of the episodes are comedies **and** the plots seem ordinary **and** commonplace,* critics *unanimously* applaud the series for its contribution to the introduction of Japanese culture to the world. *For example*, most *of the devices from the magical pocket* are *fancifully* created *based on real Japanese household devices.*

　　雖然大部份的集數都是喜劇，且劇情似乎是普通又平凡，但評論家都一致<u>讚揚</u>，此連載漫畫對世界介紹日本文化的貢獻。例如，大多數來
　　　　　4
自於神奇口袋的儀器，是根據日本眞實的家用設備想像出來的。

* episode⁶ 〔'ɛpə‚sod 〕 *n.* （連續劇等的）一集
comedy⁴ 〔'kɑmədɪ 〕 *n.* 喜劇　　plot⁴ 〔 plɑt 〕 *n.* 情節
ordinary² 〔'ɔrdn̩‚ɛrɪ 〕 *adj.* 普通的
commonplace⁵ 〔'kɑmən‚ples 〕 *adj.* 普通的；平凡的
critic⁴ 〔'krɪtɪk 〕 *n.* 評論家
unanimously⁶ 〔 ju'nænəməslɪ 〕 *adv.* 全體一致地
series⁵ 〔'sɪrɪz 〕 *n.* 連續刊物；叢書；一連串
contribution⁴ 〔‚kɑntrə'bjuʃən 〕 *n.* 貢獻
introduction³ 〔‚ɪntrə'dʌkʃən 〕 *n.* 介紹
culture² 〔'kʌltʃɚ 〕 *n.* 文化
device⁴ 〔 dɪ'vaɪs 〕 *n.* 儀器；裝置
fancifully 〔'fænsɪfəlɪ 〕 *adv.* 異想天開地
【fancy³ 〔'fænsɪ 〕 *v. n.* 幻想】
create² 〔 krɪ'et 〕 *v.* 創造　　***based on*** 根據
household⁴ 〔'haʊs‚hold 〕 *adj.* 家庭的

devices

4. (**A**)　(A) ***applaud***⁵ 〔 ə'plɔd 〕 *v.* 稱讚；鼓掌
applause⁵ *n.* 鼓掌喝采；稱讚
(B) condemn⁵ 〔 kən'dɛm 〕 *v.* 譴責
(C) charge² 〔 tʃɑrdʒ 〕 *v.* 收費；控告
charge *sb.* with 控告某人（ = *accuse sb. of* ）
(D) prepare¹ 〔 prɪ'pɛr 〕 *v.* 準備
prepare for 爲…做準備

In addition, the moral lessons *conveyed in the series* are values *like*

honesty, *courage*, *family* ***and*** *perseverance*, <u>all of **which**</u> *are highly*
5

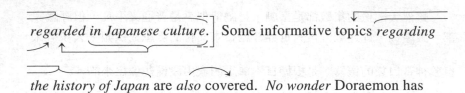

regarded in Japanese culture. Some informative topics *regarding*

the history of Japan are *also* covered. *No wonder* Doraemon has

become an essential icon *of Japanese culture.*

此外，連載漫畫中傳達的道德教訓，是誠實、勇氣、家庭以及毅力的價值觀，<u>所有這些價值觀</u>都在日本文化中受到高度重視。一些有關日本歷史的教育主題也包含其中。難怪哆啦Ａ夢已成為日本文化不可或缺的標誌。

  * in addition 此外 (= *moreover*[4])

  moral[3] 〔ˋmɔrəl 〕 *adj.* 道德的 lesson[1] 〔ˋlɛsn̩ 〕 *n.* 教訓

  convey[4] 〔 kənˋve 〕 *v.* 傳達 values[2] 〔ˋvæljuz 〕 *n. pl.* 價值觀

  honesty[3] 〔ˋɑnəstɪ 〕 *n.* 誠實

  courage[2] 〔ˋkɝɪdʒ 〕 *n.* 勇氣

  perseverance[6] 〔ˌpɝsəˋvɪrəns 〕 *n.* 毅力

  regard[2] 〔 rɪˋgard 〕 *v.* 認為；尊重

  be highly regarded 受到高度評價

  informative[4] 〔 ɪnˋfɔrmətɪv 〕 *adj.* 有教育性的；提供知識的

  regarding[4] 〔 rɪˋgardɪŋ 〕 *prep.* 關於 (= *about*[1])

  cover[1] 〔ˋkʌvɚ 〕 *v.* 涵蓋 **no wonder** 難怪

  icon 〔ˋaɪkɑn 〕 *n.* 標誌；圖像

> <u>sev</u>ere *adj.* 嚴格的
> <u>persev</u>ere *v.* 堅忍
> <u>persev</u>erance *n.* 毅力

5.(**C**) 由空格前的 ...are values 和空格後的 are highly regarded 可
    知，此處應有連接詞，而關代具有連接詞的作用，故選 (C)
    all of which。which 引導形容詞子句，修飾先行詞 values
    like honesty, courage, family and perseverance。

TEST 26

Read the following passage and choose the best answer for each blank from the choices below.

More people are meeting their future spouses online these days. ___1___, one-third of marriages in the US now begin with a digital rather than a face-to-face meeting. So what ___2___ is this making to our marital happiness?

To find out the answer, researchers at the University of Chicago and Harvard University surveyed just over 19,000 married—or previously married—people to ___3___ how blissful their marriages were. They were asked questions like "How satisfied are you with your marriage?" to which the answer was a score of 1 to 7. They were also asked to score statements such as "We have chemistry." The ___4___ "marital satisfaction" score was calculated from all these answers.

The result showed that couples who meet online are ___5___ likely to break up and are also more satisfied with their life partners. The result might be good news for those who are glued to their computers so much so that they rarely step out of their houses to have any social interaction.

1. (A) On the contrary   (B) In fact
   (C) To begin with   (D) Meanwhile
2. (A) occurrence (B) presence (C) influence (D) difference
3. (A) record   (B) assess   (C) predict   (D) wonder
4. (A) overall   (B) objective (C) obvious   (D) public
5. (A) more   (B) less   (C) much   (D) very

TEST 26 詳解

More people are meeting their future spouses *online these days*.

In fact, one-third of marriages *in the US now* begin *with a digital*

rather than a face-to-face meeting. **So** what <u>difference</u> is this

making *to our marital happiness*?

最近有更多的人在網路上認識未來的另一半。<u>事實上</u>，現在在美

國，有三分之一的婚姻，都是開始於數位的，而不是面對面的認識。所

以這對我們的婚姻幸福會有什麼影響嗎？

* meet[1] 〔 mit 〕 *v.* 認識　　future[2] 〔'fjutʃɚ〕 *adj.* 未來的

spouse[6] 〔 spaʊs 〕 *n.* 配偶

online 〔'ɑn,laɪn 〕 *adv.* 在網路上

these days 最近 (= *recently*[2] = *lately*[4])

one-third *n.* 三分之一 (= *one third*)

marriage[2] 〔'mærɪdʒ 〕 *n.* 婚姻

digital[4] 〔'dɪdʒɪtḷ 〕 *adj.* 數位的

rather than 而不是　　face-to-face *adj.* 面對面的

marital 〔'mærətḷ 〕 *adj.* 婚姻的【marital status 婚姻狀況】

happiness 〔'hæpɪnɪs 〕 *n.* 快樂；幸福

1.(**B**) (A) On the contrary 相反地

(B) *In fact* 事實上 (= *In truth* = *In reality* = *In effect*
= *As a matter of fact*)

(C) To begin with 首先 (= *First of all* = *In the first place*)

(D) Meanwhile[3] 〔'mɪn,hwaɪl 〕 *adv.* 同時

2. (**D**)　(A) occurrence⁵ 〔ə'kɝəns〕 *n.* 事件（ = *happening* ）

occur² 〔ə'kɝ〕 *v.* 發生

(B) presence² 〔'prɛzns〕 *n.* 出席；在場

(C) influence² 〔'ɪnfluəns〕 *n.* 影響（ = *effect²* = *impact⁴* ）

have an influence on　對…有影響

(D) *difference²* 〔'dɪfərəns〕 *n.* 不同

make a difference　有差別；有影響；關係重大

To find out the answer, researchers *at the University of Chicago*

and Harvard University surveyed just over 19,000 married—*or*

previously married—people to assess *how* blissful their marriages
　　　　　　　　　　　　　　　3

were.　They were asked questions *like "How satisfied are you with*

*your marriage?" to **which** the answer was a score of 1 to 7.*　They

were *also* asked to score statements *such as "We have chemistry."*

The overall "marital satisfaction" score was calculated *from all*
　　　4

these answers.

　　　爲了找出答案，芝加哥大學和哈佛大學的研究人員，調查了超過一
萬九千名已婚或失婚的人，來評估他們的婚姻有多幸福。他們被問到的
　　　　　　　　　　　　　　　　3
問題，像是「你對你的婚姻有多滿意？」，答題分數是一至七分。他們
也被要求對「我們很來電」這個說法打分數。整體的「婚姻滿意度」分
　　　　　　　　　　　　　　　　　　　4
數，是用這些所有答案來計算的。

　　　* *find out* 查出　　　researcher⁴ 〔rɪ'sɝtʃɚ〕 *n.* 研究人員

Chicago 〔ʃə'kago〕 *n.* 芝加哥【美國城市名】

Harvard〔'hɑrvəd〕*n.* 哈佛大學　　survey³〔sə've〕*v.* 調查
married¹〔'mɛrɪd〕*adj.* 已婚的
previously³〔'privɪəslɪ〕*adv.* 以前
blissful〔'blɪsfəl〕*adj.* 極幸福的
satisfied¹〔'sætɪs,faɪd〕*adj.* 感到滿意的
score²〔skor〕*n.* 分數　*v.* 給…評分
statement¹〔'stetmənt〕*n.* 敘述
chemistry⁴〔'kɛmɪstrɪ〕*n.* 化學；化學作用；男女之間的「來電」
satisfaction⁴〔,sætɪs'fækʃən〕*n.* 滿意
calculate⁴〔'kælkjə,let〕*v.* 計算

> blessing　*n.* 幸福
> bliss　*n.* 極大的幸福
> Ignorance is bliss.
> 【諺】無知便是福。

3. (**B**)　(A) record²〔rɪ'kɔrd〕*v.* 記錄
　　　　　　(B) ***assess***⁶〔ə'sɛs〕*v.* 評估（= *evaluate*⁴）
　　　　　　(C) predict⁴〔prɪ'dɪkt〕*v.* 預測
　　　　　　(D) wonder²〔'wʌndɚ〕*v.* 想知道

4. (**A**)　(A) ***overall***⁵〔'ovɚ,ɔl〕*adj.* 全面的；整體的
　　　　　　(B) objective⁴〔əb'dʒɛktɪv〕*adj.* 客觀的
　　　　　　　【subjective⁶〔səb'dʒɛktɪv〕*adj.* 主觀的】
　　　　　　(C) obvious³〔'ɑbvɪəs〕*adj.* 明顯的（= *apparent*³ = *evident*⁴
　　　　　　　= *noticable*⁵）
　　　　　　(D) public¹〔'pʌblɪk〕*adj.* 公開的；公共的

The result showed ***that*** *couples **who** meet online* are <u>less</u> likely to
break up ***and*** are *also more* satisfied *with their life partners*. The
result might be good news *for those **who** are glued to their computers*
*so much **so that** they rarely step out of their houses to have any social*
interaction.

結果顯示，在網路上認識的夫妻，<u>比較不</u>可能分手，而且對自己的
                           5
終生伴侶較滿意。此結果對整天黏著電腦的人來說，可能是個好消息，
因爲他們如此地依賴電腦，以致於很少走出家門進行任何的社交互動。

* result² (rɪˈzʌlt) *n.* 結果   show¹ (ʃo) *v.* 顯示
  couple² (ˈkʌpl̩) *v.* 一對男女；夫妻
  likely¹ (ˈlaɪklɪ) *adj.* 可能的   ***break up*** 分手
  partner¹ (ˈpɑrtnə) *n.* 夥伴；伴侶   ***life partner*** 終生伴侶
  glue¹ (glu) *v.* 黏；熱中於 < *to* >
  so that 以致於   rarely¹ (ˈrɛrlɪ) *adv.* 很少
  step out of 踏出
  social² (ˈsoʃəl) *adj.* 社交的
  interaction⁴ (ˌɪntəˈækʃən) *n.* 互動

```
inter  + action
  |         |
between + action
```

5. (**B**)   在網路上認識的夫妻「比較不」可能分手，而且對自己的終生
        伴侶較滿意，故選 (B) ***less***。

＊克漏字常考的「轉承語」：

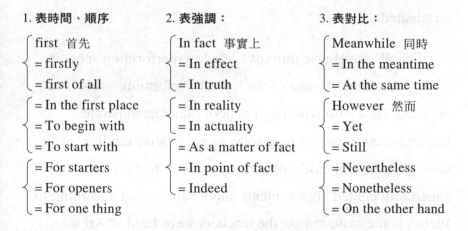

1. 表時間、順序	2. 表強調：	3. 表對比：
first 首先	In fact 事實上	Meanwhile 同時
= firstly	= In effect	= In the meantime
= first of all	= In truth	= At the same time
= In the first place	= In reality	However 然而
= To begin with	= In actuality	= Yet
= To start with	= As a matter of fact	= Still
= For starters	= In point of fact	= Nevertheless
= For openers	= Indeed	= Nonetheless
= For one thing		= On the other hand

【詳見「一口氣背同義字寫作文…①」p.223】

TEST 27

Read the following passage and choose the best answer for each blank from the choices below.

Usually, when students don't perform well, they get a failing grade. Yet in one California school district, ___1___ was the teachers who got an "F"—as in, fired. The East Palo Alto school board voted to fire the teachers after they ___2___ the addition of extra duties to their workload without extra pay. One point to consider: the average teaching salary in East Palo Alto is one of the highest in the country. But now it seems Superintendent Charles E. Weiss is willing to compromise. He has agreed to talk with the teachers' union, but many parents of children in the system say the teachers were deservedly terminated.

One White House initiative lets low-performing schools ___3___ funding. As one of the lowest-performing schools in the state, East Palo Alto High School must demonstrate improvement in one of four areas to get federal funding. The most obvious and easily obtainable—better test scores—has apparently eluded both students and teachers, and according to Weiss, is the main reason the teachers were fired. "All we asked [from the teachers] was to spend an extra hour each day

helping students prepare for standardized testing," Weiss said.
"Their unwillingness to __4__ not only does a disservice to
the students, but severely damages our chances of receiving
federal funding."

However, the situation in East Palo Alto is not unique.
Philadelphia has implemented a similar program to reposition
low-performing schools. Houston teachers __5__ their jobs if
students perform poorly on tests. As an incentive to improve,
Houston teachers can get bonuses for students' good
performance.

1. (A) there   (B) so
   (C) it   (D) that
2. (A) imposed   (B) proposed
   (C) opposed   (D) disposed
3. (A) compete for   (B) pay for
   (C) account for   (D) go in for
4. (A) comply   (B) affirm
   (C) violate   (D) decline
5. (A) will loose   (B) loss
   (C) could lose   (D) are lost

TEST 27 詳解

Usually, ***when** students don't perform well*, they get a failing grade. ***Yet** in one California school district*, <u>it</u> was the teachers ***who*** got an "F"—*as in*, *fired*. The East Palo Alto school board voted to fire the teachers |***after** they <u>opposed</u> the addition of extra duties to their workload without extra pay.|

通常學生表現不好的時候，他們就會拿到不及格的成績。但在加州有個學區，反而是老師拿到「不及格」——就像被炒魷魚一般。東帕洛阿爾托的老師們<u>反對</u>沒有加薪卻增加工作量後，學校的董事會投票表決要開除老師。

* perform³ [pə`fɔrm] v. 表現　　fail² [fel] v. 不及格
grade² [gred] n. 成績　　yet¹ [jɛt] conj. 但是 (= but)
California [͵kælə`fɔrnjə] n. 加州
district⁴ [`dɪstrɪkt] n. 地區　　*as in* 就像
fire¹ [faɪr] v. 解僱；炒魷魚
board² [bord] n. 董事會　　vote² [vot] v. 投票
addition² [ə`dɪʃən ] n. 增加　　extra² [ `ɛkstrə] adj. 額外的
duty² [`djutɪ] n. 責任；職務
workload [`wɜk͵lod] n. 工作量
pay³ [pe] n. 薪水

1. (**C**)　本句爲強調句型：It is/was + 強調部份 + that + 其餘部份，
又強調的是「老師」，所以 that 可用 who 代替，故選 (C) *it*。

2. (**C**)　(A) impose[5] 〔 ɪm'poz 〕 *v.* 強加 < *to* >

　　(B) propose[2] 〔 prə'poz 〕 *v.* 提議

　　(C) ***oppose***[4] 〔 ə'poz 〕 *v.* 反對

　　(D) dispose[5] 〔 dɪ'spoz 〕 *v.* 處置

　　Man proposes, God disposes.

　　【諺】謀事在人，成事在天。

One point *to consider*: the average teaching salary *in East Palo Alto*

is one *of the highest in the country*. **But** *now* it seems *Superintendent*

Charles E. Weiss is willing to compromise. He has agreed to talks

with the teachers' union, **but** many parents *of children in the school*

say *the teachers were deservedly terminated*.

要考慮的重點是：在東帕洛阿爾托教書的平均薪水，是國內最高的。但
是現在學校負責人查理斯・E・衛斯似乎願意妥協。他已同意跟教師聯
盟對話，但該校的許多學生家長說，那些老師應該被解僱。

　* point[1] 〔 pɔɪnt 〕 *n.* 重點　　consider[2] 〔 kən'sɪdɚ 〕 *v.* 考慮
　average[3] 〔'ævərɪdʒ 〕 *adj.* 平均的
　salary[4] 〔'sælərɪ 〕 *n.* 薪水　　seem[1] 〔 sim 〕 *v.* 似乎
　superintendent 〔,suprɪn'tɛndənt 〕 *n.* 負責人；管理者
　willing[2] 〔'wɪlɪŋ 〕 *adj.* 願意的
　compromise[5] 〔'kɑmprə,maɪz 〕 *v.* 妥協
　agree to sth. 同意某事　　talks[1] 〔 tɔk 〕 *n. pl.* 會談；協商
　union[3] 〔'junjən 〕 *n.* 聯盟；公會
　deservedly 〔 dɪ'zɝvɪdlɪ 〕 *adv.* 應當地
　【deserve[4] 〔 dɪ'zɝv 〕 *v.* 應得】
　terminate[6] 〔'tɝmə,net 〕 *v.* 終結；免職；解僱

One White House initiative lets low-performing schools compete *for funding*. *As one of the lowest-performing schools in the state*, East Palo Alto High School must demonstrate improvement *in one of four areas to get federal funding*. The *most* obvious *and easily* obtainable—better test scores—has *apparently* eluded both students *and* teachers, *and according to Weiss*, is the main reason *the teachers were fired.*

白宮有一項措施，要讓一些表現不佳的學校爭取資金。東帕洛阿爾托高中是全州表現最差的學校之一，必須在四個領域的其中之一有所改進，才能得到聯邦的資金。最明顯而且最容易達到的，就是更好的考試成績，但這好像難倒學生跟老師了，而且根據衛斯的說法，這就是老師被解僱的主要原因。

* ***the White House*** 白宮
initiative[6]〔ɪˈnɪʃɪ‚etɪv〕*n.* 措施；主動權
perform[3]〔pəˈfɔrm〕*v.* 表現
funding〔ˈfʌndɪŋ〕*n.* 資金；基金　　state[1]〔stet〕*n.* 州
demonstrate[4]〔ˈdɛmən‚stret〕*v.* 表現；證明
improvement[2]〔ɪmˈpruvmənt〕*n.* 改善
area[1]〔ˈɛrɪə〕*n.* 領域；地區　　federal[5]〔ˈfɛdərəl〕*adj.* 聯邦的
obvious[3]〔ˈɑbvɪəs〕*adj.* 明顯的
obtainable[4]〔əbˈtenəb!〕*adj.* 可得到的
score[2]〔skor〕*n.* 分數；成績
apparently[3]〔əˈpærəntlɪ〕*adv.* 似乎；好像
elude〔ɪˈlud〕*v.* 躲避；把…難倒

3. (**A**) (A) ***compete for*** 為…競爭　　compete[3] 〔 kəm'pit 〕 *v.* 競爭
　　　　　(B) pay for 付…的錢；為…付出代價
　　　　　(C) account for 說明
　　　　　(D) go in for 對…有興趣

"All we asked [from the teachers] was to spend an extra hour *each*

day helping students prepare for standardized testing," Weiss said.

"Their unwillingness *to comply **not only*** does a disservice *to the*
　　　　　　　　　　　　　　　4

students, **but** *severely* damages our chances *of receiving federal*

funding."

「我們只是要求老師，每天多花一個小時，幫助學生準備標準化的

測驗，」衛斯說。「他們不願意遵從，這不僅讓學生受害，而且嚴
　　　　　　　　　　　　　　　　　4

重損害我們得到聯邦資金的機會。」

　　　* ***prepare for*** 為…做準備　　extra[2] 〔'ɛkstrə 〕 *adj.* 額外的
　　　　standardize 〔'stændə,daɪz 〕 *v.* 使標準化
　　　　unwillingness 〔 ʌn'wɪlɪŋnɪs 〕 *n.* 不願意
　　　　not only…but also~ 不僅…而且~
　　　　disservice 〔 dɪs's3vɪs 〕 *n.* 損害
　　　　severely[4] 〔 sə'vɪrlɪ 〕 *adv.* 嚴重地
　　　　receive[1] 〔 rɪ'siv 〕 *v.* 收到；得到

4. (**A**) (A) ***comply*** 〔 kəm'plaɪ 〕 *v.* 遵從；順從
　　　　　(B) affirm[6] 〔 ə'f3m 〕 *v.* 斷言
　　　　　(C) violate[4] 〔'vaɪə,let 〕 *v.* 違反
　　　　　(D) decline[6] 〔 dɪ'klaɪn 〕 *v.* 拒絕；衰退

However, the situation *in East Palo Alto* is not unique.

Philadelphia has implemented a similar program *to reposition*

low-performing schools. Houston teachers <u>could lose</u> their jobs *if*

　　　　　　　　　　　　　　　　　　　　　　　　　5

students perform poorly on tests. As an incentive to improve, Houston

teachers can get bonuses *for students' good performance.*

　　然而，東帕洛阿爾托這樣的情況並不特殊。費城也實行類似的計畫，以改變表現差的學校的排名。如果學生考試考不好的話，休士頓的老師<u>可能會失去</u>他們的工作。休士頓的老師會因為學生表現好，而拿到
　　　　5
獎金，這是讓他們改善的誘因。

* unique⁴〔ju'nik〕*adj.* 獨特的
  Philadelphia〔,filə'dɛlfjə〕*n.* 費城【位於美國賓州】
  implement⁶〔'ɪmplə,mɛnt〕*v.* 實施
  similar²〔'sɪmələ〕*adj.* 類似的　　program³〔'progræm〕*n.* 計劃
  reposition〔,ripə'zɪʃən〕*v.* 改變…的位置
  Houston〔'hjustən〕*n.* 休士頓【位於美國德州】
  incentive²〔ɪn'sɛntɪv〕*n.* 誘因；鼓勵；動機
  improve²〔ɪm'pruv〕*v.* 改善　　bonus⁵〔'bonəs〕*n.* 獎金；紅利
  performance³〔pə'fɔrməns〕*n.* 表現

5.(**C**)　依句意，「休士頓的老師『可能會失去』他們的工作」，選
　　　　(C) *could lose*。而 (A) will loose「將會鬆開」，不合句意；
　　　　(B) loss〔lɔs〕*n.* 損失，
　　　　是名詞，在此不合；
　　　　(D) are lost「迷路了」，
　　　　則不合句意。

lose〔luz〕*v.* 失去【lose-lost-lost】
loss〔lɔs〕*n.* 喪失；損失
loose〔lus〕*v.* 鬆開

TEST 28

Read the following passage and choose the best answer for each blank from the choices below.

A British design company has ___1___ a new product to help children concentrate at school—pre-chewed pencils. The company, called Concentrate, says the pencils look like they have already been chewed, making pupils less likely to put them in their mouths. And they say this is a cheap but effective way of encouraging youngsters to get their teeth into their lessons ___2___. Concentrate, which ___3___ making products that help kids at school and in identifying why they get distracted or are unable to focus in class, claims the chewed end encourages them to get thinking ___4___.

"We know it sounds silly but just ___5___ some ideas and who knows what might happen," said company boss Mark Champkins. "We began to look at the reasons that children might be distracted, uncomfortable or unable to focus in lessons—and we set about designing some simple, cost-effective products to address some of the problems."

1. (A) launched   (B) prosecuted
   (C) dominated   (D) terminated
2. (A) otherwise   (B) instead   (C) attentively   (D) sharply
3. (A) calls for   (B) turns over
   (C) specializes in   (D) follows up
4. (A) beyond doubt   (B) inside out
   (C) straight away   (D) out and out
5. (A) step down   (B) run back over
   (C) pull through   (D) get down to

TEST 28 詳解

A British design company has <u>launched</u> a new product *to help*
                                  1

children concentrate at school—pre-chewed pencils. The company,

called Concentrate, says *the pencils look like they have already been*

chewed, making pupils less likely to put them in their mouths. ***And***

they say *this is a cheap **but** effective way of encouraging youngsters*

to get their teeth into their lessons <u>instead</u>.
                                          2

一家英國的設計公司，已<u>發售</u>要幫助兒童在學校能專心的新產品
                              1
——先咬過的鉛筆。這家名為「專心」的公司表示，這種鉛筆看起來像
是已經被咬過了，讓學生比較不會把它們放進嘴巴裡。他們說這是一種
便宜但有效的方法，反而能讓年輕人認真致力於課業。

* British〔ˈbrɪtɪʃ〕*adj.* 英國的
  design[2]〔dɪˈzaɪn〕*n.* 設計
  product[3]〔ˈprɑdəkt〕*n.* 產品
  concentrate[4]〔ˈkɑnsn̩ˌtret〕*v.* 專心
  chew[3]〔tʃu〕*v.* 嚼
  pre-chewed *adj.* 先咬過的　　pupil[2]〔ˈpjupl̩〕*n.* 學生
  effective[2]〔əˈfɛktɪv〕*adj.* 有效的
  encourage[2]〔ɪnˈkɝɪdʒ〕*v.* 鼓勵
  youngster[3]〔ˈjʌŋstɚ〕*n.* 年輕人
  get one's ***teeth into*** sth. 認真致力於

concentrate on　專心於
= be bent on
= be absorbed in
= be preoccupied with

1. (**A**) (A) ***launch***[4] 〔 lɔntʃ 〕 *v.* 發售;發射
   (B) prosecute[6] 〔'prɑsɪ,kjut 〕 *v.* 起訴;控告
   (C) dominate[4] 〔'dɑmə,net 〕 *v.* 支配;控制
   (D) terminate[3] 〔't͏ɝmə,net 〕 *v.* 終結

2. (**B**) (A) otherwise[4] 〔'ʌðə,waɪz 〕 *adv.* 否則
   (B) ***instead***[3] 〔 ɪn'stɛd 〕 *adv.* 反而;作為代替
   (C) attentively 〔 ə'tɛntɪvlɪ 〕 *adv.* 專注地
   (D) sharply[2] 〔'ʃɑrplɪ 〕 *adv.* 尖銳地

Concentrate, *which specializes in making products that help kids*
                              3

at school and in identifying why they get distracted or are unable to

focus in class, claims *the chewed end encourages them to get thinking*

straight away.
   4

「專心」公司專門製造各種能幫助學童的產品,並確認他們為何會
              3
分心或為何在課堂上無法專心,他們宣稱,被咬過的那一端會鼓勵學童
立刻去動腦思考。
   4

* identify[4] 〔 aɪ'dɛntə,faɪ 〕 *v.* 辨認;確認
  distract[6] 〔 dɪ'strækt 〕 *v.* 使分心
  be unable to V. 無法…
  focus[2] 〔'fokəs 〕 *v.* 專心   claim[2] 〔 klem 〕 *v.* 宣稱

dis	+	tract
away	+	draw

3. (**C**) (A) call for 需要   (B) turn over 移交
   (C) ***specialize in*** 專攻;專精於
      specialize[6] 〔'spɛsəl,aɪz 〕 *v.* 專攻
   (D) follow up 追查;採取後續行動

4. (**C**)　(A) beyond doubt　毋庸置疑

　　　　(B) inside out　由裏向外地；徹底地；完全地

　　　　(C) ***straight away***　立刻；馬上

　　　　(D) out and out　完全地；徹底地

"We know *it sounds silly **but** just* <u>get down to</u> some ideas ***and***
　　　　　　　　　　　　　　　　　　　5

who *knows **what** might happen*," said company boss Mark

Champkins.　"We began to look at the reasons ***that children might***

*be distracted, uncomfortable **or** unable to focus in lessons*—***and*** we

set about designing some simple, cost-effective products *to address*

some of the problems."

　　　「我們知道這聽起來很愚蠢，但就<u>認眞處理</u>一些構想，誰知道會發
　　　　　　　　　　　　　　　　　　　5
生什麼事情呢？」「專心」公司的老闆馬克・查普金斯說。「我們開始
研究兒童可能會分心、不自在，或是在課程中無法專注的原因——我們
著手設計一些簡單又經濟實惠的產品，來處理這些問題。」

　　*　silly¹〔'sɪlɪ〕adj.* 愚蠢的　　　***look at*** 研究；仔細檢查
　　set about 著手　　design²〔dɪ'zaɪn〕*v.* 設計
　　cost-effective *adj.* 經濟實惠的；有成本效益的
　　address²〔ə'drɛs〕*v.* 處理（問題）

5. (**D**)　(A) step down　辭職；退休

　　　　(B) run back over　重新討論或研究

　　　　(C) pull through　度過難關

　　　　(D) ***get down to***　認眞處理；開始做

TEST 29

Read the following passage and choose the best answer for each blank from the choices below.

Traditional medicine includes many different practices and remedies, and varies from one country to another. While some practices seem to offer benefits, others remain __1__.

There is some evidence that seems to support the use of traditional medicine—for example, acupuncture in __2__ pain, yoga to reduce asthma attacks, and Taiji techniques to help the elderly diminish their fear of falls.

Unfortunately, in some cases, the __3__ use of certain herbal remedies can give rise to harm—even death. The herb Ma Huang (ephedra) is traditionally used in China to treat short-term respiratory congestion. In the United States of America, the herb was marketed as a dietary aid, __4__ long-term use led to at least a dozen deaths, heart attacks and strokes.

In developing countries, where more than one-third of the population lacks access to essential medicines, the __5__ of safe and effective traditional and alternative remedies could become an important way of increasing access to health care.

1. (A) memorable   (B) sustainable
   (C) questionable   (D) indispensable
2. (A) inducing   (B) relieving (C) groaning   (D) notifying
3. (A) monotonous (B) notable   (C) individual (D) improper
4. (A) which   (B) whose   (C) that   (D) those
5. (A) provision   (B) prosperity
   (C) projection   (D) procession

TEST 29 詳解

Traditional medicine includes many different practices *and*
remedies, *and* varies *from one country to another*. *While some*
practices seem to offer benefits, others remain <u>questionable</u>.
                                                                    1

　　傳統醫學包含許多不同的做法與治療方法，而且每個國家都不同。
有的方法看似有好處，但有些方法仍然<u>令人質疑</u>。

1

* traditional[2] 〔 trəˈdɪʃənḷ 〕 *adj.* 傳統的
  medicine[2] 〔ˈmɛdəsn̩ 〕 *n.* 醫學
  include[2] 〔 ɪnˈklud 〕 *v.* 包括
  practice[1] 〔ˈpræktɪs 〕 *n.* 做法；慣例
  remedy[4] 〔ˈrɛmədɪ 〕 *n.* 治療方法
  vary[3] 〔ˈvɛrɪ 〕 *v.* 不同；改變
  vary from country to country 每個國家都不同
  while[1] 〔 hwaɪl 〕 *conj.* 雖然　　offer[2] 〔ˈɔfɚ 〕 *v.* 提供
  benefit[3] 〔ˈbɛnəfɪt 〕 *n.* 利益；好處
  remain[3] 〔 rɪˈmen 〕 *v.* 仍然

「包括」的幾種用法：
① S. + include…
② ~, { including / inclusive of } …
③ ~, …included.

1. (**C**)　(A) memorable[4] 〔ˈmɛmərəbḷ 〕 *adj.* 難忘的
　　　　　　(B) sustainable[5] 〔 səˈstenəbḷ 〕 *adj.* 可支持的；可持續的
　　　　　　(C) *questionable*[1] 〔ˈkwɛstʃənəbḷ 〕 *adj.* 可疑的；有問題的
　　　　　　(D) indispensable[5] 〔ˌɪndɪˈspɛnsəbḷ 〕 *adj.* 不可或缺的

There is some evidence [*that seems to support the use of*
traditional medicine—for example, acupuncture in <u>relieving pain</u>,
                                                                    2

yoga to reduce asthma attacks, **and** *Taiji techniques to help the elderly*

diminish their fear of falls.

　　有些證據似乎是支持傳統醫學的——例如，用針灸來減輕疼痛，瑜

珈可減少氣喘發作，還有太極拳技術能幫助年長者，減少他們對跌倒的

恐懼。

* evidence[4] 〔'ɛvədəns 〕 n. 證據　　support[2] 〔 sə'port 〕 v. 支持
acupuncture 〔'ækjʊˌpʌŋktʃɚ 〕 n. 針灸　　yoga[5] 〔'jogə 〕 n. 瑜珈
reduce[3] 〔 rɪ'djus 〕 v. 減少　　asthma[6] 〔'æzmə 〕 n. 氣喘
attack[2] 〔 ə'tæk 〕 n. 發作　　Taiji 〔'taɪ'dʒi 〕 n. 太極拳
technique[3] 〔 tɛk'nik 〕 n. 技術；技巧　　*the elderly* 年長者；老人
diminish[6] 〔 dɪ'mɪnɪʃ 〕 v. 減少　　fall[1] 〔 fɔl 〕 n. 跌倒

2. (**B**)　(A) induce[5] 〔 ɪn'djus 〕 v. 引起；導致
　　　　　(B) **relieve**[4] 〔 rɪ'liv 〕 v. 減輕
　　　　　(C) groan[5] 〔 gron 〕 v. (因痛苦、悲傷等) 呻吟
　　　　　(D) notify[5] 〔'notəˌfaɪ 〕 v. 通知

Unfortunately, in some cases, the improper use *of certain herbal*

remedies can give rise to harm—*even* death.　The herb *Ma Huang*

(ephedra) is *traditionally* used *in China to treat short-term respiratory*

congestion.　In the United States of America, the herb was marketed

as a dietary aid, **_whose_** *long-term use led to at least a dozen deaths,*

heart attacks **and** *strokes.*

　　不幸的是，在一些案例中，<u>不當</u>使用某些藥草療法，可能會造成傷
害，甚至死亡。麻黃是一種藥草，在中國傳統上是用來治療短期的呼吸
困難。在美國，這種藥草被當作飲食輔助品來販售，<u>此藥草的</u>長期使用
已導致至少十二起死亡、心臟病發作，以及中風。　　　　　4

* unfortunately⁴〔ʌnˈfɔrtʃənɪtlɪ〕 *adv.* 不幸地；遺憾地
　certain¹〔ˈsɝtn̩〕 *adj.* 某種；某些
　herbal〔ˈhɝbl̩, ˈɝbl̩〕 *adj.* 藥草的　　***give rise to*** 導致
　herb⁵〔hɝb, ɝb〕 *n.* 藥草　　***Ma Huang*** 麻黃
　ephedra〔ˈɛfədrə〕 *n.* 麻黃【中藥常用的藥材，可治療氣喘、感冒等
　　症狀，但其含有的麻黃素（ephodrine）有讓血管收縮、血壓升高、
　　中樞神經興奮等副作用。因麻黃與其他合成物可做成安非他命，故
　　用量有嚴格規定】
　short-term〔ˈʃɔrtˈtɝm〕 *adj.* 短期的
　respiratory〔rɪˈspaɪrəˌtorɪ〕 *adj.* 呼吸的【respire *v.* 呼吸】
　congestion〔kənˈdʒɛstʃən〕 *n.* 阻塞
　market¹〔ˈmɑrkɪt〕 *v.* （在市場上）銷售
　dietary³〔ˈdaɪəˌtɛrɪ〕 *adj.* 飲食的
　【diet³〔ˈdaɪət〕 *n.* 飲食】
　aid²〔ed〕 *n.* 輔助品
　long-term〔ˈlɔŋˈtɝm〕 *adj.* 長期的
　at least 至少　　***lead to*** 導致
　dozen¹〔ˈdʌzn̩〕 *n.* 一打；十二個
　heart attack 心臟病發
　stroke⁴〔strok〕 *n.* 中風

lead to 導致
= contribute to
= give rise to
= account for
= be responsible for
= bring about
= result in
= cause

3.(**D**)　(A) monotonous⁵〔məˈnɑtn̩əs〕 *adj.* 單調的
　　　　(B) notable⁵〔ˈnotəbl̩〕 *adj.* 值得注意的；著名的
　　　　(C) individual⁵〔ˌɪndəˈvɪdʒuəl〕 *adj.* 個別的　 *n.* 個人
　　　　(D) ***improper***〔ɪmˈprɑpɚ〕 *adj.* 不適當的
　　　　　（ ↔ proper³〔ˈprɑpɚ〕 *adj.* 適當的 ）

4. (**B**)　依句意，「這種草藥的」長期使用，須用關代 which 的所有
　　　　格 **whose**，引導形容詞子句，故選 (B)。而 (A) which 不合句
　　　　意，(C) that 前面不可有逗點，且句意不合，(D) those 爲普通
　　　　代名詞，無連接詞作用，用法與句意皆不合。

In developing countries, ***where*** *more than one-third of the*

population lacks access to essential medicines, the provision *of safe*
　　　　　　　　　　　　　　　　　　　　　　　　　5

and *effective traditional* ***and*** *alternative remedies* could become an

important way *of increasing access to health care.*

　　　在開發中國家，有超過三分之一的人口，都缺乏使用基本藥物的管
道，供應安全又有效的傳統和替代性療法，可能會變成增加醫療管道的
　5
一種重要方式。

* ***developing country***　開發中國家
one-third *n.* 三分之一
population[2] (͵pɑpjə'leʃən) *n.* 人口
lack[1] (læk) *v.* 缺乏
access[4] ('æksɛs) *n.* 接近或使用權
essential[4] (ə'sɛnʃəl) *adj.* 必要的；基本的
effective[2] (ɪ'fɛktɪv) *adj.* 有效的
alternative[6] (ɔl'tɝnətɪv) *adj.* 替代的
health care　醫療保健服務

英文分數的幾點提醒：
① 分子大於 1 時，分母加 s。
② 分母爲 2 時，用 half 表示；
　 分母爲 4 時，用 quarter 表示。
③ 務必約分。

5. (**A**)　(A) ***provision***[5] (prə'vɪʒən) *n.* 供應【provide[2] *v.* 提供】
　　　　(B) prosperity[4] (prɑ'spɛrətɪ) *n.* 繁榮
　　　　(C) projection[6] (prə'dʒɛkʃən) *n.* 投射；投影
　　　　(D) procession[5] (prə'sɛʃən) *n.* 行列；（隊伍的）行進

TEST 30

Read the following passage and choose the best answer for each blank from the choices below.

To attain convenience, we have gone too deep into a world of grotesqueness. I do believe that a reduction in our quality of life can __1__ materialism. When people become too short-sighted, they tend to overlook the importance of taste and quality. By quality, I __2__ quiet, neatness, space, composure, etc. Instances of convenience versus quality can be found everywhere in our society. Take road building for example. Many cities are trying to build as many roads as possible, as they think that will effectively solve most traffic problems. But I think the quiet of our living environment is __3__. Another example is the abuse of plastic bags. Years ago, plastic bags were thought of as the handiest containers. But now we have to admit that we are incapable of treating this poison of the century. Therefore, I am firmly persuaded that good quality and taste, once __4__, are extremely hard to restore. Convenience, on the other hand, can wait until we find it vital to our daily life. If we believe in the value of good quality in all aspects of life, then we should __5__ enjoying too much convenience.

1. (A) result from (B) be good for (C) happen to (D) make up
2. (A) am taking up   (B) am referring to
   (C) am summing up   (D) am paying off
3. (A) sacrificed   (B) transformed
   (C) improved   (D) privileged
4. (A) impairment (B) impaired   (C) impairing (D) impair
5. (A) derive from   (B) refrain from
   (C) devote to   (D) look forward to

TEST 30 詳解

To attain convenience, we have gone *too deep into a world of*

grotesqueness. I do believe *that a reduction in our quality of life can*

<u>result from</u> *materialism.* **When** *people become too short-sighted*, they
1

tend to overlook the importance *of taste* **and** *quality.* *By quality*, I

<u>am referring to</u> quiet, neatness, space, composure, etc.
2

　　爲了獲得便利，我們已經深深地進入一個古怪的世界。我的確相
信我們生活品質的降低，可能<u>起因於</u>物質主義。當人們變得太短視近
　　　　　　　　　　　　　　　　1
利時，他們傾向於忽略品味和品質的重要性。所謂的品質，我<u>指的是</u>
安靜、整潔、空間、沉著冷靜等。　　　　　　　　　　　　　　2

　　* attain[6] 〔ə'ten 〕 *v.* 達到；獲得
　　convenience[4] 〔kən'vinjəns 〕 *n.* 方便
　　go too deep into 深入（某地）【引申爲「太過火」】
　　grotesqueness 〔gro'tɛsknɪs 〕 *n.* 怪異；可笑
　　reduction[4] 〔rɪ'dʌkʃən 〕 *n.* 減少；降低
　　quality[2] 〔'kwɑlətɪ 〕 *n.* 品質　　***quality of life*** 生活品質
　　materialism[6] 〔mə'tɪrɪəlˌɪzəm 〕 *n.* 物質主義

materialism *n.* 物質主義	quality of life 生活品質
capitalism *n.* 資本主義	standard of living 生活水準

　　short-sighted 〔'ʃɔrt'saɪtɪd 〕 *adj.* 短視近利的
　　tend to 易於；傾向於（ = *be inclined to* ）

overlook[4] (ˌovɚˈlʊk) v. 忽視
taste[1] (test) n. 品味；欣賞力
quiet[1] (ˈkwaɪət) n. 安靜
neatness (ˈnitnɪs) n. 乾淨；整潔
【neat[2] (nit) adj. 整潔的】
composure (kəmˈpoʒɚ) n. 沉著；冷靜
etc. ···等等 (= *et cetera* (ɛtˈsɛtrə))

overlook[4] v. 忽視
= ignore[2]
= neglect[4]
= disregard[6]

1. (**A**)　(A) *result from* 起因於　　(B) be good for 對···有好處
　　　　　　(C) happen to 碰巧　　　　(D) make up 組成

2. (**B**)　(A) take up 開始從事　　(B) *refer to* 是指
　　　　　　(C) sum up 總結　　　　(D) pay off 得到；回報；還清

Instances *of convenience versus quality* can be found *everywhere in our society*. Take road building *for example*. Many cities are trying to build *as* many roads *as possible*, *as they think **that** will effectively solve most traffic problems.* **But** I think the quiet *of our living environment* is <u>sacrificed</u>.

3

在我們的社會中，隨處可見便利與品質相抗衡的實例。就以建造道路為例好了，很多城市都想要儘可能建造很多道路，因為人們認為這能有效解決大多數的交通問題。但我認為我們平靜的生活環境被犧牲了。

3

* instance[2] (ˈɪnstəns) n. 實例　　versus[5] (ˈvɝsəs) prep. ···對···
　society[2] (səˈsaɪətɪ) n. 社會　　*take···for example* 以···為例
　as···as possible 儘可能···

effectively⁶〔ə'fɛktɪvlɪ〕*adv.* 有效地　　solve²〔sɑlv〕*v.* 解決
environment²〔ɪn'vaɪrənmənt〕*n.* 環境

3. (**A**)　(A) ***sacrifice***⁴〔'sækrə‚faɪs〕*v.* 犧牲
　　　　(B) transform⁴〔træns'fɔrm〕*v.* 使轉變
　　　　(C) improve²〔ɪm'pruv〕*v.* 改善
　　　　(D) privilege⁴〔'prɪvḷɪdʒ〕*v.* 給予…特權　*n.* 特權

Another example is the abuse *of plastic bags*. *Years ago*, plastic

bags were thought of as the handiest containers. ***But*** *now* we have

to admit ***that*** *we are incapable of treating this poison of the century.*

Therefore, I am *firmly* persuaded ***that*** *good quality and taste, once*

impaired, are *extremely* hard to restore.
4

另一個例子是塑膠袋的濫用。很多年以前，塑膠袋被認為是最方便的容器。但現在我們必須承認，我們無法處理這個世紀毒物。因此，我非常確信，良好的品質和品味，一旦被損害，就非常難以恢復。
4

＊abuse⁶〔ə'bjus〕*n.* 濫用　　plastic³〔'plæstɪk〕*adj.* 塑膠的
be thought of as 被認為是
handy³〔'hændɪ〕*adj.* 在手邊的；方便的
container⁴〔kən'tenɚ〕*n.* 容器　　admit³〔əd'mɪt〕*v.* 承認
be incapable of 無法　　treat⁵〔trit〕*v.* 處理
poison²〔'pɔɪzn̩〕*n.* 毒藥　　century²〔'sɛntʃərɪ〕*n.* 世紀
firmly²〔'fɝmlɪ〕*adv.* 堅定地
persuade³〔pɚ'swed〕*v.* 說服；使相信
once¹〔wʌns〕*conj.* 一旦
extremely³〔ɪk'strimlɪ〕*adv.* 極度地；非常
restore⁴〔rɪ'stor〕*v.* 恢復

4.(**B**)　副詞子句中，句意很明顯，主詞和 be 動詞可同時省略，依句意，「良好的品質和品味一旦被損害，…」，…good quality and taste, once they are impaired,…，可將 they are 省略，簡化成 …, once *impaired*,…，故選 (B)。

　　　　impair〔ɪmˋpɛr〕v. 損害

Convenience, *on the other hand*, can wait *until we find it vital to our*

daily life. *If we believe in the value of good quality in all aspects of*

life, then we should <u>refrain from</u> enjoying *too* much convenience.
　　　　　　　　　　　　　5

從另一個角度來看，除非便利對我們日常生活非常重要，否則就不應該擺在第一位。如果我們相信，在生活中各方面都有良好品質的價值，那麼我們就應該克制自己不要享受太多的便利。
　　　　　　　5

　　* *on the other hand* 另一方面；從另一個角度來看
　　can wait （事情、工作）可以延緩；延後
　　find[1]〔faɪnd〕v. 覺得　　vital[4]〔ˋvaɪtl̩〕adj. 非常重要的
　　daily life 日常生活　　*believe in* 相信（～的價值）
　　aspect[4]〔ˋæspɛkt〕n. 方面

5.(**B**)　(A) derive from 起源於（= *originate from*）
　　　　(B) *refrain from* 克制不要
　　　　(C) devote *oneself* to 致力於（= *dedicate oneself to*
　　　　　　= *commit oneself to*）
　　　　(D) look forward to + V-ing 期待～
　　　　　　I'm looking forward to seeing you.
　　　　　（我期待見到你。）

TEST 31

Read the following passage and choose the best answer for each blank from the choices below.

Capsule hotels are unique accommodations developed in Japan. They usually cost from 2,500 yen to 4,500 yen per night. __1__ they are cheap, many businessmen who can't go home will choose to stay at capsule hotels. Capsule hotels are also popular among foreign travelers. In a capsule hotel, each guest stays in a small sleeping space in which there is a TV, an alarm clock, a light, __2__. Almost everything is provided. Guests close a thin curtain between them and the ten to seventy other men sleeping in the same area. __3__ the noise in capsule hotels, earplugs might be helpful. Sometimes there's a hole providing some air circulation. Shower rooms and restrooms are __4__ by all guests. and some capsule hotels may offer a large public bath or a sauna. Women aren't often allowed in capsule hotels __5__ security reasons. Flexible, at times strange, and self-contained, they are, however, after two weeks, a bit depressing.

1. (A) When   (B) Before   (C) Though   (D) Since
2. (A) on the contrary   (B) nothing else
    (C) and so on   (D) name a few
3. (A) To block   (B) Blocked
    (C) Block   (D) Having blocked
4. (A) divided   (B) shared   (C) combined   (D) adapted
5. (A) in addition to   (B) due to
    (C) in spite of   (D) except for

TEST 31 詳解

Capsule hotels are unique accommodations *developed in Japan.*

They *usually* cost *from 2,500 yen to 4,500 yen per night.* __Since__ they
1

are cheap, many businessmen *who* can't go home will choose to stay

at capsule hotels. Capsule hotels are *also* popular *among foreign*

travelers.

膠囊旅館是日本研發出的獨特住宿設備。住宿一晚的價格通常是
2,500 到 4,500 日元。因為很便宜，所以許多無法回家的商務人士，會
1
選擇住膠囊旅館。膠囊旅館也很受外國旅客的歡迎。

* capsule⁶ ('kæps!̩) *n.* 膠囊
  capsule hotel 膠囊旅館
  unique⁴ (ju'nik) *adj.* 獨特的
  accommodations⁶ (ə,kɑmə'deʃənz)
      n. pl. 住宿設備
  develop² (dɪ'vɛləp) *v.* 研發   cost¹ (kɔst) *v.* 花費
  per² (pə‚ pɝ) *prep.* 每   stay¹ (ste) *v.* 暫住
  foreign¹ ('fɔrɪn) *adj.* 外國的

┌─────────────────────────────┐
│ capsule ('kæps!̩) *n.* 膠囊 │
│ tablet ('tæblɪt) *n.* 藥錠 │
│ pill (pɪl) *n.* 藥丸   │
└─────────────────────────────┘

1. (**D**)　依句意，選 (D) *Since*「因為」(= *Because*)。
　　而 (A) When「當…的時候」，(B) Before「在…之前」，
　　(C) Though「雖然」，皆不合句意。

In a capsule hotel, each guest stays *in a small sleeping space in which there is a TV, an alarm clock, a light, and so on.* Almost everything is provided. Guests close a thin curtain *between them and the ten to seventy other men sleeping in the same area.* *To block the noise in capsule hotels*, earplugs might be helpful. *Sometimes* there's a hole *providing some air circulation.*

在膠囊旅館中，每位房客都住在一個裡面有一台電視、一個鬧鐘、一盞燈等等的小型睡眠空間。幾乎所有東西都有提供。房客會關上一扇薄的簾子，把自己和其他十到七十個睡在同樣地方的人隔開。為了阻絕膠囊旅館中的噪音，耳塞也許能幫得上忙。有時候膠囊旅館中，會有個洞提供一些空氣流通。

* guest[1] 〔 gɛst 〕 *n.* (旅館的) 旅客　　*alarm clock* 鬧鐘
  provide[2] 〔 prə'vaɪd 〕 *v.* 提供　　thin[2] 〔 θɪn 〕 *adj.* 薄的
  curtain[2] 〔'kɝtn̩ 〕 *n.* 窗簾；布簾
  earplug 〔'ɪrˌplʌg 〕 *n.* 耳塞【plug[3] *n.* (塞住水管等管口的) 塞子；
  　栓子 】　　hole[1] 〔 hol 〕 *n.* 洞
  circulation[4] 〔ˌsɝkjə'leʃən 〕 *n.* 循環；流通

2. (**C**)　(A) on the contrary 相反地
　　　　(B) nothing else 沒有別的
　　　　(C) **and so on** ⋯等等 (*= and so forth = and the like = etc.*)
　　　　(D) name a few 舉出一些

3. (**A**)　不定詞可表「目的」，故選 (A) **To block**「為了阻絕」。
而 (B) Blocked「被阻絕」，(C) Block[1]〔blɑk〕*v.* 阻擋；
阻絕，(D) Having blocked「已經阻絕」，皆不合句意。

表「目的」的說法有：

to V. 為了⋯
= in order to V.
= so as to V.

with an eye to N/V-ing 為了⋯
= with a view to N/V-ing
= for the purpose of N/V-ing

so that 子句　所以；以便於
= in order that 子句

Shower rooms *and* restrooms are <u>shared</u> *by all guests*, *and* some
₄
capsule hotels may offer a large public bath *or* a sauna.　Women

aren't *often* allowed *in capsule hotels <u>due to</u> security reasons*.
₅

[*Flexible*, *at times strange*, *and self-contained*,] they are, *however*,

after two weeks, *a bit* depressing.

淋浴間和廁所是所有房客<u>共用</u>的，而有些膠囊旅館可能會提供大型公共
　　　　　　　　　　　4
澡堂或是桑拿。<u>基於</u>安全的理由，女性通常不允許在膠囊旅館入住。膠
　　　　　5
囊旅館很有彈性，有時奇怪，且設施齊全，然而入住超過兩週後，可能
會讓人有點沮喪。

* shower[2] 〔'ʃauɚ〕*n.* 淋浴
restroom[2] 〔'rɛst,rum〕*n.* 廁所 (= *rest room*)
bath[1] 〔bæθ〕*n.* 浴室；澡堂
sauna 〔'saunə〕*n.* 桑拿；三溫暖

restroom[2] *n.* 廁所
= bathroom[1]
= lavatory

allow[1] 〔ə'lau〕*v.* 允許

security[3] 〔 sɪˈkjʊrətɪ 〕 *n.* 安全（ = *safety*[2] ）

flexible[4] 〔ˈflɛksəbḷ 〕 *adj.* 有彈性的

commendably 〔 kəˈmɛndəblɪ 〕 *adv.* 值得稱讚地；很好地

modular 〔ˈmɑdʒʊlɚ 〕 *adj.* 積木式的；組合式的

self-contained 〔ˌsɛlfkənˈtend 〕 *adj.* 設施齊全的；自給自足的

【contain[2] 〔 kənˈten 〕 *v.* 包含 】

depressing[4] 〔 dɪˈprɛsɪŋ 〕 *adj.* 令人沮喪的

4. (**B**)　(A) divide[2] 〔 dəˈvaɪd 〕 *v.* 分割；劃分

　　　　　(B) *share*[2] 〔 ʃɛr 〕 *v.* 分享；共用

　　　　　(C) combine[3] 〔 kəmˈbaɪn 〕 *v.* 結合

　　　　　(D) adapt[4] 〔 əˈdæpt 〕 *v.* 適應；改編

5. (**B**)　(A) in addition to　除了…之外（還有）（ = *besides*[2] ）

　　　　　(B) *due to*　因為；由於

$$
\text{I was late}
\left\{
\begin{array}{l}
\textit{due to} \\
\textit{owing to} \\
\textit{thanks to} \\
\textit{on account of} \\
\textit{because of}
\end{array}
\right\}
\text{heavy traffic.}
$$

　　　　　（我因為交通繁忙，所以遲到了。）

　　　　　1. thanks to 多用在好的方面，作「幸虧；由於」解，用在
　　　　　　　壞的方面，作「歸咎於；由於」解，有諷刺的意味。

　　　　　2. 一般人以為 *due to* 只能放在句子後面，但現代英語 due
　　　　　　　to 也可放在句首。

　　　　　　　Due to heavy traffic, I was late.

　　　　　　　（因為繁忙的交通，我遲到了。）

　　　　　(C) in spite of　儘管（ = *despite*[4] ）

　　　　　(D) except for　除了…之外

TEST 32

Read the following passage and choose the best answer for each blank from the choices below.

You may think that you feel most alert and energetic in the morning after eight hours of sleeping and resting. ___1___, it is actually the time when you may feel dizzy and disoriented because of sleep inertia—the phenomenon in which the part of your brain responsible for consciousness is turned on but the part that deals with complex and advanced thinking is still ___2___. Unfortunately, this phenomenon can last up to two hours if you do not supply glucose to your brain for it to function well.

One of the best ways to get rid of this addled state of mind is to have a bowl of oatmeal with skim milk, ___3___ can provide a steady glucose infusion and enhance information processing in the brain. Actually, any type of whole grain with milk or soybean milk will do more good than just a cup of coffee. Using a cup of coffee to replace a real meal is just ___4___ low blood sugar by temporarily stimulating the brain with caffeine. That will not only do nothing to meet the need for energy, but also lead to malnutrition ___5___.

1. (A) In addition (B) However (C) Even (D) By contrast
2. (A) warming up   (B) winning out
   (C) taking the lead   (D) springing up
3. (A) it   (B) that   (C) which (D) also
4. (A) manipulating   (B) masking
   (C) mastering   (D) mistaking
5. (A) for the time being   (B) in any case
   (C) on the whole   (D) in the long run

TEST 32 詳解

You may think *that you feel most alert and energetic in the morning after eight hours of sleeping and resting.* <u>However</u>, it is
1
actually the time *when you may feel dizzy and disoriented because of sleep inertia—the phenomenon* [*in which the part of your brain responsible for consciousness is turned on but the part that deals with complex and advanced thinking is still <u>warming up</u>.*] *Unfortunately,*
2
this phenomenon can last *up to two hours if you do not supply glucose to your brain for it to function well.*

　　你可能會認為，在經過八小時的睡眠和休息之後的早晨，你會感到非常機警且精力充沛。<u>然而</u>，這其實正是你可能會覺得頭昏，且失去判
1
斷力的時候，原兇就是睡眠惰性——此種現象是你頭腦負責意識的區塊已經啟動，但處理複雜高階思考的區塊還在<u>暖機</u>。不幸的是，如果你不
2
供給葡萄糖來讓你的大腦順利運作的話，這個現象可能會持續達兩個小時之久。

* alert⁴ (ə'lɜt) *adj.* 機警的；靈活的
  energetic³ (ˌɛnɚ'dʒɛtɪk) *adj.* 充滿活力的
  rest¹ (rɛst) *v.* 休息
  actually³ ('æktʃʊəlɪ) *adv.* 實際上

dizzy[2] (ˈdɪzɪ) *adj.* 頭昏的

disoriented (dɪsˈorɪˌɛntɪd) *adj.* 失去方向的；失去判斷力的

inertia (ɪˈnɝʃə) *n.* 無力症　　***sleep inertia*** 睡眠惰性

phenomenon[4] (fəˈnɑməˌnɑn) *n.* 現象【複數形爲 phenomen<u>a</u>】

responsible[2] (rɪˈspɑnsəbḷ) *adj.* 負責的 < *for* >

consciousness (ˈkɑnʃəsnɪs) *n.* 意識

【conscious[3] (ˈkɑnʃəs) *adj.* 知道的；察覺到的】

turn on 啟動　　***deal with*** 處理 (= *cope with*)

complex[3] (ˈkɑmplɛks) *adj.* 複雜的

advanced[3] (ədˈvænst) *adj.* 高階的；先進的

thinking[1] (ˈθɪŋkɪŋ) *n.* 思考；思想

unfortunately[4] (ʌnˈfɔrtʃənɪtlɪ) *adv.* 不幸地；遺憾地

last[1] (læst) *v.* 持續　　supply[2] (səˈplaɪ) *v.* 供給

glucose (ˈglukos) *n.* 葡萄糖　　function[2] (ˈfʌŋkʃən) *v.* 運作

1. (**B**) 依句意，選 (B) ***However*** 「然而」。

　　而 (A) In addition 「此外」，(C) Even 「甚至」，

　　(D) By contrast 「對比之下」，皆不合句意。

2. (**A**) (A) ***warm up*** 暖身

　　(B) win out 勝出

　　(C) take the lead 領先；率先

　　(D) spring up 突然出現；迅速增長

One *of the best ways to get rid of this addled state of mind* is to

have a bowl *of oatmeal with skim milk,* ***which*** *can provide a steady*

3

glucose infusion ***and*** *enhance information processing in the brain.*

Actually, any type *of whole grain with milk* ***or*** *soybean milk* will do

more good ***than*** *just a cup of coffee.* Using a cup of coffee *to replace a real meal* is *just* <u>masking</u> low blood sugar *by temporarily stimulating*
4

the brain with caffeine. That will ***not only*** do nothing to meet the

need *for energy,* ***but also*** lead to malnutrition *in the long run.*
5

　　要除去腦袋昏亂狀態最好的方式之一，就是吃一碗燕麥片加脫脂牛奶，這樣可以提供穩定注入的葡萄糖，增強腦內的資訊處理。事實上，任何全穀物加牛奶或豆漿，都比只喝一杯咖啡來得好。用一杯咖啡來取代正餐，只是藉由暫時用咖啡因刺激大腦，來<u>掩飾</u>低血糖的狀態。這樣
4
不僅無法滿足身體對能量的需求，而且<u>最後</u>會導致營養不良。
5

* ***get rid of*** 除去；擺脫（= *remove*[3]）
addled〔ˈædl̩d〕*adj.* 昏亂的；腐壞的　　state[1]〔stet〕*n.* 狀態
state of mind 心理狀態；心境　　have[1]〔hæv〕*v.* 吃
bowl[1]〔bol〕*n.* 碗　　oatmeal[5]〔ˈotˌmil〕*n.* 燕麥片
skim[6]〔skɪm〕*adj.*（牛奶等）脫脂的　　***skim milk*** 脫脂牛奶
steady[3]〔ˈstɛdɪ〕*adj.* 穩定的　　infusion〔ɪnˈfjuʒən〕*n.* 注入
enhance[3]〔ɪnˈhæns〕*v.* 提高；增進（= *boost*[6]〔bust〕）
processing[3]〔ˈprɑsɛsɪŋ〕*n.* 處理　　grain[3]〔gren〕*n.* 穀物
whole grain 全穀物　　soybean[2]〔ˈsɔɪˌbin〕*n.* 大豆；黃豆
soybean milk 豆漿　　***do good*** 有好處
replace[3]〔rɪˈples〕*v.* 取代　　meal[2]〔mil〕*n.* 一餐
blood suagr 血糖　　temporarily[3]〔ˈtɛmpəˌrɛrɪlɪ〕*adv.* 暫時地
stimulate[6]〔ˈstɪmjəˌlet〕*v.* 刺激
coffeine[6]〔ˈkæfiɪn〕*n.* 咖啡因
not only…but also 不僅…而且

meet¹〔mit〕v. 滿足（需求）

energy²〔ˈɛnɚdʒɪ〕n. 能量

malnutrition〔͵mælnuˈtrɪʃən〕n. 營養不良【mal（=*bad*）】

lead to 導致

Hard work $\left\{ \begin{array}{l} \textit{leads to} \\ \textit{results in} \\ \textit{brings about} \\ \textit{gives rise to} \end{array} \right\}$ successs.

（努力就會成功。）

3. (**C**) 關代 which 代替前面的先行詞 to have...milk，引導補述用法的形容詞子句，故選 (C)。而 (B) 關代 that 前面不可有逗點，在此不合；(A) it 是代名詞，(D) also「也」是副詞，無連接詞作用，在此不合。

4. (**B**) (A) manipulate⁶〔məˈnɪpjəͺlet〕v. 操縱
    (B) ***mask***²〔mæsk〕v. 掩飾；偽裝   *n.* 面具
    (C) master¹〔ˈmæstɚ〕v. 精通
    (D) mistake²〔məˈstek〕v. 誤解；弄錯

5. (**D**) (A) for the time being 暫時（= *temporarily*³）
    (B) in any case 無論如何
    (C) on the whole 整體而言
    (D) ***in the long run*** 最後（= *at length* = *at last*）

【劉毅老師的話】

　　把這本克漏字測驗當課本讀，每天朗誦，等於複習了 7000 字。唯有閱讀 7000字範圍內的書，才能把 7000 字背得滾瓜爛熟。

TEST 33

Read the following passage and choose the best answer for each blank from the choices below.

One in 10 new fathers may have the baby blues, US researchers believe, based on their search of medical literature. Lack of sleep and new responsibilities, or supporting a wife with post-natal depression can be ___1___, they say. The Eastern Virginia Medical School team based their findings on 43 studies involving 28,004 parents from 16 different countries ___2___ the UK and the US. They found new fathers were generally happiest in the early weeks after the birth of their baby, with depression kicking in after three to six months. And depression appeared to be shared—men were far more ___3___ be depressed if their partner also had post-natal depression. Dr. James Paulson and Sharnail Bazemore, who ___4___ the study, said more efforts should be made to improve screening and referral of at-risk fathers, particularly as mounting evidence suggests that early paternal depression may have ___5___ emotional, behavioral and developmental effects on children.

1. (A) trifles   (B) triggers   (C) trophies   (D) troops
2. (A) to include   (B) included   (C) inclusive of (D) include
3. (A) possible to (B) likely to   (C) willing to   (D) eager to
4. (A) carried out   (B) carried on
   (C) carried off   (D) carried over
5. (A) superficial   (B) superior
   (C) subordinate   (D) substantial

TEST 33 詳解

One *in 10 new fathers* may have the baby blues, *US researchers believe, based on their search of medical literature.* Lack *of sleep and* new responsibilities, *or* supporting a wife *with post-natal depression* can be <u>triggers</u>, they say. The Eastern Virginia Medical School team
1
based their findings *on 43 studies involving 28,004 parents from 16 different countries <u>inclusive of</u> the UK and the US.* They found *new*
2
fathers were generally happiest in the early weeks after the birth of their baby, with depression kicking in after three to six months.

　　美國的研究人員根據他們對醫學文獻的搜尋，認為十個新手父親中，就有一個可能有產後憂鬱症。研究人員表示，缺乏睡眠和新的責任到來，或要安慰有產後憂鬱症的妻子，都可能是新手父親得產後憂鬱症的<u>起因</u>。東維吉尼亞醫學院團隊的研究結果，是根據43項研究，其中
1
有28,004位父母親，來自<u>包括</u>英國和美國在內的16個不同的國家。
2
他們發現，新手父親通常在寶寶出生後，最初的幾個星期是最快樂的，憂鬱症會在三到六個月後發生。

　　* *baby blues* 產後憂鬱症【是在產前產後，因為內外在環境、心理及生
　　理的改變，讓新手父母在照顧第一胎寶寶時亂了手腳，承受不住龐大
　　的壓力而產生憂鬱症症狀】

based on 根據

search[2] 〔 sɝtʃ 〕 *n.* 搜尋

medical[3] 〔'mɛdɪkļ〕 *adj.* 醫學的

literature[4] 〔'lɪtərətʃə〕 *n.* 文學；文獻

lack[1] 〔 læk 〕 *n.* 缺乏

responsibility[3] 〔 rɪ,spɑnsə'bɪlətɪ 〕 *n.* 責任

support[2] 〔 sə'port 〕 *v.* 支持；鼓勵；安慰

post-natal 〔'post'netļ〕 *adj.* 產後的；出生後的

depression[4] 〔 dɪ'prɛʃən 〕 *n.* 沮喪；憂鬱（症）

Eastern Virginia Medical School 東維吉尼亞醫學院【1973 年建

立，雖然歷史不算悠久，但卻是美國東部相當著名的醫學大學】

base A on B 使 A 以 B 爲基礎

findings 〔'faɪndɪŋz〕 *n. pl.* 研究發現

involve[1] 〔 ɪn'vɑlv 〕 *v.* 包含　　***kick in*** 開始起作用

> "post-" 表 "after"，如：
>
> <u>post</u> ¦ <u>nat</u> ¦ <u>al</u> *adj.* 產後的
> after ¦ born ¦ *adj.*
>
> <u>post</u> ¦ <u>pone</u> *v.* 延期
> after ¦ put
>
> <u>post</u> ¦ <u>script</u> *n.* 後記
> after ¦ write

---

1. (**B**)　(A) trifle[5] 〔'traɪfļ〕 *n.* 瑣事；不重要的小事

　　　　　(B) ***trigger***[6] 〔'trɪgə〕 *n.* 板機；誘因；起因

　　　　　(C) trophy[6] 〔'trofɪ〕 *n.* 戰利品；獎盃

　　　　　(D) troops[3] 〔 trups 〕 *n. pl.* 軍隊；部隊

2. (**C**)　依文法和句意，選 (C) ***inclusive of*** 「包括」（ = *including* ）。
　　　　而 (A) to include 「爲了包括」，不合句意，(B) included 「被
　　　　包括在內的」，須置於名詞之後，在此不合，(D) include 「包
　　　　括」，是原形動詞，和主要動詞之間無連接詞，故用法不合。

> 「包括」的幾種用法：
>
> ① S. + include…
>
> ② ~, { including / inclusive of } …
>
> ③ ~, …included.

And depression appeared to be shared—men were *far more* <u>likely to</u>
3
be depressed *if their partner also had post-natal depression.* Dr.

James Paulson *and* Sharnail Bazemore, *who* <u>carried out</u> the study,
4
said more efforts should be made *to improve screening and referral*

of at-risk fathers, │*particularly as mounting evidence suggests that*

early paternal depression may have <u>substantial</u> *emotional, behavioral*
5
and developmental effects on children.│

憂鬱似乎是會共同擁有的——如果男士的伴侶也有產後憂鬱症，他們就
更加有可能會情緒低落。<u>執行</u>這項研究的詹姆士・保羅森和沙內爾・貝
　　　　　　　　　　4
茲摩爾博士說，應該要更加努力，改善有產後憂鬱症危機的父親篩檢和
轉診，特別是當越來越多的證據顯示，早期父親產後憂鬱症，可能會對
小孩情緒上、行為上，及身心發展方面，有<u>相當大的</u>影響。
　　　　　　　　　　　　　　　　5

* appear[1] 〔ə'pɪr〕 v. 似乎（= seem[1]）
  share[2] 〔ʃɛr〕 v. 分享；共同擁有
  depressed[4] 〔dɪ'prɛst〕 adj. 沮喪的　　*make efforts* 努力
  improve[2] 〔ɪm'pruv〕 v. 改善
  screening 〔'skrinɪŋ〕 n. 篩選；審查
  referral 〔rɪ'fɝəl〕 n. 轉診介紹
  【refer[4] v. 提到；參考；囑咐（病人）轉診於】
  at-risk 〔ət'rɪsk〕 adj. 處於危險的
  particularly[2] 〔pə'tɪkjələlɪ〕 adv. 尤其；特別是
  mount[5] 〔maʊnt〕 v. 增加

evidence[4] ('ɛvədəns) *n.* 證據
suggest[3] (səg'dʒɛst) *v.* 顯示
paternal (pə'tɜnl) *adj.* 父親的
emotional[4] (ɪ'moʃənl) *adj.* 情緒的；
　感情的
behavioral[4] (bɪ'hevjərəl) *adj.* 行為的
developmental[2] (dɪ,vɛləp'mɛntl) *adj.* 身心發展的

pater ¦ nal *adj.* 父親的
father ¦ *adj.*
mater ¦ nal *adj.* 母親的
mother ¦ *adj.*

3. (**B**) 　依句意，選 (B) *likely to*。*be likely to V.* 可能…
　　而 (A) possible「可能的」，只能修飾事物，不可修飾人；
　　而 (C) be willing to「願意」，(D) be eager to「急著要；
　　渴望」，則不合句意。

4. (**A**) 　(A) *carry out* 執行
　　(B) carry on　繼續
　　(C) carry off　成功地應付 (難事)；獲 (獎)
　　(D) carry over　(使) 繼續下去；(使) 延伸

5. (**D**) 　(A) superficial[5] (,supɚ'fɪʃəl) *adj.* 表面的；膚淺的
　　(B) superior[3] (sə'pɪrɪɚ) *adj.* 較優秀的
　　(C) subordinate[6] (sə'bɔrdṇɪt) *adj.* 下級的；次要的
　　(D) *substantial*[5] (sʌb'stænʃəl) *adj.* 實質的；相當大的
　　　Your English is pretty good.

$$\text{You have made} \left\{\begin{array}{l} \text{substantial} \\ \text{significant} \\ \text{considerable} \end{array}\right\} \text{progress.}$$

　　　(你的英文很棒。你已經有相當大的進步。)

TEST 34

Read the following passage and choose the best answer for each blank from the choices below.

For those who love the thrill of danger and who are willing to take risks, becoming a stuntman might sound like the perfect career choice. The most important qualities ___1___ to become a stuntman are strength, stamina and coordination. Physical ___2___ is an essential element of this job, and it can be very helpful to have a background in martial arts or gymnastics. Typically, no specific degree or certification is required to become a stuntman. ___3___, not everyone can be a stuntman. To become a stuntman, one has to become ___4___ at a wide variety of daredevil sports, such as scuba diving, rock climbing and high-performance driving and motorcycling. Every stunt is executed exactly as planned, practiced, rehearsed, and reviewed. With the advancement of technology and computer simulation, the need for stuntmen in the movie industry is ___5___. Instead of hiring stuntmen, many films use computer generated images to portray the dangerous scenes.

1. (A) which needed   (B) to need
   (C) needed   (D) needing
2. (A) mold   (B) transformation
   (C) fitness   (D) challenge
3. (A) Therefore   (B) However   (C) Besides   (D) Otherwise
4. (A) adopt   (B) adapt   (C) adjust   (D) adept
5. (A) on the decline   (B) on the increase
   (C) on the edge   (D) on the record

TEST 34 詳解

For those ***who** love the thrill of danger **and who** are willing to take risks*, becoming a stuntman might sound like the perfect career choice. The *most* important qualities <u>*needed* to become a stuntman</u>
1
are strength, stamina ***and*** coordination. Physical <u>fitness</u> is an
2
essential element *of this job*, **and** it can be *very* helpful to have a background *in martial arts **or** gymnastics*.

對於那些喜歡危險刺激，和願意冒險的人而言，成為一位特技演員，可能聽起來像是完美的職業選擇。成為特技演員所<u>需要的</u>重要特
1
質，是力量、耐力，以及協調性。身體<u>健康</u>是這項工作的基本要素，
而且有武術或體操背景會非常有幫助。 2

* thrill[5] (θrɪl) *n.* 刺激
willing[2] ('wɪlɪŋ) *adj.* 願意的　　***take a risk*** 冒險
stuntman ('stʌntmæn) *n.* 特技演員；替身演員
【stunt[6] (stʌnt) *n.* 特技】
perfect[2] ('pɜfɪkt) *adj.* 完美的　　career[4] (kə'rɪr) *n.* 職業；生涯
quality[2] ('kwɑlətɪ) *n.* 特質　　strength[3] (strɛŋθ) *n.* 力量
stamina ('stæmənə) *n.* 耐力；毅力
coordination (ko,ɔrdn̩'eʃən) *n.* 協調
【coordinate[6] (ko'ɔrdn̩,et) *v.* 使協調】
physical[4] ('fɪzɪkl̩) *adj.* 身體的
essential[4] (ə'sɛnʃəl) *adj.* 必要的；非常重要的
element[2] ('ɛləmənt) *n.* 要素

background[3] 〔'bæk,graʊnd 〕 n. 背景　　***martial arts***　武術
gymnastics 〔 dʒɪm'næstɪks 〕 n. 體操

1. (**C**)　依句意,「所需要的重要技能」important qualities which are needed,可將關代與 be 動詞 which are 同時省略,簡化成過去分詞 ***needed*** 修飾 qualities,故選 (C)。

2. (**C**)　(A) mold[6] 〔 mold 〕 n. 模子
　　　　(B) transformation[6] 〔,trænsfə'meʃən 〕 n. 轉變
　　　　(C) ***fitness***[2] 〔'fɪtnɪs 〕 n. 健康【 fit[2] 〔 fɪt 〕 adj. 健康的 】
　　　　(D) challenge[3] 〔'tʃælɪndʒ 〕 n. 挑戰

Typically, no specific degree ***or*** certification is required *to become a stuntman. However*, not everyone can be a stuntman. *To become a stuntman*, one has to become adept [4] *at a wide variety of daredevil sports, such as scuba diving, rock climbing **and** high-performance driving **and** motorcycling.* Every stunt is executed *exactly **as** planned, practiced, rehearsed, **and** reviewed.*

通常要成為特技演員,不需要特定的學位或證書。然而,不是每個人都可以成為特技演員。要成為一位特技演員,必須熟練很多各式各樣的大膽冒險運動,像是水肺潛水、攀岩,和駕駛高性能汽車和騎機車。每項特技都完全按照之前計劃、演練、彩排,以及審核的執行。

　　* typically[3] 〔'tɪpɪk̩lɪ 〕 adv. 通常 (= *usually*[2])
　　specific[3] 〔 spɪ'sɪfɪk 〕 adj. 特定的　　degree[2] 〔 dɪ'gri 〕 n. 學位

certification〔,sɜtəfə'keʃən〕*n.* 證明書;檢定
【certificate⁵〔sə'tɪfəkɪt〕*n.* 證書】
require²〔rɪ'kwaɪr〕*v.* 需要
variety³〔və'raɪətɪ〕*n.* 多樣性;種類
a wide variety of 很多各式各樣的
daredevil〔'dɛr,dɛv!〕*adj.* 魯莽大膽的【dare³ *v.* 敢】
scuba〔'kub〕*n.* 水肺   dive³〔daɪv〕*v.* 潛水
scuba diving 水肺潛水   *rock climbing* 攀岩
high-performance *adj.* 高性能的;大馬力的
motorcycle²〔'motə,saɪk!〕*v.* 騎摩托車
execute⁵〔'ɛksɪ,kjut〕*v.* 執行
exactly²〔ɪg'zæktlɪ〕*adv.* 確切地;完全
rehearse⁴〔rɪ'hɜs〕*v.* 預演;排練
review²〔rɪ'vju〕*v.* 再檢查;複習;審查

3. (**B**)   依句意,選 (B) *However*「然而」。
而 (A) Therefore「因此」,(C) Besides「此外」,
(D) Otherwise「否則」,皆不合句意。

4. (**D**)   (A) adopt³〔ə'dɑpt〕*v.* 採用;領養
(B) adapt⁴〔ə'dæpt〕*v.* 適應;改編
(C) adjust⁴〔ə'dʒʌst〕*v.* 調整
(D) *adept*〔ə'dɛpt〕*adj.* 熟練的;精通的 *< in/at >*

*With the advancement of technology **and** computer simulation*, the

need *for stuntmen in the movie industry* is <u>on the decline</u>. *Instead of*
5

hiring stuntmen, many films use computer generated images *to*

portray the dangerous scenes.

隨著科技的進步和電腦模擬的出現，電影業對特技演員的需求正在<u>下滑</u>
₅
中。許多電影使用電腦產生的圖像去描繪危險場景，而不是僱用特技演員。

* advancement^2〔əd'vænsmənt〕*n.* 進步
technology^1〔tɛk'nɑlədʒɪ〕*n.* 科技
simulation〔‚saɪmjə'leʃən〕*n.* 模擬
industry^2〔'ɪndʌstrɪ〕*n.* …業
instead of 而不是；不…而~　　hire^2〔haɪr〕*v.* 僱用
generate^6〔'dʒɛnə‚ret〕*v.* 產生
image^3〔'ɪmɪdʒ〕*n.* 影像；圖像
portray^4〔por'tre〕*v.* 描繪；表現　　scene^1〔sin〕*n.* 場景

simulation *n.* 模擬
<u>s</u>timulation^6 *n.* 刺激

5. (**A**)　(A) *decline*^{6}〔dɪ'klaɪn〕*n.* 下滑；衰退
　　　　　　　on the decline 在衰退中

decline 也可當動詞，如：
I'm getting old. My memory is { on the decline. / declining.
（我的年齡越來越大。我的記憶力正在衰退中。）

　　(B) increase^2〔'ɪnkris〕*n.* 增加
　　　　on the increase 在增加中
　　　　（↔ on the decrease 在減少中）
　　(C) edge^1〔ɛdʒ〕*n.* 邊緣　　on the edge 在邊緣
　　(D) record^2〔'rɛkəd〕*n.* 記錄
　　　　on the record 公開的；正式的
　　　　（↔ off the record 不公開的；非正式的）

TEST 35

*Read the following passage and choose the best answer for each blank
from the choices below.*

The early bird catches the worm, so the saying goes.
___1___ recent studies, there are actual benefits to waking up
early. Studies have shown that morning people are actually
happier than night owls. This does not mean they are happier
for the first 15 minutes in the morning, ___2___ that they are
happier with life overall. Also, morning people are often in
better shape than night owls. The reasoning behind this is
simple. Waking up early ___3___ people extra time to exercise
before the family is awake or before their work day begins.
This morning exercise helps to boost mood and provides
energy for the rest of the day. Additionally, ___4___ night owls,
morning people are more likely to exhibit traits like optimism,
satisfaction and conscientiousness. Mornings aren't for
everybody. But ___5___ you are looking for a way to improve
the way you live, consider waking up earlier. You never know, it
could make a huge difference.

1. (A) According to   (B) Except for
   (C) In spite of   (D) Aside from
2. (A) rather than   (B) instead of
   (C) so that   (D) but rather
3. (A) makes   (B) takes   (C) lets   (D) gives
4. (A) in comparison with   (B) compare
   (C) comparing to   (D) comparison
5. (A) though   (B) because   (C) if   (D) while

TEST 35 詳解

The early bird catches the worm, *so the saying goes.* <u>According</u>
                                                              1
<u>to recent studies</u>, there are actual benefits *to waking up early.* Studies

have shown *that morning people are actually happier than night owls.*

This does not mean *they are happier for the first 15 minutes in the*

*morning, **but rather** that they are happier with life overall.*
           2

　　俗話說，早起的鳥兒有蟲吃。<u>根據最近的研究</u>，早點醒來真的是有
                                        1
好處。研究顯示，晨型人實際上比夜貓子更快樂。這並不表示他們在早
晨那最初的 15 分鐘比較快樂，<u>而是</u>就整體來說，他們對生活更滿意。
                                    2

　　* worm¹〔wɜm〕*n.* 蟲　　saying¹〔ˋseɪŋ〕*n.* 諺語
　　actual³〔ˋæktʃʊəl〕*adj.* 實際的；真實的
　　benefit³〔ˋbɛnəfɪt〕*n.* 利益；好處
　　wake up 醒來　　owl²〔aʊl〕*n.* 貓頭鷹
　　night owl 夜貓子；夜間工作者；熬夜的人
　　overall⁵〔ˋovɚˏɔl〕*adv.* 就整體來說
　　be happy with 對…滿意

1. (**A**)　(A) ***according to*** 根據　　(B) except for 除了…之外
　　　　　(C) in spite of 儘管　　　　(D) aside from 除了…之外

2. (**D**)　(A) rather than 而不是　　(B) instead of 而不是
　　　　　(C) so that 以便於　　　　(D) ***but rather*** 而是

Also, morning people are *often* in better shape *than night owls*.　The

reasoning *behind this* is simple.　Waking up *early* <u>gives</u> people extra
                                                            3
time to exercise *before the family is awake or before their work day*

begins.　This morning exercise helps to boost mood *and* provides

energy *for the rest of the day*.

而且，晨型人往往比夜貓子身體更健康。這背後的理由很簡單。早點醒
來<u>給</u>人們有額外的時間，在家人醒過來之前或工作日開始前運動。晨間
    3
運動有助於振奮情緒，並提供接下來一整天所需的活力。

> * shape[1] 〔 ʃep 〕 *n.* 形狀；（健康）狀況
> ***be in good shape*** 健康狀況良好
> reasoning 〔'riznɪŋ 〕 *n.* 理由；推論　　extra[2] 〔'ɛkstrə 〕 *adj.* 額外的
> awake[3] 〔 ə'wek 〕 *adj.* 醒著的　　boost[6] 〔 bust 〕 *v.* 振奮；振作
> mood[3] 〔 mud 〕 *n.* 心情；情緒　　provide[2] 〔 prə'vaɪd 〕 *v.* 提供
> energy[2] 〔'ɛnədʒ 〕 *n.* 活力；精力　　rest[1] 〔 rɛst 〕 *n.* 其餘的部份

3. (**D**)　依句意，選 (D) ***gives*** 「給」。而 (A) make 「做」，
　　　　　　(B) take 「拿」，(C) let 「讓」，皆不合句意。

Additionally, <u>*in comparison with* night owls</u>, morning people are *more*
                                              4
likely to exhibit traits *like optimism, satisfaction and conscientiousness*.

Mornings aren't for everybody.　***But if** you are looking for a way to*
                                                                    5
improve the way you live, consider waking up *earlier*.　You *never*

know, it could make a huge difference.

此外，<u>與</u>夜貓子<u>相比</u>，晨型人比較可能會表現出樂觀、滿足，和認真負
    4   4
責的特質。早晨並不適合每個人。但<u>如果</u>你正在尋找一種方法，要改善
                               5
你的生活方式的話，就考慮早點醒來。說不定早起可能會產生巨大的影
響。

> * additionally³ (ə'dıʃənlı) *adv.* 此外
> exhibit⁴ (ıg'zıbıt) *v.* 展現；展示　　trait⁶ (tret) *n.* 特質
> optimism⁵ ('aptə,mızəm) *n.* 樂觀
> satisfaction⁴ (,sætıs'fækʃən) *n.* 滿足
> conscientiousness⁵ (,kanʃı'ɛnʃəsnıs) *n.* 認真負責
> for¹ (fɔr) *prep.* 適合　　***look for*** 尋找
> improve² (ım'pruv) *v.* 改善　　consider² (kən'sıdə) *v.* 考慮
> ***you never know*** 說不定；很難說　　huge¹ (hjudʒ) *adj.* 巨大的
> ***make a difference*** 有影響；有關係

4. (**A**)　依句意，選 (A) ***in comparison with***「與…相比」。
        而 (B) compare² (kəm'pɛr) *v.* 比較，不合句意，
        (C) 須改成 compared to「和…相比」，才能選，
        (D) comparison³ (kəm'pɛrısən) *n.* 比較，是名詞，在此用法
        不合。

5. (**C**)　依句意，選 (C) ***if***「如果」。而 (A) though「雖然」，
        (B) because「因為」，(D) while「當…時候」，皆不合句意。

孩子們，趁現在記憶力最好的時候，
藉著考大學的機會，把7000字背好，
就等於把英文字學好。

TEST 36

Read the following passage and choose the best answer for each blank from the choices below.

Though *typhoon* and *cyclone* are synonyms describing the same formations, the word *hurricane* refers only to violent wind-and-rain-filled storms that develop over the western Atlantic and rage across North America and the Caribbean. A storm won't be defined as a hurricane ___1___ its winds exceed 72 miles per hour. Warm ocean water ___2___ low atmospheric pressure leads to the development of such gigantic and fast-moving storms. In fact, the low-pressure area ___3___ a chimney: the warm air ascends, cools, condenses into rain, and spreads, forming a thunderstorm that grows larger ___4___ more air is drawn in. At the hurricane's center ___5___ the eye, an area of intensely low pressure ___5___, surprisingly, the air is calm and the sky is clear. Around this eye, however, winds are raging. Property may be destroyed either by strong winds or by the terrible flooding they provoke. Under such circumstances, lives and homes are at the mercy of the formidable forces of nature.

1. (A) only if   (B) when   (C) once   (D) unless
2. (A) in comparison with   (B) combined with
   (C) by way of   (D) rather than
3. (A) uses as   (B) is equipped with
   (C) functions as   (D) used to be
4. (A) as   (B) for   (C) so   (D) with
5. (A) lies ; where   (B) locates ; that
   (C) lays ; in which   (D) situated ; when

TEST 36 詳解

Though typhoon *and* cyclone *are synonyms describing the same*
formations, the word *hurricane* refers *only* to violent
wind-and-rain-filled storms *that develop over the western Atlantic*
and rage across North America and the Caribbean. A storm won't
be defined as a hurricane **_unless_** *its winds exceed 72 miles per hour.*
1
Warm ocean water *combined with low atmospheric pressure* leads to
2
the development *of such gigantic and fast-moving storms.*

雖然颱風和氣旋是描述相同結構的同義詞,但颶風這個字,僅指在
大西洋西部上方所形成的充滿狂風暴雨的暴風雨,肆虐橫跨北美洲和加
勒比海地區。暴風雨不會被定義爲颶風,除非它的風速每小時超過72
1
英里。溫暖的海水結合了低氣壓,導致如此巨大和快速移動暴風雨的形
成。
2

   * typhoon[2] 〔 taɪˈfun 〕 *n.* 颱風
   cyclone 〔ˈsaɪklon 〕 *n.* 氣旋;旋風;暴風
   synonym[6] 〔ˈsɪməˌnɪm 〕 *n.* 同義字
   describe[2] 〔 dɪˈskraɪb 〕 *v.* 描述
   formation[4] 〔 fɚˈmeʃən 〕 *n.* 構成物;結構;形成
   hurricane[4] 〔ˈhɝɪˌken 〕 *n.* 颶風   ***refer to*** 是指
   violent[3] 〔ˈvaɪələnt 〕 *adj.* 劇烈的;暴力的
   storm[2] 〔 stɔrm 〕 *n.* 暴風雨   develop[2] 〔 dɪˈvɛləp 〕 *v.* 形成;發展
   Atlantic 〔 ætˈlæntɪk 〕 *adj.* 大西洋的

rage[4] 〔 redʒ 〕 v. (暴風雨、戰爭、疾病、熱情等) 肆虐；狂暴

the Caribbean 〔͵kærɪ'biən 〕 n. 加勒比海地區

define[3] 〔 dɪ'faɪn 〕 v. 下定義　　exceed[5] 〔 ɪk'sid 〕 v. 超過

atmospheric 〔͵ætməs'fɛrɪk 〕 adj. 大氣的；空氣的

【 atmosphere[4] 〔'ætməs͵fɪr 〕 n. 大氣層；氣氛 】

pressure[3] 〔'prɛʃɚ 〕 n. 壓力　　*lead to*　導致；造成

gigantic[4] 〔 dʒaɪ'gæntɪk 〕 adj. 巨大的

1. (**D**)　依句意，選 (D) *unless*「除非」。

　　　　　而 (A) only if「只要；只有」，(B) when「當…的時候」，

　　　　　(C) once「一旦」，皆不合句意。

2. (**B**)　(A) in comparison with　與…相比

　　　　　(B) *combine with*　和…結合

　　　　　(C) by way of　經由

　　　　　(D) rather than　而不是 (= *instead of*)

In fact, the low-pressure area functions *as a chimney*: the warm air

ascends, cools, condenses into rain, *and* spreads, *forming a*

*thunderstorm **that** grows larger **as** more air is drawn in.*

事實上，低壓區域像煙囪般運作：暖空氣上升、冷卻、凝結成雨，然後

擴散，形成隨著更多空氣被吸入而變得更大的雷雨。

　* *in fact* 事實上　　chimney[3] 〔'tʃɪmnɪ 〕 n. 煙囪

　　ascend[5] 〔 ə'sɛnd 〕 v. 上升　　cool[1] 〔 kul 〕 v. 冷卻

　　condense[6] 〔 kən'dɛns 〕 v. 凝結；濃縮

　　spread[2] 〔 sprɛd 〕 v. 擴散；散播

　　grow[1] 〔 gro 〕 v. (逐漸) 變成　　draw[1] 〔 drɔ 〕 v. 拉；吸引

3. (**C**)　依句意，選 (C) ***functions as*** 「充當；當作；如…運作」。
　　　　　　而 (A) use as 文法與句意皆不合；
　　　　　　(B) be equipped with 「配備有…」，
　　　　　　(D) used to be 「以前是」，則不合句意。

4. (**A**)　依句意與文法，選可做連接詞的 (A) ***as*** 「隨著」。
　　　　　　而 (B) for 可當連接詞，作「因為」解，但前面須有逗點，
　　　　　　(C) so 不合句意，而 (D) with 「隨著」，則是文法不合。

At the hurricane's center <u>lies</u> the eye, *an area of intensely low pressure*
　　　　　　　　　　　　　5

<u>*where*</u>, *surprisingly, the air is calm* **and** *the sky is clear.* *Around this*
　5

eye, however, winds are raging. Property may be destroyed *either*

by strong winds **or** *by the terrible flooding they provoke.* *Under such*

circumstances, lives **and** homes are at the mercy *of the formidable*

forces of nature.

<u>位於</u>颶風中心的是颶風眼，令人驚訝的是，這個強烈低壓區域，氣流平
　5
靜，而且天空晴朗。然而，在颶風眼周圍，風正在狂吹。身家財產可能
會被強風或被強風引起的可怕洪水所破壞。在這種情況下，生命和家園
就任由令人畏懼的大自然力量所擺佈了。

* intensely[4] 〔ɪnˈtɛnslɪ〕 *adv.* 強烈地　　　clear[1] 〔klɪr〕 *adj.* 晴朗的
property[3] 〔ˈprɑpɚtɪ〕 *n.* 財產；房屋及院落
destroy[3] 〔dɪˈstrɔɪ〕 *v.* 破壞　　***either*** A ***or*** B　A 或 B
flooding[2] 〔ˈflʌdɪŋ〕 *n.* 氾濫；淹水
provoke[6] 〔prəˈvok〕 *v.* 引起

circumstances[4]〔'sɝkəm͵stænsɪz〕*n. pl.* 情況
under such circumstances 在這種情況下
mercy[4]〔'mɝsɪ〕*n.* 慈悲；仁慈
at the mercy of 任由…擺佈；在…的掌握中
formidable[6]〔'fɔrmɪdəbḷ〕*adj.* 可怕的；令人畏懼的
force[1]〔fors〕*n.* 力量

5. (**A**)　依句意與文法，選 (A) *lies*；*where*。lie[1]〔laɪ〕*v.* 位於；躺；
　　　　　而 where 是表「地點」的關係副詞，在此等於 in which。
　　　(B) locates; that，locate[2]〔'loket〕*v.* 使位於；that 是關代，
　　　　　在子句中須做主詞或受詞，在此不合。
　　　(C) lays; in which，lay[1]〔le〕*v.* 下（蛋）；放置，不合句
　　　　　意。
　　　(D) situated; when，situate〔'sɪtʃu͵et〕*v.* 使位於；when 是
　　　　　表「時間」的關係副詞。在此不合。

考試常考「位於」，sit, stand, lie 是不及物動詞，無
被動，只能用主動；locate and situate 是及物動詞，
「非人」做主詞，就要用被動。例如：

Taiwan $\begin{cases} \textbf{\textit{sists}} \\ \textbf{\textit{stands}} \\ \textbf{\textit{lies}} \\ \textbf{\textit{is located}} \\ \textbf{\textit{is situated}} \end{cases}$ to the southwest of Japan.

（台灣位於日本的西南方。）

TEST 37

Read the following passage and choose the best answer for each blank from the choices below.

What are the causes of sleep disorders? Although the answer is often unknown, we are slowly learning what might ___1___ the various disruptions of sleep.

Snoring is simply a sound produced by the vibration of soft tissues in the nose, throat, and mouth. It occurs ___2___ universally. However, it may also be associated with conditions that narrow the upper airway. These may include obesity and nasal congestion. In severe cases, snoring may also coexist with a complete cessation of breathing called sleep apnea. It is a chronic disorder ___3___ one repeatedly stops breathing during the night. Apnea literally means "no breath." These events last 10 seconds or longer and may occur hundreds of times during a night. Someone with sleep apnea may be aware of snorting, gasping, or waking up short of breath. ___4___ they are asleep, many may not realize anything is happening at all. This disorder can have ___5___ health consequences and can be life threatening.

1. (A) influence on   (B) identify with
   (C) focus on   (D) contribute to
2. (A) hardly   (B) nearly   (C) barely   (D) considerably
3. (A) in which   (B) when   (C) and   (D) that
4. (A) Although   (B) Because   (C) Unless   (D) Even
5. (A) slight   (B) efficient   (C) intensive   (D) major

TEST 37 詳解

What are the causes *of sleep disorders*? ***Although*** *the answer is often unknown*, we are *slowly* learning ***what*** *might* <u>contribute to</u> *the various disruptions of sleep.*
                                          1

　　睡眠障礙的原因是什麼？雖然答案通常是未知的，但我們正慢慢地知道，什麼可能<u>促成</u>各種不同的睡眠中斷。
　　　　　　　　　　1

* cause¹〔kɔz〕*n.* 原因
  disorder⁴〔dɪsˋɔrdɚ〕*n.* 失調；障礙；疾病
  unknown〔ʌnˋnon〕*adj.* 不知道的；未知的
  learn¹〔lɝn〕*v.* 得知　　various³〔ˋvɛrɪəs〕*adj.* 各種不同的
  disruption〔dɪsˋrʌpʃən〕*n.* 中斷

1. (**D**)　(A) influence²〔ˋɪnflʊəns〕*v.* 影響【是及物動詞，不可加介系詞，當名詞時，才會加 on】
　　　　(B) identify⁴〔aɪˋdɛntəˏfaɪ〕*v.* 視…爲同一事物；與…融爲一體 <*with*>
　　　　　　 identify with　理解並同情…的感受
　　　　(C) focus on　專注於
　　　　(D) ***contribute***⁴〔kənˋtrɪbjʊt〕*v.* 貢獻
　　　　　　 contribute to　促成；造成

contribute to 造成
= lead to
= give rise to
= result in
= bring about
= cause

Snoring is *simply* a sound *produced by the vibration of soft tissues in the nose, throat,* ***and*** *mouth.* It occurs <u>*nearly*</u> *universally.*
                                                                    2

However, it may *also* be associated with conditions **that** *narrow the upper airway*. These may include obesity **and** nasal congestion.

In severe cases, snoring may *also* coexist *with a complete cessation of breathing called sleep apnea*. It is a chronic disorder *in which* 3 *one repeatedly stops breathing during the night*.

　　打呼就是鼻子、喉嚨和嘴巴中的軟組織振動，所產生的聲音。它幾乎到處都有。然而，它也可能和會使上呼吸道狹窄的症狀有關。這2些症狀可能包括肥胖症和鼻塞。在嚴重的情況下，打呼也可能和所謂的「睡眠呼吸中止症」的呼吸完全中斷同時存在。睡眠呼吸中止症是一種慢性疾病，患者會在夜間反覆地停止呼吸。

* snore⁵〔snor〕v. 打呼　　simply²〔'sɪmplɪ〕adv. 不過；僅僅
produce²〔prə'djus〕v. 產生
vibration⁶〔vaɪ'breʃən〕n. 振動　　tissue³〔'tɪʃu〕n. 組織
throat²〔θrot〕n. 喉嚨　　occur²〔ə'kɝ〕v. 存在；發生
universally⁴〔ˌjunə'vɝslɪ〕adv. 普遍地；到處
be associated with 和…有關
condition³〔kən'dɪʃən〕n. 狀況；症狀
narrow²〔'næro〕v. 使變窄　　upper²〔'ʌpɚ〕adj. 上面的
airway〔'ɛrˌwe〕n.（呼吸系統的）氣道
include²〔ɪn'klud〕v. 包括　　obesity〔o'bisətɪ〕n. 肥胖
nasal〔'nezl̩〕adj. 鼻子的　　congestion〔kən'dʒɛstʃən〕n. 阻塞
severe⁴〔sɪ'vɪr〕adj. 嚴重的　　case¹〔kes〕n. 情況；案例
coexist〔ˌkoɪg'zɪst〕v. 同時存在【exist²v. 存在】
cessation〔sɛ'seʃən〕n. 中止；中斷【cease⁴〔siz〕v. 停止】
breathe³〔brið〕v. 呼吸　　apnea〔æp'niə〕n. 呼吸暫停；窒息

sleep apnea 睡眠呼吸中止症

chronic[6] 〔'krɑnɪk 〕 *adj.* 慢性的（ ↔ acute[6] 〔 ə'kjut 〕 *adj.* 急性的）

repeatedly 〔 rɪ'pitɪdlɪ 〕 *adv.* 反覆地【repeat[2] *v.* 重複】

2. (**B**)　(A) hardly[2] 〔'hɑrdlɪ 〕 *adv.* 幾乎不

　　　　　(B) ***nearly***[2] 〔'nɪrlɪ 〕 *adv.* 幾乎（ = *almost*[1]）

　　　　　(C) barely[3] 〔'bɛrlɪ 〕 *adv.* 幾乎不

　　　　　(D) considerably[3] 〔 kən'sɪdərəblɪ 〕 *adv.* 相當大地

3. (**A**)　空格後是完整句，故空格應填關係副詞或「介詞 + 關代」，引
　　　　　導形容詞子句，修飾先行詞 disorder，(B) when 表「時間」，
　　　　　在此不合，故選 (A) ***in which*** 表「在這種情況中」。
　　　　　而 (C) and「而且」，不合句意，(D) that 是關代，須在子句中
　　　　　做主詞或受詞，在此用法不合。

Apnea *literally* means "no breath."　These events last *10 seconds **or***

*longer **and*** may occur *hundreds of times during a night*.　Someone

with sleep apnea may be aware of snorting, gasping, ***or*** waking up

short of breath.　***Because*** *they are asleep*, many may not realize
　　　　　　　　　　　　　　　4

anything is happening at all.　This disorder can have <u>major</u> health
　　　　　　　　　　　　　　　　　　　　　　　　　　5

consequences ***and*** can be life threatening.

呼吸暫停的字面意思是「無呼吸」。這些情況會持續 10 秒或更久，並
且可能在一夜之間發生數百次。有睡眠呼吸中止症的人可能會意識到噴
鼻息、喘氣，或上氣不接下氣而醒來。<u>因為睡著了</u>，所以許多人可能一
　　　　　　　　　　　　　　　　　　　　　　　　　　4
點都不知道發生了什麼事。這種病症可能會對健康有<u>重大的</u>影響，並
可能會危及生命。
　　　　　　　　　　　　　　　　　　　　　　5

* literally⁶〔ˈlɪtərəlɪ〕*adv.* 照字面意義地
breath³〔brɛθ〕*n.* 呼吸
event²〔ɪˈvɛnt〕*n.* 事件;(可能的)情況
last¹〔læst〕*v.* 持續　　***be aware of*** 知道;察覺到
snort⁵〔snɔrt〕*v.* 噴鼻息　　gasp⁵〔gæsp〕*v.* 喘氣
wake up 醒來　　***short of breath*** 喘著氣;上氣不接下氣
asleep²〔əˈslip〕*adj.* 睡著的
consequence⁴〔ˈkɑnsəˌkwɛns〕*n.* 後果;結果
threaten³〔ˈθrɛtn̩〕*v.* 威脅　　***life threatening*** 威脅生命的

4.(**B**)　依句意,選 (B) ***Because***「因為」。
　　　　而 (A) Although「雖然」,(C) Unless「除非」,
　　　　(D) Even「甚至」,皆不合句意。

5.(**D**)　(A) slight⁴〔slaɪt〕*adj.* 輕微的
　　　　(B) efficient³〔əˈfɪʃənt〕*adj.* 有效率的
　　　　(C) intensive⁴〔ɪnˈtɛnsɪv〕*adj.* 密集的
　　　　(D) ***major***³〔ˈmedʒɚ〕*adj.* 重大的

　　準備大考,要背「高中常用7000字」,它是命題的範圍。千萬不要做超出範圍的試題,因為英文單字無限多,第一份有60個生字,做到第10份,還是有60多個單字不合。惟有限制在7000字範圍內,才會越做越順,越有信心。

TEST 38

*Read the following passage and choose the best answer for each blank
from the choices below.*

You have probably heard that yoga is good for you.
Maybe you have tried yoga and discovered that it makes you
feel better. But what are the specific health __1__ you can expect
to enjoy from doing yoga regularly? Simply stretching your tight
body in new ways will help it to become more
flexible, __2__ greater range of motion to muscles and joints.
Such increased flexibility and strength can help prevent the
causes of some types of back pain, especially nowadays. Many
people __3__ a lot of time sitting at a computer or driving a
car, so they suffer from tightness and spinal compression.

Yoga also helps in mental calmness and body awareness.
Concentrating on what your body is doing has the effect of
bringing calmness to the mind. It introduces you __4__
meditation techniques, such as watching how you breathe and
disengagement from your thoughts. __5__, doing yoga gives
you an increased awareness of your own body, as you are often
called upon to make small and subtle movements.

1. (A) disadvantages   (B) benefits
   (C) requirements   (D) matters
2. (A) bring   (B) bringing   (C) to bring   (D) brought
3. (A) cost   (B) lose   (C) make   (D) spend
4. (A) on   (B) for   (C) to   (D) with
5. (A) In addition   (B) For this reason
   (C) On the contrary   (D) By contrast

TEST 38 詳解

You have *probably* heard *that yoga is good for you.* *Maybe* you
have tried yoga *and* discovered *that it makes you feel better.* *But*
what are the specific health <u>benefits</u> *you can expect to enjoy from*
₁
doing yoga regularly? *Simply* stretching your tight body *in new ways*
will help it to become *more* flexible, <u>*bringing*</u> *greater range of*
₂
motion to muscles *and* joints.

你可能聽說做瑜伽對你有好處。也許你已經試過瑜伽,而且發現它
讓你感覺更好。但是,定期做瑜伽,你可以預期能享受到什麼具體的健
康<u>益處</u>嗎?只是用新的方式伸展你緊繃的身體,就會幫助你的身體變得
₁
更<u>靈活</u>,<u>使</u>你的肌肉和關節<u>產生</u>更大的活動範圍。
₂   ₂

    * yoga⁵ (ˋjogə) *n.* 瑜珈   specific³ (spɪˋsɪfɪk) *adj.* 特定的
      expect² (ɪkˋspɛkt) *v.* 預期;期待
      regularly² (ˋrɛgjələlɪ) *adv.* 定期地   stretch² (strɛtʃ) *v.* 伸展
      tight³ (taɪt) *adj.* 緊繃的   flexible⁴ (ˋflɛksəbḷ) *adj.* 有彈性的
      range² (rendʒ) *n.* 範圍   motion² (ˋmoʃən) *n.* 動作
      muscle³ (ˋmʌsḷ) *n.* 肌肉   joint² (dʒɔɪnt) *n.* 關節

1. (**B**)   (A) disadvantage⁴ (ˌdɪsədˋvæntɪdʒ) *n.* 缺點
         (B) ***benefit***³ (ˋbɛnəfɪt) *n.* 利益;好處
         (C) requirement² (rɪˋkwaɪrmənt) *n.* 需要;必備條件
         (D) matter¹ (ˋmætɚ) *n.* 事情

2. (**B**)　兩動詞之間無連接詞，第二個動詞須改爲現在分詞，故選 (B) ***bringing***「使…產生」。

Such increased flexibility ***and*** strength can help prevent the causes

of some types of back pain, especially nowadays. Many people <u>spend</u>
3

a lot of time *sitting at a computer* ***or*** *driving a car,* ***so*** they suffer

from tightness ***and*** spinal compression.

這樣增加的柔軟度和強度，可以幫助防止某些背痛的成因，特別是在現
今。因爲許多人<u>花</u>大量的時間，坐在電腦前或駕駛汽車，所以他們遭受
　　　　　　　3
緊繃和脊椎壓迫之苦。

* increased[2] 〔ˈɪnkrist〕 *adj.* 增加的
  flexibility[4] 〔ˌflɛksəˈbɪlətɪ〕 *n.* 彈性　　***suffer from*** 因…而受苦
  strength[3] 〔strɛŋθ〕 *n.* 力量；強度
  prevent[3] 〔prɪˈvɛnt〕 *v.* 防止；預防
  cause[1] 〔kɔz〕 *n.* 起因；原因　　type[2] 〔taɪp〕 *n.* 類型
  especially[2] 〔əˈspɛʃəlɪ〕 *adv.* 尤其；特別是
  nowadays[4] 〔ˈnɑʊəˌdez〕 *adv.* 現今
  tightness 〔ˈtaɪtnɪs〕 *n.* 緊繃；僵硬　　spinal 〔ˈspaɪnl̩〕 *adj.* 脊椎的
  compression 〔kəmˈprɛʃən〕 *n.* 壓縮；壓緊

3. (**D**)　依句意，很多人「花」大量的時間，選 (D) ***spend***「花（錢/時
　　　　間）」。

Yoga ***also*** helps *in mental calmness* ***and*** *body awareness.*

Concentrating on ***what*** *your body is doing* has the effect *of bringing*

calmness to the mind. It introduces you to meditation techniques,
4

*such as watching **how** you breathe **and** disengagement from your*

thoughts. *In addition*, doing yoga gives you an increased awareness
5

of your own body, *as you are often called upon to make small **and***

subtle movements.

　　瑜伽也有助於心理平靜和身體意識。專注於你的身體正在做的動作，有使心靈平靜的效果。它使你認識冥想的技巧，像是觀察呼吸和脫
　　　　　　　　　　　　　　　　　　4　　4
離思緒。此外，因爲做瑜伽經常會被要求做細微的動作，所以會增加自
　　　　5
己對身體的意識。

　　* mental³ (ˈmɛntl̩) *adj.* 心理的；精神的
　　calmness (ˈkɑmnɪs) *n.* 平靜【calm² (kɑm) *v.* 平靜】
　　awareness (əˈwɛrnɪs) *n.* 察覺；意識【aware³ (əˈvɛr) *adj.* 知道的】
　　concentrate on 專心於　　effect² (ɪˈfɛkt) *n.* 影響
　　meditation⁶ (ˌmɛdəˈteʃən) *n.* 沉思；冥想
　　technique³ (tɛkˈnik) *n.* 技術；技巧
　　disengagement (ˌdɪsɪnˈgedʒmənt) *n.* 脫離；分開
　　【engagement³ (ɪnˈgedʒmənt) *n.* 約定；關注】
　　call upon 要求　　subtle⁶ (ˈsʌtl̩) *adj.* 微妙的；細微的
　　movement¹ (ˈmuvmənt) *n.* 動作

4. (**C**)　introduce² (ˌɪntrəˈdjus) *v.* 引進；介紹
　　　　introduce *sb.* ***to*** *sth.* 使某人體驗某事；使某人接受某事

5. (**A**)　(A) *In addition* 此外　　　(B) For this reason 因此
　　　　(C) On the contrary 相反地　　(D) By contrast 對比之下

TEST 39

Read the following passage and choose the best answer for each blank from the choices below.

There are many different ways to manage stress. Basically, it is best to eliminate ___1___ stressors as you can, and find practical and less emotional ways to better handle the stressors that are left.

Much of your experience of stress ___2___ your attitude and the way you perceive your life's events. So you must change your thoughts and maintain a stress-relieving ___3___. The way you think about an event can shape the emotional response that you have in a given situation. ___4___, if you perceive a situation to be a "threat," you will have a different emotional, and therefore physical, response than if you viewed the same situation as a "challenge." Looking at a situation through a new lens, ___5___ just dwelling on negative thoughts, can help with anger management and lower your stress response. Once you understand how your thoughts color your experiences, you can use this information to reduce your stress.

1. (A) so many   (B) how many   (C) as many (D) very many
2. (A) keeps up with   (B) catches hold of
   (C) comes up with   (D) has to do with
3. (A) diagnosis (B) appearance (C) attitude (D) excellence
4. (A) For example   (B) At first
   (C) On average   (D) In fact
5. (A) together with   (B) rather than
   (C) different from   (D) let alone

TEST 39 詳解

There are many different ways *to manage stress*. *Basically*, it is
best to eliminate *as* many stressors *as you can*, *and* find practical
and less emotional ways *to better handle the stressors that are left*.

有許多不同的方法能處理壓力。基本上,最好盡可能多消除壓力
源,然後找到實用又較不情緒化的方式,去更安善地處理剩下的壓力
源。

* manage[3] 〔'mænɪdʒ〕 v. 管理;處理
  stress[2] 〔strɛs〕 n. 壓力 (= *pressure*[3] 〔'prɛʃɚ〕)
  basically[1] 〔'besɪklɪ〕 adv. 基本上【basic[1] adj. 基本的】
  eliminate[4] 〔ɪ'lɪmə,net〕 v. 除去
  practical[3] 〔'præktɪkl〕 adj. 實用的;實際的
  emotional[4] 〔ɪ'moʃənl〕 adj. 情緒激動的
  handle[2] 〔'hændl〕 v. 處理
  stressor 〔'strɛsɚ〕 n. 壓力源【即引發壓力反應的事件】

1. (**C**) *as…as one can* 盡可能…

Much *of your experience of stress* has to do with your attitude
and the way *you perceive your life's events*. *So* you must change
your thoughts *and* maintain a stress-relieving attitude. The way *you*
think about an event can shape the emotional response *that you have*

in a given situation. <u>*For example*</u>, **if** *you perceive a situation to be a*
4

"threat," you will have a different emotional, **and** *therefore* physical,

response **than if** *you viewed the same situation as a "challenge."*

　　許多壓力的經歷，都和你的態度以及你理解生活事件的方式有關。
所以你必須改變你的想法，並保有能緩解壓力的<u>態度</u>。你對事件的思考
3
方式，會塑造你在特定情況下的情緒反應。<u>例如</u>，如果你把某種情況看
4
成是一種「威脅」，或你把它看成是「挑戰」，將會有不同的情緒和身
體的反應。

* perceive[5] 〔 pɚ'siv 〕 v. 察覺；認為；理解
   relieve[4] 〔 rɪ'liv 〕 v. 減輕　　shape[1] 〔 ʃep 〕 v. 塑造
   response[3] 〔 rɪ'spɑns 〕 n. 反應　given 〔'gɪvən 〕 adj. 特定的
   perceive A to be B 認為 A 是 B　　threat[3] 〔 θrɛt 〕 v. 威脅
   physical[4] 〔'fɪzɪkl̩ 〕 adj. 身體的　　**view A as B** 視 A 為 B
   challenge[3] 〔'tʃælɪndʒ 〕 n. 挑戰

2. (**D**)　(A) keep up with 和…並駕齊驅；不落後
　　　　　(B) catch hold of 抓住；握住
　　　　　(C) come up with 提出；想出
　　　　　(D) **have to do with** 和…有關

3. (**C**)　(A) diagnosis[6] 〔,daɪəg'nosɪs 〕 n. 診斷
　　　　　(B) appearance[2] 〔 ə'pɪrəns 〕 n. 外表
　　　　　(C) **attitude**[3] 〔'ætə,tjud 〕 n. 態度
　　　　　(D) excellence[3] 〔'ɛksḷəns 〕 n. 優秀

4. (**A**)　(A) **For example** 例如
　　　　　(B) At first 起初
　　　　　(C) On average 平均而言
　　　　　(D) In fact 事實上

{ for example　例如
  = for instance
{ = let's say
  = say

Looking at a situation *through a new lens*, <u>*rather than*</u> just dwelling
5
on negative thoughts, can help with anger management *and* lowering
your stress response. ***Once** you understand **how** your thoughts color
your experiences, you can use this information *to reduce your stress*.

透過新觀點來看某個情況，<u>而非</u>只是想著負面思維，可以有助於處理憤
5
怒和降低你的壓力反應。一旦你了解你的想法會如何影響你的經驗，就
可以利用這資訊來減輕壓力。

* lens[3] 〔 lɛnz 〕 *n.* 鏡片；鏡頭【在此引申為「觀點」】
  dwell[5] 〔 dwɛl 〕 *v.* 思索；細想　　***dwell on*** 老是想著
  negative[2] 〔 'nɛgətɪv 〕 *adj.* 負面的
  thought[1] 〔 θɔt 〕 *n.* 思維；想法
  help with 幫忙；幫助　　anger[1] 〔 'æŋgɚ 〕 *n.* 憤怒
  management[3] 〔 'mænɪdʒmənt 〕 *n.* 管理
  lower[2] 〔 'loɚ 〕 *v.* 降低　　color[1] 〔 'kʌlɚ 〕 *v.* 將…上色；影響
  information[4] 〔 ͵ɪnfɚ'meʃən 〕 *n.* 資訊　　reduce[3] 〔 rɪ'djus 〕 *v.* 減少

5. (**B**)　(A) together with 連同（ = *along with* ）
　　　　　(B) ***rather than*** 而不是（ = *instead of* ）

> 原則上，***rather than*** 通常接原形動詞，如 She
> would die ***rather than*** tell you.（她寧願死，
> 也不願告訴你。）但在這裡，前面有 Looking
> at a situation....，後面用 dwelling on....，所
> 以 ***rather than*** 在這裡是反義對等連接詞。

　　　　　(C) different from 和…不同
　　　　　(D) let alone 更別提；更不用說（ = *not to mention* ）

TEST 40

Read the following passage and choose the best answer for each blank from the choices below.

Listening is actually difficult. One reason is a natural tendency to immediately evaluate or judge __1__ the other person says without truly listening. This tendency to evaluate is even stronger when emotions are involved. Active listening occurs when you __2__ this tendency to judge and evaluate. You see the other people's point of view, sense how it feels to them, and experience their frame of reference. This is called empathy. Empathy is not __3__ agreeing with the other person, but is recognizing and understanding their point of view. It is different from sympathy. It is not feeling sorry for them or pitying them. It is putting yourself in their __4__ and feeling what they are feeling.

Truly empathic listening is your feeling the issue as the other person feels it, sensing and understanding the emotions of the other person. It __5__ releases powerful forces of communication.

1. (A) when   (B) what   (C) how   (D) that
2. (A) embrace   (B) avoid   (C) escort   (D) tackle
3. (A) ironically   (B) necessarily
   (C) frequently   (D) reluctantly
4. (A) hats   (B) gloves   (C) shoes   (D) pants
5. (A) hence   (B) instead   (C) nevertheless (D) contrary

TEST 40 詳解

Listening is *actually* difficult. One reason is a natural tendency *to immediately evaluate **or** judge __what__ the other person says without truly listening.* This tendency *to evaluate* is *even* stronger ***when** emotions are involved.* Active listening occurs *__when__ you __avoid__ this tendency to judge **and** evaluate.*

傾聽其實是很困難的。原因之一就是沒有眞正傾聽別人說**什麼**，就立即評估或判斷的天性。當情感涉入時，這種評估別人的傾向就會更強烈。當你能**避免**判斷和評估的傾向時，才能積極傾聽。

* listening[1] ('lɪsənɪŋ) *n.* 傾聽
actually[3] ('æktʃʊəlɪ) *adv.* 事實上
natural[2] ('nætʃərəl) *adj.* 自然的；天生的
tendency[4] ('tɛndənsɪ) *n.* 傾向
natural tendency 自然傾向；天性
immediately (ɪ'midɪɪtlɪ) *adv.* 立刻
evaluate[4] (ɪ'væljʊ,et) *v.* 評估　　judge[2] (dʒʌdʒ) *v.* 判斷
truly[1] ('trulɪ) *adv.* 眞地　　emotion[2] (ɪ'moʃən) *n.* 情感；情緒
involve[4] (ɪn'vɑlv) *v.* 牽涉
active[2] ('æktɪv) *adj.* 積極的；主動的　　occur[2] (ə'kɝ) *v.* 發生

1. (**B**)　依句意與文法，to immediately evaluate or judge ***the thing*(s) *which*** the other person says，故空格應選有兼做先行詞的複合關係代名詞，選 (B) *what*。

2. (**B**)　(A) embrace⁵ 〔 ɪmˋbres 〕 v. 擁抱
　　　　(B) ***avoid***² 〔 əˋvɔɪd 〕 v. 避免
　　　　(C) escort⁵ 〔 ɪˋskɔrt 〕 v. 護衛
　　　　(D) tackle⁵ 〔 ˋtækl̩ 〕 v. 處理；應付

You see the other people's point of view, sense ***how** it feels to them*,

and experience their frame *of reference*. This is called empathy.

Empathy is not *necessarily* agreeing with the other person, ***but*** is
　　　　　　　　3

recognizing ***and*** understanding their point of view. It is different

from sympathy. It is not feeling sorry *for them **or*** pitying them. It is

putting yourself *in their underline{shoes} **and*** feeling ***what** they are feeling*.
　　　　　　　　4

理解別人的見解、感受他們的感覺，並且體會他們的觀點，這就叫作同
理心。同理心不一定是同意對方，而是認同及理解他們的觀點。這跟同
　　　　　3
情心不同。同理心不是為他人感到難過或憐憫，而是站在他人的立場，
對他們的感覺感同身受。
　　　　　　　　　　　　　　　　　　4

　　* ***point of view*** 觀點；見解　　sense¹ 〔 sɛns 〕 v. 感受；感覺
　　experience² 〔 ɪkˋspɪrɪəns 〕 v. 經歷；經驗
　　frame⁴ 〔 frem 〕 n. 心情；結構　　reference⁴ 〔 ˋrɛfrəns 〕 n. 參考
　　frame of reference　（作為個人的判斷、行為等的依據的）參考
　　　　架構；觀點；理論
　　empathy 〔 ˋɛmpəθɪ 〕 n. 同理心　　recognize³ 〔 ˋrɛkəgˌnaɪz 〕 v. 認同
　　understand¹ 〔 ˌʌndəˋstænd 〕 v. 了解；同情
　　be different from　和…不同
　　sympathy⁴ 〔 ˋsɪmpəθɪ 〕 n. 同情　　pity³ 〔 ˋpɪtɪ 〕 v. 憐憫；同情

3. (**B**) (A) ironically⁶〔 aɪˈrɑnɪkḷɪ 〕 *adv.* 諷刺地

(B) ***necessarily***²〔ˈnɛsəˌsɛrəlɪ 〕 *adv.* 必定；必然

not necessarily 未必；不一定（ = *not always* ）

(C) frequently³〔ˈfrikwəntlɪ 〕 *adv.* 經常

(D) reluctantly⁴〔 rɪˈlʌktəntlɪ 〕 *adv.* 不情願地；勉強地

4. (**C**) ***put*** *oneself* ***in*** *one's* ***shoes/place/position***
站在他人立場思考；換位思考

Truly empathic listening is your feeling the issue ***as*** *the other*
person feels it, sensing ***and*** understanding the emotions *of the other*
person. It <u>hence</u> releases powerful forces *of communication.*
5

眞正有同理心的傾聽，是你對問題的感受和對方的感受一樣，體會
並理解對方的情緒，<u>因此</u>就能釋放出強大的溝通力量。
5

* empathetic〔 ɛmˈpæθɪk 〕 *adj.* 同理心的
issue⁵〔ˈɪʃʊ 〕 *n.* 問題；議題　　release³〔 rɪˈlis 〕 *v.* 釋放
powerful²〔ˈpaʊəfəl 〕 *adj.* 強有力的　　force¹〔 fors 〕 *n.* 力量
communication⁴〔 kəˌmjunəˈkeʃən 〕 *n.* 溝通

5. (**A**) (A) ***hence***⁵〔 hɛns 〕 *adv.* 因此（ = *therefore*² ）

(B) instead³〔 ɪnˈstɛd 〕 *adv.* 作爲代替；取而代之

(C) nevertheless⁴〔ˌnɛvəðəˈlɛs 〕 *adv.* 然而（ = *nonetheless*⁵
= *however*² ）

(D) contrary⁴〔ˈkɑntrɛrɪ 〕 *adj.* 相反的　 *adv.* 相反地

TEST 41

Read the following passage and choose the best answer for each blank from the choices below.

Everyone must have heard of the temperature increases due to greenhouse gas ___1___. But geographers have recently reached the conclusion that climate zones will shift and some climates will disappear completely by 2100. Large climate changes worldwide are anticipated. Global warming could change our current world climate zones, which would affect where crops are grown and even drive some plant and animal species to ___2___, all in the next 100 years.

___3___ their new analyses of climate forecasting models, tropical highlands and polar regions might be the first to disappear, and large swaths of the tropics and subtropics would reach ___4___ hotter temperatures. The eastern United States would have a mild, humid, temperate climate, ___5___ the western United States would have a dry climate.

1. (A) permissions   (B) commissions
   (C) emissions   (D) transmissions
2. (A) attraction   (B) conviction
   (C) distinction(D) extinction
3. (A) In contrast with   (B) On top of
   (C) According to   (D) Along with
4. (A) even   (B) more   (C) quite   (D) pretty
5. (A) lest   (B) while   (C) since   (D) unless

TEST 41 詳解

Everyone must have heard of the temperature increases *due to*

greenhouse gas *emissions*. **But** geographers have *recently* reached
1

the conclusion **that** *climate zones will shift* **and** *some climates will*

disappear completely by 2100.

　　每個人都一定聽說過，因為溫室氣體的排放而引起的氣溫上升。但
　　　　　　　　　　　　　　　　　　1
最近地理學家已經下了結論，認為氣候區會轉移，而且某些氣候型態在
2100 年之前會完全消失。

* must[1] 〔 mʌst 〕 *aux.* 一定　　***hear of*** 聽說
  temperature[2] 〔ˋtɛmpərətʃɚ 〕 *n.* 溫度；氣溫
  increase[2] 〔ˋɪnkris 〕 *n.* 增加　　***due to*** 由於
  greenhouse[3] 〔ˋgrinˌhaʊs 〕 *n.* 溫室　　gas[1] 〔 gæs 〕 *n.* 氣體
  geographer 〔 dʒiˋɑgrəfɚ 〕 *n.* 地理學家
  recently[2] 〔ˋrisn̩tlɪ 〕 *adv.* 最近
  conclusion[3] 〔 kənˋkluʒən 〕 *n.* 結論

geo	+ graph	+	er
earth	+ write	+	person

  reach a conclusion 下結論
  climate[2] 〔ˋklaɪmɪt 〕 *n.* 氣候　　zone[3] 〔 zon 〕 *n.* 地區
  shift[4] 〔 ʃɪft 〕 *v.* 轉移　　disappear[2] 〔ˌdɪsəˋpɪr 〕 *v.* 消失
  completely[2] 〔 kəmˋplitlɪ 〕 *adv.* 完全地

1. (**C**)　(A) permission[3] 〔 pɚˋmɪʃən 〕 *n.* 許可；准許
　　　　　(B) commission[5] 〔 kəˋmɪʃən 〕 *n.* 委員會；佣金
　　　　　(C) ***emission*** 〔 ɪˋmɪʃən 〕 *n.* 排放
　　　　　(D) transmission[6] 〔 trænsˋmɪʃən 〕 *n.* 傳送；傳達

Large climate changes *worldwide* are anticipated.　Global warming

could change our current world climate zones, ***which*** *would affect*

where *crops are grown* ***and*** *even drive some plant* ***and*** *animal species*

to extinction, all in the next 100 years.

在世界各地大型的氣候改變是可以預期的。全球暖化會改變我們現在世
界的氣候區，這將影響農作物生長，甚至使得某些動植物品種滅絕，這
些在接下來的一百年內都會發生。

* worldwide〔'wɝld'waɪd〕*adv.* 在世界各地
  anticipate[6]〔æn'tɪsə,pet〕*v.* 預期；期待
  global[3]〔'globḷ〕*adj.* 全球的

anti	+ cip	+ ate
before	+ *take*	+ *v.*

  current[3]〔'kɝənt〕*adj.* 現在的；目前的
  affect[3]〔ə'fɛkt〕*v.* 影響　　crop[2]〔krɑp〕*n.* 農作物
  drive[1]〔draɪv〕*v.* 驅使　　species[4]〔'spiʃɪz〕*n.* 物種【單複數同形】

2. (**D**)　(A) attraction[4]〔ə'trækʃən〕*n.* 吸引力
　　　　　(B) conviction[6]〔kən'vɪkʃən〕*n.* 信念；定罪
　　　　　(C) distinction[5]〔dɪ'stɪŋkʃən〕*n.* 區別；差別
　　　　　(D) ***extinction***[5]〔ɪk'stɪŋkʃən〕*n.* 滅絕；絕種
　　　　　　　【extinct[5] *adj.* 絕種的】

According to *their new analyses of climate forecasting models,*

tropical highlands ***and*** polar regions might be the first *to disappear,*

and *large swaths* *of the tropics* ***and*** *subtropics* would reach *even*

hotter temperatures.

　　根據地理學家氣候預測模型的最新分析，熱帶高地和極地區域可
　　3
能會是最早消失的氣候區，以及在熱帶及副熱帶大型帶狀區域的氣溫，
甚至會更熱。
4

> * analysis[4] 〔 ə'næləsɪs 〕 *n.* 分析【複數形為 analyses】
> forecast[4] 〔 for'kæst 〕 *v.* 預報；預測　　model[2] 〔'mɑdḷ 〕 *n.* 模型
> tropical[3] 〔'trɑpɪkḷ 〕 *adj.* 熱帶的
> highland 〔'haɪlənd 〕 *n.* 高原；高地　　polar[5] 〔'polɚ 〕 *adj.* 極地的
> region[2] 〔'rɪdʒən 〕 *n.* 地區　　swath 〔 swɑθ 〕 *n.* 帶狀地區
> *the tropics* 熱帶地區　　*the subtropics* 副熱帶地區

3. (**C**)　(A) in contrast with 和…成對比
　　　　　　(B) on top of 在…上面　　　(C) *according to* 根據
　　　　　　(D) along with 連同 (= *together with*)

4. (**A**)　空格應為能修飾比較級形容詞 hotter 的副詞 much, *even*, still
　　　　　　或 far，故選 (A)。而 (B) more「更加」，(C) quite「相當地」，
　　　　　　(D) pretty「相當地」，都用於修飾原級形容詞，在此不合。

The eastern United States would have a mild, humid, temperate

climate, *while* the western United States would have a dry climate.
　　　　　5
美國東部將會有溫和、潮濕、不極端的氣候，而美國西部則會有乾燥的
　　　　　　　　　　　　　　　　　　　　　5
氣候。

> * eastern[2] 〔'istɚn 〕 *adj.* 東部的　　mild[4] 〔 maɪld 〕 *adj.* 溫和的
> humid[2] 〔'hjumɪd 〕 *adj.* 潮濕的
> temperate 〔'tɛmpərɪt 〕 *adj.* 溫和的；不極端的
> western[2] 〔'wɛstɚn 〕 *adj.* 西部的　　dry[1] 〔 draɪ 〕 *adj.* 乾燥的

5. (**B**)　表「對比」，用 *while*「然而」(= *whereas*)，選 (B)。
　　　　　　而 (A) lest[5] 〔 lɛst 〕 *conj.* 以免，(C) since[1] 〔 sɪns 〕 *conj.* 自從，
　　　　　　(D) unless[3] 〔 ən'lɛs 〕 *conj.* 除非，皆不合句意。

TEST 42

Read the following passage and choose the best answer for each blank from the choices below.

Psychology is the scientific study of behavior and the mind. The term __1__ two Greek words: psyche, which means "soul," and logos, "the study of." These root words were first combined in the 16th century, __2__ the human soul, spirit, or mind was seen as distinct from the body.

Many people think of psychologists as individuals who dispense advice, analyze personality, and help those who are mentally ill. But psychology is __3__ the treatment of personal problems. With its broad scope, psychology investigates an enormous range of phenomena. Psychologists examine them from a variety of complementary perspectives. Some conduct detailed biological studies of the brain; others explore how we process information; others analyze the role of evolution, and __4__ study the influence of culture and society. Their goal is to understand the mysteries of human nature. Their discoveries can help people understand themselves, __5__ better to others, and solve the problems that confront them.

1. (A) consists in (B) calls for (C) comes from (D) relies on
2. (A) which   (B) unless   (C) until   (D) when
3. (A) in turn   (B) without doubt
   (C) more than   (D) on average
4. (A) still others (B) other   (C) the others   (D) another
5. (A) detect   (B) resist   (C) accuse   (D) relate

TEST 42 詳解

Psychology is the scientific study *of behavior **and** the mind*. The term comes *from two Greek words*: psyche, **which** means "soul," **and** logos, "*the study of*." These root words were *first* combined *in the 16th century*, **when** *the human soul, spirit, **or** mind was seen as distinct from the body*.

心理學是對行為與心智所做的科學研究。這個名詞起源於兩個希臘字：psyche 意思是「靈魂」，而 logos 意思是「…的研究」。這兩個字根最初組合於十六世紀，那時人類的靈魂、精神或心智，被看成是與身體分開的東西。

* psychology [saɪˈkɑlədʒɪ] *n.* 心理學
scientific [ˌsaɪənˈtɪfɪk] *adj.* 科學的　　study [ˈstʌdɪ] *n.* 研究
behavior [bɪˈhevjɚ] *n.* 行為　　mind [maɪnd] *n.* 心智；精神
term [tɝm] *n.* 名詞；用語　　Greek [grik] *adj.* 希臘的
psyche [ˈsaɪkɪ] *n.* 靈魂；精神　　soul [sol] *n.* 靈魂
logos [ˈlɑgɑs] *n.* 理法；宇宙法則　　root [rut] *adj.* 根的
root word 字根　　combine [kəmˈbaɪn] *v.* 結合
century [ˈsɛntʃərɪ] *n.* 世紀　　***been seen as*** 被視為
distinct [dɪˈstɪŋkt] *adj.* 分開的；不同的

1. (**C**)　(A) consist in 在於 (= *lie in*)
　　　　(B) call for 需要；要求
　　　　(C) ***come from*** 起源於
　　　　(D) rely on 依賴 (= *depend on*)

> come from 起源於
> = originate from
> = derive from

2. (**D**)　表「時間」，關係副詞用 ***when***，選 (D)。

而 (A) which 應改爲 in which，(B) unless「除非」，

(C) until「直到」，則不合句意。

Many people think of psychologists as individuals *who dispense*

advice, analyze personality, **and** *help those* **who** *are mentally ill.* ***But***

psychology is <u>more than</u> the treatment *of personal problems.* *With*
　　　　　　　　 3

its broad scope, psychology investigates an enormous range of

phenomena.

　　許多人認爲心理學家是提供建議、剖析人格，並幫助那些有精神疾
病的人。但心理學<u>不只</u>是個人問題的治療。心理學有著廣大的範圍，研
　　　　　　　 3
究很多各式各樣的現象。

　　* ***think of A as B*** 認爲 A 是 B
　　　psychologist[4]〔saɪˋkɑlədʒɪst〕*n.* 心理學家
　　　individual[3]〔͵ɪndəˋvɪdʒʊəl〕*n.* 人；個人
　　　dispense[5]〔dɪˋspɛns〕*v.* 分發；分送
　　　advice[3]〔ədˋvaɪs〕*n.* 建議；勸告　　analyze[4]〔ˋænl͵aɪz〕*v.* 分析
　　　personality[3]〔͵pɝsn̩ˋælətɪ〕*n.* 性格
　　　mentally[3]〔ˋmɛntl̩ɪ〕*adv.* 精神上；心理上
　　　treatment[5]〔ˋtrimənt〕*n.* 治療
　　　personal[2]〔ˋpɝsn̩l〕*adj.* 個人的
　　　broad[2]〔brɔd〕*adj.* 寬的　　scope[6]〔skop〕*n.* 範圍
　　　investigate[3]〔ɪnˋvɛstə͵get〕*v.* 調查；研究
　　　enormous[4]〔ɪˋnɔrməs〕*adj.* 巨大的
　　　range[2]〔rendʒ〕*n.* 範圍

an enormous range of 很多各式各樣的（ = *a wide range of* ）

phenomena〔 fə'nɑmənə 〕 *n. pl.* 現象

【單數是 phenomenon[4]〔 fə'nɑmə,nɑn 〕】

名詞若是 -on 或 -um 結尾，則複數型變成 -a，如：

phenomen<u>on</u> → phenomen<u>a</u> *n.* 現象

criteri<u>on</u> → criteri<u>a</u> *n.* 標準

medi<u>um</u> → medi<u>a</u> *n.* 媒介

bacteri<u>um</u> → bacteri<u>a</u> *n.* 細菌

dat<u>um</u> → dat<u>a</u> *n.* 資料

curricul<u>um</u> → curricul<u>a</u> *n.* 課程

---

3. (**C**) (A) in turn 依次地

      (B) without doubt 無疑地（ = *undoubtedly* ）

      (C) ***more than*** 不只是

      (D) on average 平均而言

Psychologists examine them *from a variety of complementary perspectives.* Some conduct detailed biological studies *of the brain*; others explore **how** *we process information*; others analyze the role *of evolution*, **and** <u>still others</u> study the influence *of culture **and** society.*

Their goal is to understand the mysteries *of human nature*. Their discoveries can help people understand themselves, <u>relate</u> *better* to others, **and** solve the problems **that** *confront them.*

心理學家從各種互補的觀點來檢視這些現象。有些心理學家對大腦做了詳細的生物學研究；有些探討我們如何處理資訊；有些分析演化的角色；還有一些心理學家研究文化與社會的影響。他們的目標是要理解人
      4
類本性的奧秘。他們的發現可以幫助人們了解自己、和他人相處得更融洽，並解決人們面臨的問題。
         5

  * examine[1] 〔 ɪgˈzæmɪn 〕 v. 檢查；檢視
  a variety of 各種的；各式各樣的
  complementary 〔ˌkɑmpləˈmɛntərɪ 〕 *adj.* 互補的；補充的
  【complement[6] 〔ˌkɑmpləˈmɛnt 〕 v. 補充】
  perspective[6] 〔 pɚˈspɛktɪv 〕 *n.* 觀點 (= *point of view*)；正確的眼光
  conduct[5] 〔 kənˈdʌkt 〕 v. 進行；做
  detailed 〔ˈditeld 〕 *adj.* 詳細的【detail[3] *n.* 細節】
  biological[6] 〔 baɪəˈlɑdʒɪkl̩ 〕 *adj.* 生物學的
  explore[4] 〔 ɪkˈsplor 〕 v. 探討   process[3] 〔ˈprɑsɛs 〕 v. 處理
  role[2] 〔 rol 〕 *n.* 角色   evolution[6] 〔ˌɛvəˈluʃən 〕 *n.* 進化；演化
  influence[2] 〔ˈɪnfluəns 〕 *n.* 影響   culture[2] 〔ˈkʌltʃɚ 〕 *n.* 文化
  mystery[3] 〔ˈmɪstərɪ 〕 *n.* 奧秘；謎   ***human nature*** 人性
  discovery[3] 〔 dɪˈskʌvərɪ 〕 *n.* 發現   solve[2] 〔 sɑlv 〕 v. 解決
  confront[5] 〔 kənˈfrʌnt 〕 v. 使面臨

4. (**A**) some…others…others…and ***still others***
      有些…有些…有些…還有一些
      而 (B) other「其他的」，(C) the others「其餘的人或物」
      (= *the rest*)，(D) another「（三者以上）另一個」，
      句意及用法皆不合。

5. (**D**) (A) detect[2] 〔 dɪˈtɛkt 〕 v. 偵測；發現
      (B) resist[3] 〔 rɪˈzɪst 〕 v. 抵抗
      (C) accuse[4] 〔 əˈkjuz 〕 v. 控告   accuse *sb.* of 控告某人…
      (D) ***relate***[3] 〔 rɪˈlet 〕 v. (與他人) 友好地相處；(互相) 合
          得來；使有關聯 < *to* >

TEST 43

Read the following passage and choose the best answer for each blank from the choices below.

Domesticated honeybee populations are suffering a devastating collapse all over the world, and Taiwan is no exception. The local bee population has declined by about 30 percent in the last two years. Local scientists __1__ the population loss to a combination of factors, such as climate change, __2__ use of pesticides and a virus spread by parasites.

According to Chen Yue-wen, a professor from National Ilan University, bees face two major problems in Taiwan. Many are killed directly by the irresponsible use of pesticides and herbicides, and __3__ die of viruses spread by parasitic mites that have grown __4__ to sprays. The fact that the bee population is declining here is alarming because without bees to pollinate crops, Taiwan's production of fruit and vegetables could suffer a severe __5__.

1. (A) contribute (B) attribute   (C) tribute   (D) distribute
2. (A) excessive   (B) successive
   (C) progressive   (D) aggressive
3. (A) the others (B) other   (C) another (D) others
4. (A) assistant (B) consistent (C) resistant (D) persistent
5. (A) poke   (B) pinch   (C) blow   (D) tickle

TEST 43 詳解

Domesticated honeybee populations are suffering a devastating collapse *all over the world*, ***and*** Taiwan is no exception. The local bee population has declined *by about 30 percent in the last two years.* Local scientists <u>attribute</u> the population loss *to a combination of*
                    1
factors, *such as climate change*, <u>*excessive*</u> *use of pesticides* ***and*** *a virus*
                                2
spread by parasites.

世界各地的養殖蜜蜂的總數，正驚人地大幅減少中，而台灣也不例外。在過去兩年內，台灣的蜜蜂總數已經減少了大約百分之三十。本地的科學家把蜜蜂數量的減少，<u>歸因於</u>幾種因素，像是氣候變遷、<u>過度的</u>
                    1   2
使用殺蟲劑，以及由寄生蟲傳播的病毒。

* domesticated〔də'mɛstə,ketɪd〕*adj.* 被馴養的
  【domestic³〔də'mɛstɪk〕*adj.* 馴養的；國內的】
  honeybee〔'hʌnɪ,bi〕*n.* 蜜蜂
  population²〔,pɑpjə'leʃən〕*n.* 人口；（動植物的）總數
  suffer³〔'sʌfɚ〕*v.* 遭受；經歷
  devastating〔'dɛvəs,tetɪŋ〕*adj.*
    毀滅性的；驚人的

  | dom- 表示 rule 之意，如： |
  | domesticate *v.* 馴服 |
  | dominate *v.* 統治 |
  | domain *n.* 領土 |
  | kingdom *n.* 王國 |

  collapse⁴〔kə'læps〕*n.* 崩塌；暴跌
  all over the world 在世界各地
  exception⁴〔ɪk'sɛpʃən〕*n.* 例外
  local²〔'lokḷ〕*adj.* 當地的   decline⁶〔dɪ'klaɪn〕*v.* 下降；衰退
  by 表「差距」。   percent⁴〔pɚ'sɛnt〕*n.* 百分之…
  loss²〔lɔs〕*n.* 損失   combination⁴〔,kɑmbə'neʃən〕*n.* 結合

factor[3]〔'fæktɚ〕*n.* 因素　　***such as*** 像是
climate[2] 〔'klaɪmɪt〕*n.* 氣候　　pesticide[6] 〔'pɛstɪ,saɪd〕*n.* 殺蟲劑
virus[4] 〔'vaɪrəs〕*n.* 病毒　　spread[2] 〔sprɛd〕*v.* 散播
parasite 〔'pærə,saɪt〕*n.* 寄生蟲

1. (**B**)　(A) contribute[4] 〔kən'trɪbjut〕*v.* 貢獻
　　　　　(B) ***attribute*** 〔ə'trɪbjut〕*v.* 歸因於
　　　　　attribute A to B 把 A 歸因於 B
　　　　　(C) tribute[5] 〔'trɪbjut〕*n.* 貢物；頌辭
　　　　　(D) distribute[4] 〔dɪ'strɪbjut〕*v.* 分配；分發

2. (**A**)　(A) ***excessive***[6] 〔ɪk'sɛsɪv〕*adj.* 過度的
　　　　　(B) successive[6] 〔sək'sɛsɪv〕*adj.* 連續的
　　　　　(C) progressive[6] 〔prə'grɛsɪv〕*adj.* 進步的；漸進的
　　　　　(D) aggressive[4] 〔ə'grɛsɪv〕*adj.* 有攻擊性的

According to Chen Yue-wen, a professor from National Ilan University, bees face two major problems *in Taiwan.* Many are killed *directly by the irresponsible use of pesticides **and** herbicides,* **and** others die of viruses *spread by parasitic mites **that** have grown resistant to sprays.*

根據國立宜蘭大學的陳裕文教授的說法，台灣的蜜蜂面臨兩個主要的問題。許多蜜蜂直接死於殺蟲劑和除草劑的濫用，而其他的蜜蜂，則死於逐漸對噴霧殺蟲劑有抵抗力的寄生小蟲所傳播的病毒。

* ***according to*** 根據　　professor[4] 〔prə'fɛsɚ〕*n.* 教授
national[2] 〔'næʃənḷ〕*adj.* 國立的
university[4] 〔,junə'vɝsətɪ〕*n.* 大學

major[3] 〔 'medʒɚ 〕 *adj.* 主要的　　directly[1] 〔 də'rɛktlɪ 〕 *adv.* 直接地

irresponsible[3] 〔 ˌɪrɪ'spɑnsəbḷ 〕 *adj.* 不負責任的

herbicide 〔'hɝbəˌsaɪd 〕 *n.* 除草劑

【herb[5] *n.* 草藥】　　*die of* 因…而死

parasitic 〔 ˌpærə'sɪtɪk 〕 *adj.* 寄生的

mite 〔 maɪt 〕 *n.* 小蟲

spray[3] 〔 spre 〕 *n.* 噴霧劑

> -cide 表示 kill 之意，如：
> herbi<u>cide</u> *n.* 除草劑
> pesti<u>cide</u> *n.* 殺蟲劑
> germi<u>cide</u> *n.* 殺菌劑
> sui<u>cide</u> *n.* 自殺

3. (**D**)　***many…others*** 很多…其他的【*some…others* 有些…有些】
　　　　而 (A) the others「其餘的人或物」(= *the rest*) 有限定範圍；
　　　　在此不合；(B) other「其他的」是形容詞，(C) another「（三
　　　　個以上）另一個」，用法與句意皆不合。

4. (**C**)　(A) assistant[2] 〔 ə'sɪstənt 〕 *n.* 助理
　　　　(B) consistent[4] 〔 kən'sɪstənt 〕 *adj.* 一致的
　　　　(C) ***resistant***[6] 〔 rɪ'zɪstənt 〕 *adj.* 有抵抗力的 < *to* >
　　　　(D) persistent[6] 〔 pɚ'zɪstənt 〕 *adj.* 持續的

The fact ***that*** the bee population is declining here is alarming |***because***

without bees to pollinate crops, *Taiwan's production of fruit **and***

vegetables could suffer a severe <u>blow</u>.
　　　　　　　　　　　　　　　　5

這裡的蜜蜂數量正在減少的事實令人擔憂，因爲沒有蜜蜂爲農作物傳授
花粉，台灣的蔬果產量可能會遭受到嚴重的<u>打擊</u>。
　　　　　　　　　　　　　　　　5

　　* alarming[2] 〔 ə'lɑrmɪŋ 〕 *adj.* 令人擔憂的；驚人的
　　　pollinate 〔'pɑləˌnet 〕 *v.* 授粉【pollen 〔'pɑlən 〕 *n.* 花粉】
　　　crop[2] 〔 krɑp 〕 *n.* 農作物　　production[4] 〔 prə'dʌkʃən 〕 *n.* 生產
　　　severe[4] 〔 sə'vɪr 〕 *adj.* 嚴重的

5. (**C**)　(A) poke[5] 〔 pok 〕 *v. n.* 刺；戳　　(B) pinch[5] 〔 pɪntʃ 〕 *v. n.* 捏；擰
　　　　(C) ***blow***[1] 〔 blo 〕 *v. n.* 打擊　　(D) tickle[3] 〔'tɪkḷ 〕 *v. n.* 搔癢

TEST 44

Read the following passage and choose the best answer for each blank from the choices below.

Pet owners know their pets are able to do all sorts of incredible things. Dogs seem to prick up their ears when their owners mention the word walk. Cats have many creative ways of ___1___ their owners to feed them in the morning. So ___2___ how intelligent are animals? Scientists as well as pet owners are interested in the question of animal intelligence. In recent years, animal researchers have learned a lot about the cognitive abilities of animals.

Some of the most exciting investigations into the cognitive abilities of animals ___3___ their ability to use tools. Through observation of animals in the wild and in zoos, animal researchers know that several animal species apparently use tools. Perhaps the most notable investigation of this kind is the work of Jane Goodall in Africa. She observed chimpanzees in their native environment ___4___ small sticks to catch termites. Great apes in zoos have been seen to use tools. Scientists have trained crows to use small sticks to spear insects in the bark of trees.

Another aspect of animal cognition is solving problems. Some species of birds, such as ravens, are particularly clever. Ravens are able to solve many different problems, such as untying a knot to get at food. Besides, orangutans can learn complex tasks, such as washing clothes by hand, ___5___ just a few tries. Dolphins, too, can follow complex instructions.

1. (A) remind   (B) reminding
   (C) reminded   (D) reminder
2. (A) definitely   (B) curiously
   (C) exactly   (D) undeniably
3. (A) look after   (B) take over
   (C) result in   (D) look at
4. (A) to use   (B) using
   (C) use to   (D) by using
5. (A) by   (B) for
   (C) without   (D) after

【劉毅老師的話】

　　和大考中心一樣，克漏字測驗都取材自現成的文章。要把超出 7000 字範圍的難字改成簡單的，很不容易，非一般外國老師能夠更改。有這本書，同學太幸福了！

TEST 44 詳解

Pet owners know *their pets are able to do all sorts of incredible things*. Dogs seem to prick up their ears ***when** their owners mention the word walk*. Cats have many creative ways *of <u>reminding</u> their*
1

owners to feed them in the morning. ***So** <u>exactly</u> **how** intelligent* are
2

animals? Scientists ***as well as*** pet owners are interested in the question *of animal intelligence*. *In recent years*, animal researchers have learned a lot about the cognitive abilities *of animals*.

　　寵物主人知道，自己的寵物能做出各種不可思議的事情。當主人提到散步這個詞時，狗似乎會豎起牠們的耳朵。貓會用很多有創意的方式，<u>提醒</u>主人在早晨餵食牠們。所以，動物<u>到底</u>有多聰明？科學家對於
1　　　　　　　　　　　2

動物智力的問題，和寵物主人一樣感興趣。在最近幾年，動物研究人員對於動物的認知能力已經了解很多。

　　* pet[1] (pɛt) *n.* 寵物　　　owner[2] ('onɚ) *n.* 擁有者
　　be able to V. 能夠…　　　sort[2] (sɔrt) *n.* 種類
　　incredible (ɪn'krɛdəbḷ) *adj.* 令人難以置信的；驚人的
　　prick up 豎起
　　mention[3] ('mɛnʃən) *v.* 提到
　　creative[3] (krɪ'etɪv) *adj.* 有創意的
　　feed[1] (fid) *v.* 餵
　　intelligent[4] (ɪn'tɛlədʒənt) *adj.* 聰明的
　　as well as 以及　　　***be interested in*** 對…感興趣

> cred- (believe)
> in**cred**ible *adj.* 令人難以置信的
> in**cred**ulous *adj.* 不肯輕信的

intelligence[4] 〔ɪnˋtɛlədʒəns 〕 *n.* 智力

recent[2] 〔ˋrisn̩t 〕 *adj.* 最近的　　researcher[4] 〔rɪˋsɝtʃɚ 〕 *n.* 研究人員

cognitive 〔ˋkɑgnətɪv 〕 *adj.* 認知的　　ability[2] 〔əˋbɪlətɪ 〕 *n.* 能力

1. (**B**)　介系詞 of 後應接名詞或動名詞，依句意，選 (B) ***reminding***
　　　　「提醒」。remind[3] 〔rɪˋmaɪnd 〕 *v.* 提醒；使想起
　　　　而 (D) reminder[5] 〔rɪˋmaɪndɚ 〕 *n.* 提醒的人或物，則不合句意。

2. (**C**)　(A) definitely[4] 〔ˋdɛfənɪtlɪ 〕 *adv.* 確定地
　　　　(B) curiously[2] 〔ˋkjʊrɪəslɪ 〕 *adv.* 好奇地
　　　　(C) ***exactly***[2] 〔ɪgˋzæktlɪ 〕 *adv.* 確切地；究竟；到底
　　　　(D) undeniably 〔ˌʌndɪˋnaɪəblɪ 〕 *adv.* 不可否認地
　　　　【deny[2] 〔dɪˋnaɪ 〕 *v.* 否認 】

Some *of the most exciting investigations into the cognitive*

abilities of animals look at *their ability to use tools. Through*
　　　　　　　　　　　3

*observation of animals in the wild **and** in zoos*, animal researchers

know ***that** several animal species apparently use tools. Perhaps* the

most notable investigation *of this kind* is the work *of Jane Goodall in*

Africa. She observed chimpanzees *in their native environment* *using*
　　　　　　　　　　　　　　　　　　　　　　　　　　　　　4

small sticks to catch termites. Great apes *in zoos* have been seen to

use tools. Scientists have trained crows to use small sticks *to spear*

insects in the bark of trees.

有些最令人興奮的動物認知能力的調查，<u>著眼於</u>他們使用工具的能
　　　　　　　　　　　　　　　　　3
力。透過觀察在野外和動物園的動物，動物研究人員得知，有好幾種動
物似乎會使用工具。這樣的研究調查工作當中，也許最著名的，就是珍
古德在非洲的調查。她觀察到，黑猩猩在牠們的原生環境中，會<u>使用</u>小
　　　　　　　　　　　　　　　　　　　　　　　　　　　　　4
樹枝來抓白蟻。也有人看到動物園裡的類人猿會使用工具。科學家已經
訓練烏鴉，用小樹枝來叉起樹皮裡的昆蟲。

　　　* exciting² 〔 ɪkˋsaɪtɪŋ 〕adj. 令人興奮的
　　　　investigation⁴ 〔 ɪn͵vɛstəˋgeʃən 〕n. 調查；研究 < into >
　　　　tool¹ 〔 tul 〕n. 工具　　observation⁴ 〔͵ɑbzɚˋveʃən 〕n. 觀察
　　　　wild² 〔 waɪld 〕n. 野外　　zoo¹ 〔 zu 〕n. 動物園
　　　　species⁴ 〔ˋspiʃɪz 〕n. 物種【單複數同形】
　　　　apparently³ 〔 əˋpærəntlɪ 〕adv. 似乎；顯然
　　　　perhaps¹ 〔 pɚˋhæps 〕adv. 也許
　　　　notable⁵ 〔ˋnotəb!〕adj. 值得注意的；著名的
　　　　Jane Goodall 珍古德　　Africa 〔ˋæfrɪkə 〕n. 非洲
　　　　observe³ 〔 əbˋzɝv 〕v. 觀察；看到
　　　　chimpanzee⁵ 〔͵tʃɪmpænˋzi 〕n. 黑猩猩
　　　　native³ 〔ˋnetɪv 〕adj. 出生地的；本地的
　　　　environment² 〔 ɪnˋvaɪrənmənt 〕n. 環境
　　　　stick² 〔 stɪk 〕n. 枝條；棍子　　termite 〔ˋtɝmaɪt 〕n. 白蟻
　　　　ape¹ 〔 ep 〕n. 猿　　***great ape*** 類人猿　　train¹ 〔 tren 〕v. 訓練
　　　　crow² 〔 kro 〕n. 烏鴉　　spear⁴ 〔 spɪr 〕v. 叉住
　　　　insect² 〔ˋɪnsɛkt 〕n. 昆蟲　　bark² 〔 bɑrk 〕n. 樹皮

3. (**D**)　(A) look after 照顧　　　　　(B) take over 接管
　　　　　　(C) result in 導致　　　　　　(D) ***look at*** 著眼於

4. (**B**)　observe「看到」是感官動詞，其用法為：
　　　　感官動詞 + O. + { V-ing 或 V. 表「主動」
　　　　　　　　　　　　 { p.p. 表「被動」
　　　　依句意，「用」小樹枝，是主動，故選 (B) ***using***。

Another aspect *of animal cognition* is solving problems. Some

species *of birds*, *such as ravens*, are *particularly* clever. Ravens are

able to solve many different problems, *such as untying a knot to get at*

food. *Besides*, orangutans can learn complex tasks, *such as washing*

clothes by hand, <u>*after just a few tries*</u>. Dolphins, *too*, can follow
            5

complex instructions.

　　動物認知的另一個層面，是解決問題。某些品種的鳥，例如渡鴉，
就特別聰明。渡鴉能解決許多不同的問題，像是爲了拿到食物而解開繩
結。此外，紅毛猩猩能學會複雜的工作，像是<u>在嘗試幾次之後</u>，就能用
手洗衣服。海豚也可以服從複雜的指令。　　5　　　　　5

* aspect⁴〔'æspɛkt〕 *n.* 方面　　cognition〔kɑg'nɪʃən〕 *n.* 認知
　solve²〔salv〕 *v.* 解決　　raven〔'revən〕 *n.* 渡鴉
　particularly²〔pə'tɪkjələlɪ〕 *adv.* 特別地；尤其
　clever²〔'klɛvə〕 *adj.* 聰明的　　***such as*** 像是
　untie〔ʌn'taɪ〕 *v.* 解開【tie¹ *v.* 綁；打 (結)】
　knot³〔nɑt〕 *n.* 結　　***get at*** 拿得到；接近
　orangutan〔o'ræŋʊˌtæn〕 *n.* (紅毛) 猩猩
　complex³〔kəm'plɛks〕 *adj.* 複雜的
　task²〔tæsk〕 *n.* 任務；工作　　***a few*** 一些
　try¹〔traɪ〕 *n.* 嘗試　　dolphin²〔'dɑlfɪn〕 *n.* 海豚
　follow¹〔'falo〕 *v.* 遵守；聽從；服從
　instructions³〔ɪn'strʌkʃənz〕 *n. pl.* 命令；指示

5. (**D**)　依句意，選 (D) ***after***「在…之後」。而 (A) by「藉由」，
　　　　　 (B) for「爲了」，(C) without「沒有」，皆不合句意。

TEST 45

Read the following passage and choose the best answer for each blank from the choices below.

Technology is becoming increasingly important to restaurants and tabletop ordering devices only stand to multiply, according to Darren Tristano, executive vice president at the Chicago-based restaurant consulting firm Technomic. "It's cool and trendy and kids love it," he explained. "It ___1___ other opportunities with applications."

Chicago-based restaurant Au Bon Pain uses iPads at six of its 220 locations, with plans to expand. Ed Frechette, the company's vice president of marketing in Boston, said diners usually fill out pieces of paper with their orders at the cafés, but iPads have ___2___ the process. "One of our employees has an iPad ___3___ a menu loaded in it and they'll take your order," Frechette said. "You still see a menu board with all the information on it. We have handheld laminated menus for a reference, but all the paper pads are ___4___."

At 4Food in New York, ___5___ diners can make and name their own burgers, customers order and enter credit card information into an iPad to pay. Managing partner Adam Kidron said ordering food electronically will eventually be the norm.

1. (A) gives way to   (B) make way for
   (C) paves the way for   (D) has a way with

2. (A) strengthened   (B) clarified
   (C) undergone   (D) simplified

3. (A) as   (B) with
   (C) of   (D) than

4. (A) gone   (B) available
   (C) left   (D) free

5. (A) where   (B) since
   (C) there   (D) while

【劉毅老師的話】

　　傳統的模擬試題，克漏字、文意選填、閱讀測驗，甚至連詞彙測驗，都超出 7000 字，同學做題目會受到艱深單字的影響，無法進步。我們每一個單字都有標明級數，嚴格控制在 7000 字範圍內，同學越做，生字越少。

TEST 45 詳解

Technology is becoming *increasingly* important *to restaurants*

and tabletop ordering devices *only* stand to multiply, *according to*

Darren Tristano, executive vice president at the Chicago-based

restaurant consulting firm Technomic. "It's cool *and* trendy *and*

kids love it," he explained. "It <u>paves the way</u> *for other opportunities*

1

with applications."

根據芝加哥的餐廳顧問公司 Technomic 的執行副總德倫·崔斯塔
諾的說法，對於餐廳來說，科技變得越來越重要，而且桌上型的點餐裝
置，只會倍數成長。「這很酷、很潮，而且小孩子很愛，」他解釋道。
「這爲其他應用程式的機會鋪了路。」

1

* technology³ (tɛkˈnɑlədʒɪ) *n.* 科技
  increasingly (ɪnˈkrisʊŋlɪ) *adv.* 越來越 (= *more and more*)
  tabletop (ˈtɛblˌtɑp) *adj.* 桌上型的
  order¹ (ˈɔrdə) *v. n.* 點餐　　device⁴ (dɪˈvaɪs) *n.* 裝置
  stand¹ (stænd) *v.* 處於…狀態
  multiply² (ˈmʌltəˌplaɪ) *v.* 增加；繁殖
  executive⁵ (ɪgˈzɛkjʊtɪv) *adj.* 執行的
  vice president³ (ˈvaɪs ˈprɛzədənt) *n.* 副總
  Chicago (ʃɪˈkɑgo) *n.* 芝加哥【美國城市名】
  -based¹ (best) *adj.* 以…爲根據地的
  consulting⁴ (kənˈsʌltɪŋ) *adj.* 顧問的
  firm² (fɝm) *n.* 公司

cool[1] 〔kul〕 *adj.* 酷的
trendy[3] 〔'trɛndɪ〕 *adj.* 流行的；時髦的
explain[2] 〔ɪk'splen〕 *v.* 解釋；說明
opportunity[3] 〔ˌɑpə'tjunətɪ〕 *n.* 機會
application[4] 〔ˌæplə'keʃən〕 *n.* 應用程式

1. (**C**)　(A) give way to　對…讓步
　　　　(B) make way for　讓路給
　　　　(C) **pave the way for**　爲…鋪路；爲…作準備；使…容易
　　　　(D) have a way with　善於處理；有能力對付

Chicago-based restaurant Au Bon Pain uses iPads *at six of its*

220 locations, with plans to expand.　Ed Frechette, *the company's vice*

president of marketing in Boston, said *diners usually fill out pieces of*

paper with their orders at the cafés, **but** iPads have <u>simplified</u> the
　　　　　　　　　　　　　　　　　　　　2

process.　"One *of our employees* has an iPad <u>*with*</u> *a menu loaded in it*
　　　　　　　　　　　　　　　　　3

and they'll take your order," Frechette said.　"You *still* see a menu

board *with all the information on it.*　We have handheld laminated

menus *for a reference*, **but** all the paper pads are <u>gone</u>."
　　　　　　　　　　　　　　　　4

　　總部位於芝加哥的餐廳 Au Bon Pain，在其兩百二十個據點中的六個點使用 iPad 點餐，並且計畫擴大使用。該公司在波士頓的行銷副總艾迪・弗切特說，顧客通常在咖啡廳填寫點菜的單子，而 iPad <u>簡化</u>了

這個過程。「我們的員工<u>有</u>台已經下載菜單的 iPad，他們可以幫你點
3
餐，」弗切特說。「你還是看得到包含所有資訊的菜單板。我們有手持
的壓膜菜單給你參考，但是所有的便條紙簿都<u>沒了</u>。」
4

* location⁴〔loˈkeʃən〕n. 地點
expand⁴〔ɪkˈspænd〕v. 擴大
marketing¹〔ˈmarkɪtɪŋ〕n. 行銷
diner〔ˈdaɪnɚ〕n. 用餐的人

dine³ v. ①用餐 ②宴請
diner n. ①用餐者 ②餐館

fill out 填寫　　café²〔kəˈfe〕n. 咖啡廳
process³〔ˈprɑsɛs〕n. 過程　　employee³〔ˌɛmplɔɪˈi〕n. 員工
menu²〔ˈmɛnju〕n. 菜單　　load³〔lod〕v. 下載
take one's order 接受某人點菜
board²〔bord〕n.（布告）板
information⁴〔ˌɪnfɚˈmeʃən〕n. 資訊；資料
handheld〔ˈhændˌhɛld〕adj. 手持式的
laminated〔ˈlæməˌnetɪd〕adj. 薄片狀的；壓膜的
reference⁴〔ˈrɛfərəns〕n. 參考
pad³〔pæd〕n. 便條紙簿

2. (**D**)　(A) strengthen⁴〔ˈstrɛŋθən〕v. 加強
　　　　　(B) clarify⁴〔ˈklærəˌfaɪ〕v. 清楚說明
　　　　　(C) undergo⁶〔ˌʌndɚˈgo〕v. 經歷
　　　　　(D) *simplify*⁶〔ˈsɪmpləˌfaɪ〕v. 簡化

3. (**B**)　依句意，選 (B) *with*「有」。

4. (**A**)　(A) *gone*〔gɔn〕adj. 消失的
　　　　　(B) available³〔əˈveləbḷ〕adj. 可獲得的
　　　　　(C) left¹〔lɛft〕adj. 左邊的
　　　　　(D) free¹〔fri〕adj. 自由的；免費的

At 4Food in New York, ___**where**___ diners can make **and** name their
5

own burgers, customers order **and** enter credit card information

into an iPad to pay. Managing partner Adam Kidron said *ordering*

food electronically will eventually be the norm.

在紐約的 4Food 餐廳裡，用餐者可以<u>在那</u>創造並命名屬於自己的
5

漢堡，並且點餐後，可以在 iPad 上輸入信用卡資料付款。餐廳合夥人
Adam Kidron 說，電子點餐終將成爲常態。

* customer² 〔'kʌstəmɚ〕 *n.* 顧客　　***credit card*** 信用卡
manage³ 〔'mænɪdʒ〕 *n.* 管理
partner² 〔'pɑrtnɚ〕 *n.* 夥伴
managing partner 經營合夥人；執行業務股東
electronically 〔ɪ,lɛk'trɑnɪklɪ〕 *adv.* 通過電子手段
eventually⁴ 〔ɪ'vɛntʃuəlɪ〕 *adv.* 最後
norm⁶ 〔nɔrm〕 *n.* 常態

5. (**A**)　表「地點」，關係副詞用 ***where***，選 (A)。

未經仔細校對，錯誤的文章無法做
句子分析。學會分析句子，有助於
增進閱讀的能力。

TEST 46

Read the following passage and choose the best answer for each blank from the choices below.

According to research conducted by the Debenhams department store in 2009, the length of the skirts that women wear is related to their age. People may generally ___1___ that the older a woman becomes, the longer her skirt is. This hypothesis, however, is only ___2___ correct as there are other factors that influence women's decisions on the length of their skirts, such as their dating or marital ___3___.

In the study, it was found that women's skirts reach their shortest when they are 23 years old. Between the ages of 23 and 27, skirt lengths increase due to the fact that women are in their first stable relationships at this ___4___ of their lives and have no desire to attract male attention. Between the ages of 27 and 34, however, short skirts ___5___ after old relationships fail and new ones begin to form. Then, after the age 34, the trend for longer skirts becomes unstoppable.

1. (A) consume   (B) assume   (C) resume   (D) costume
2. (A) entirely   (B) fundamentally
   (C) similarly   (D) partially
3. (A) stereotype   (B) stimulation   (C) status   (D) shortage
4. (A) stack   (B) station   (C) stage   (D) statue
5. (A) become a river of no return   (B) make a comeback
   (C) get in the way   (D) make a scene

TEST 46 詳解

According to research conducted by the Debenhams department store in 2009, the length of the skirts *that* women wear is related to their age. People may *generally* <u>assume</u> *that* the older a woman becomes, *the longer her skirt is.*

根據德班漢姆斯百貨公司在 2009 年所做的研究，女性穿著裙子的長度與其年齡有關。一般來說，人們可能會<u>認為</u>，女性年紀愈大，裙子的長度就會愈長。

* research⁴ (ˈrɪsɜtʃ) *n.* 研究　conduct⁵ (kənˈdʌkt) *v.* 進行；做
  Debenhams (ˈdɛbnəms) *n.* 德班漢姆斯【英國知名百貨公司，在英國本土及愛爾蘭、丹麥等歐洲國家開設許多直營店】
  department store 百貨公司　length² (lɛŋθ) *n.* 長度
  be related to 和…有關
  generally² (ˈdʒɛnərəlɪ) *adv.* 一般來說；通常
  「the + 比較級…the +比較級」表「越…就越～」。

1. (**B**)　(A) consume⁴ (kənˈsum) *v.* 消耗；吃（喝）
　　　　(B) *assume*⁴ (əˈsum) *v.* 假定；認為
　　　　(C) resume⁵ (rɪˈzum) *v.* 恢復；再繼續
　　　　(D) costume⁴ (ˈkɑstjum) *n.* 服裝；戲服

This hypothesis, *however*, is only <u>partially</u> correct *as there are other factors **that** influence women's decisions on the length of their skirts, such as their dating **or** marital <u>status</u>.*

然而，這假設僅<u>部分</u>正確，因為有其他影響女性決定她們裙子長度的因
₂
素，例如她們約會或婚姻的<u>狀態</u>。
₃

* hypothesis〔haɪˈpɑθəsɪs〕*n.* 假設
correct[1]〔kəˈrɛkt〕*adj.* 正確的　　factor[1]〔ˈfæktɚ〕*n.* 因素
influence[2]〔ˈɪnfluəns〕*v.* 影響　　decision[2]〔dɪˈsɪʒən〕*n.* 決定
date[1]〔det〕*v.* 約會　　marital〔ˈmærətl̩〕*adj.* 婚姻的

2. (**D**)　(A) entirely[2]〔ɪnˈtaɪrlɪ〕*adv.* 完全地
　　　　　(B) fundamentally[4]〔ˌfʌndəˈmɛntl̩ɪ〕*adv.* 基本上
　　　　　(C) similarly[2]〔ˈsɪmələlɪ〕*adv.* 同樣地
　　　　　(D) ***partially***[4]〔ˈparʃəlɪ〕*adv.* 部分地

3. (**C**)　(A) stereotype[5]〔ˈstɛrɪəˌtaɪp〕*n.* 刻版印象
　　　　　(B) stimulation[6]〔ˌstɪmjəˈleʃən〕*n.* 刺激
　　　　　(C) ***status***[4]〔ˈstetəs〕*n.* 狀態　***marital status*** 婚姻狀態
　　　　　(D) shortage[5]〔ˈʃɔrtɪdʒ〕*n.* 短缺

In the study, it was found *that women's skirts reach their shortest*

when they are 23 years old. Between the ages of 23 and 27, skirt

lengths increase *due to the fact that women are in their first stable*

relationships at this <u>stage</u> *of their lives and have no desire to attract*
₄
male attention.

這項研究發現，女性裙子的長度，當她們二十三歲時是最短的。
在二十三歲到二十七歲這段期間，裙子的長度會增加，因為在這個人
生<u>階段</u>的女性，正好處於她們第一段穩定關係，所以沒有吸引男性注
₄
意的慾望。

* study[1]〔'stʌdɪ〕 *n.* 研究　　increase[2] 〔ɪn'kris〕 *v.* 增加

due to 由於　　stable[3] 〔'stebḷ〕 *adj.* 穩定的

relationship[2] 〔rɪ'leʃən,ʃɪp〕 *n.* 關係

desire[2] 〔dɪ'zaɪr〕 *n.* 慾望　　attract[3] 〔ə'trækt〕 *v.* 吸引

male[2] 〔mel〕 *adj.* 男性的　　attention[2] 〔ə'tɛnʃən〕 *n.* 注意力

4. (**C**)　(A) stack[5] 〔stæk〕 *n.* 乾草堆

　　　　(B) station[1] 〔'steʃən〕 *n.* 車站

　　　　(C) **stage**[2] 〔stedʒ〕 *n.* 階段

　　　　(D) statue[3] 〔'stætʃʊ〕 *n.* 雕像

*Between the ages of 27 **and** 34, however,* short skirts make a comeback
[5]
***after** old relationships fail **and** new ones begin to form. Then, after*

age 34, the trend *for longer skirts* becomes unstoppable.

然而，在二十七歲到三十四歲這段期間，在舊戀情失敗，而新的感情正
開始成形時，短裙會捲土重來。然後，在三十四歲之後，長裙就變得勢
不可擋。
[5]

* fail[2] 〔fel〕 *v.* 失敗　　form[2] 〔fɔrm〕 *v.* 形成

trend[3] 〔trɛnd〕 *n.* 時尚；趨勢

unstoppable 〔ʌn'stɑpəbḷ〕 *adj.* 擋不住的

5. (**B**)　(A) become a river of no return　如大江東去

　　　　(B) **make a comeback**　捲土重來

　　　　　comeback 〔'kʌm,bæk〕 *n.* 捲土重來；東山再起

　　　　(C) get in the way　妨礙

　　　　(D) make a scene　（當眾）大吵大鬧

TEST 47

Read the following passage and choose the best answer for each blank from the choices below.

"An eye for an eye" is a quotation from the Bible that talks about how an injured party performs the same kind of act to hurt the person that imposed pain on him. It is a classic act of ___1___. Recently, this concept was fully realized by an Australian man who hit his friend's car with a giant ax. Waking up in the morning after a wild party, Nick was ___2___ to find an ax stuck in the roof of his car. It was a ___3___ that his friend, Cal, had pulled on him. To take an eye for an eye, Nick spent all his savings and had a professional build an ax that was 13 meters tall and weighed over a ton. ___4___ the completion of the killer ax, Nick gathered a crowd of his friends and eight cameras around Cal's car. He then got Cal on Skype moments before the cable holding the ax ___5___ from a crane. Within seconds, the sharp ax landed on the car roof and almost cut it in half. The mission was accomplished when Cal shrieked in horror on the computer.

1. (A) arrange   (B) change   (C) revenge   (D) challenge
2. (A) devastated   (B) dreary   (C) dreadful   (D) drastic
3. (A) praise   (B) plain   (C) plague   (D) prank
4. (A) Among   (B) Upon   (C) Until   (D) When
5. (A) leak   (B) was released
    (C) amounted   (D) was launched

TEST 47 詳解

"An eye for an eye" is a quotation *from the Bible that* talks *about **how** an injured party performs the same kind of act to hurt the person **that** imposed pain on him.* It is a classic act *of revenge.*
                                                                                                    1

「以眼還眼」這句引述自聖經的話，說的是受到傷害的一方，如何以相同的行為，去傷害對他們施加痛苦的人。這是個經典的<u>復仇</u>之舉。
                                                                                                    1

* quotation〔kwoˈteʃən〕*n.* 引文【quote³〔kwot〕*v.* 引用】
  Bible〔ˈbaɪbḷ〕*n.* 聖經　　injured³〔ˈɪndʒəd〕*adj.* 受傷的
  party¹〔ˈpɑrtɪ〕*n.* 一方
  perform³〔pəˈfɔrm〕*v.* 執行；做
  act¹〔ækt〕*n.* 行為
  hurt¹〔hɜt〕*v.* 傷害
  impose⁵〔ɪmˈpoz〕*v.* 強加 < *on* >
  pain²〔pen〕*n.* 痛苦
  classic²〔ˈklæsɪk〕*adj.* 典型的

revenge *v.* 復仇；以眼還眼
= avenge〔əˈvɛndʒ〕
= retaliate〔rɪˈtælɪˌet〕
= take an eye for an eye
= give tit for tat
= return like for like

1. (**C**)　(A) arrange²〔əˈrendʒ〕*v.* 安排
　　　　　(B) change²〔tʃendʒ〕*n.* 改變
　　　　　(C) ***revenge***⁴〔rɪˈvɛndʒ〕*n.* 報復
　　　　　(D) challenge³〔ˈtʃælɪndʒ〕*n.* 挑戰

Recently, this concept was *fully* realized *by an Australian man **who** hit his friend's car with a giant ax.* *Waking up in the morning after a*

wild party, Nick was <u>devastated</u> to find an ax *stuck in the roof of his*
2

car. It was a <u>prank</u> *that his friend, Cal, had pulled on him. To take*
3

an eye for an eye, Nick spent all his savings *and* had a professional

build an ax *that was 13 meters tall and weighed over a ton.*

最近，這個概念被一個澳洲男人徹底實行，他用巨大的斧頭攻擊他朋友
的車子。狂歡派對後一早醒來，尼克<u>極為震驚地</u>發現，有一把斧頭插在
2

自己汽車的車頂上。這是他的朋友凱爾對他搞的<u>惡作劇</u>。為了報復，尼
3

克花掉他全部的存款，請一個專業人士打造了一把長達十三公尺、重超
過一噸的斧頭。

* recently[2] ('risṇtlı) *adv.* 最近   concept[4] ('kansɛpt) *n.* 概念
  fully[1] ('fulı) *adv.* 徹底地；完全地
  realize[2] ('rıə,laız) *v.* 實行
  Australian (ɔ'streljən) *adj.* 澳洲的   hit[1] (hıt) *v.* 打
  giant[2] ('dʒaıənt) *adj.* 巨大的   ax[3] (æks) *n.* 斧頭 (= *axe*)
  wake up 醒來   wild[2] (waıld) *adj.* 瘋狂的
  stick[2] (stık) *v.* 刺；插【三態變化：stick-stuck-stuck】
  roof[1] (ruf) *n.* 屋頂；(汽車的) 車頂
  savings[3] ('sevıŋz) *n. pl.* 存款；儲金
  professional[4] (prə'fɛʃənḷ) *n.* 專業人士
  meter[2] ('mitɚ) *n.* 公尺   weigh[1] (we) *v.* 重…
  ton[3] (tɑn) *n.* 公噸

2. (**A**)   (A) **devastated** ('dɛvəs,tetıd) *adj.* 極為震驚的
      (B) dreary[6] ('drırı) *adj.* (天氣) 陰沈的
      (C) dreadful[5] ('drɛdfəl) *adj.* 可怕的
      (D) drastic[6] ('dræstık) *adj.* 激烈的

3. (**D**)　(A) praise[2] 〔 rez 〕 *n.* 稱讚

　　(B) plain[2] 〔 plen 〕 *n.* 平原

　　(C) plague[5] 〔 pleg 〕 *n.* 瘟疫

　　(D) ***prank*** 〔 præŋk 〕 *n.* 惡作劇

　　　pull a prank (***on*** *someone*)　對某人惡作劇

Upon the completion of the killer ax, Nick gathered a crowd of his
4

friends *and* eight cameras *around Cal's car.* He *then* got Cal *on Skype*

moments *before* the cable holding the ax *was released* from a crane.
　　　　　　　　　　　　　　　　　　　5

Within seconds, the sharp ax landed *on the car roof and* almost cut it

in half. The mission was accomplished *when Cal shrieked in horror*

on the computer.

當這把殺手級巨斧一完工後，尼克就召集了一大群朋友，並且架設了八
台攝影機在凱爾的車子周圍。在固定巨斧的鋼索從起重機被鬆開之前，
　　　　　　　　　　　　　　　　　　　　　　　　　　　　5
尼克讓凱爾在 Skype 線上。幾秒之內，那把銳利的巨斧就落在車頂上，
幾乎把整台車劈成兩半。當電腦前的凱爾驚恐地失聲尖叫時，任務便大
功告成。

　　* completion[2] 〔 kəm'pliʃən 〕 *n.* 完成
　　　killer[2] 〔'kɪlɚ 〕 *n.* 殺手　　gather[2] 〔'gæðɚ 〕 *v.* 聚集
　　　crowd[2] 〔 kraʊd 〕 *n.* 群眾；人群　　*a crowd of* 一群
　　　camera[1] 〔'kæmərə 〕 *n.* 攝影機　　get[1] 〔 gɛt 〕 *v.* 使
　　　Skype *n.* 一款通訊應用軟體
　　　moment[1] 〔'momənt 〕 *n.* 片刻　　cable[2] 〔'kebḷ 〕 *n.* 鋼索

hold[1] 〔 hold 〕*v.* 握住；固定住
crane[2] 〔 kren 〕*n.* 起重機
within[2] 〔 wɪð'ɪn 〕*prep.* 在…之內　　second[1] 〔'sɛkənd 〕*n.* 秒
sharp[1] 〔 ʃɑrp 〕*adj.* 銳利的　　land[1] 〔 lænd 〕*v.* 降落
in half 成兩半地　　mission[3] 〔'mɪʃən 〕*n.* 任務
accomplish[4] 〔 ə'kɑmplɪʃ 〕*v.* 完成
shriek[5] 〔 ʃrik 〕*v.* 尖叫　　horror[3] 〔'hɔrɚ 〕*n.* 恐怖；恐懼
in horror 恐懼地

4. (**B**)　依句意，選 (B) *Upon*「一…就」。
　　而 (A) Among「在…之間」，(C) Until「直到」，不合句意；
　　(D) When「當…時候」，是連接詞，引導副詞子句，在此用
　　法不合。

5. (**B**)　依句意，選 (B) *be released*「被解開」。
　　release[3] 〔 rɪ'lis 〕*v.* 釋放；放開；解開
　　(A) leak[3] 〔 lik 〕*v.* 漏出；漏水
　　(C) amount[2] 〔 ə'maʊnt 〕*v.* 共計 < *to* >
　　(D) launch[4] 〔 lɔntʃ 〕*v.* 發射

---

* release 和 leak 不同，例如：

Please *release* my hand. (請放開我的手。)
= *Please let go of my hand.*
The faucet is *leaking*. (水龍頭在漏水。)
= *Water is dripping from the faucet.*

TEST 48

Read the following passage and choose the best answer for each blank from the choices below.

A class reunion can reach across space and time. What pops into your head when you __1__ the jolly scenario? Some shout and embrace on seeing their old friends, __2__ others may check out the names or words of love they carved on the walls to recapture some of the vitality of their youth. If this is what's in your mind, the comments of Harvard professor David E. Bell may cause you to think otherwise. He once advised that a group of graduating students __3__ attend their reunion.

Bell's reason was that reunions compel students to face their achievements or lack thereof. The moment attendees arrive, they begin checking out the model of the other cars, __4__ they assess how well their classmates have done since graduation. In his opinion, a reunion __5__ huge anxieties about one's value as an individual. The attendees' confidence can be undermined, which makes them less likely to pursue their true ambitions.

1. (A) image   (B) imagine   (C) imagination (D) imaginative
2. (A) while   (B) since
   (C) at the same time   (D) on the other hand
3. (A) to   (B) should   (C) not   (D) did not
4. (A) that   (B) then   (C) in which   (D) by which
5. (A) recites   (B) repeats   (C) triggers   (D) contributes

TEST 48 詳解

A class reunion can reach across space ***and*** time. What pops

into your head ***when*** *you* *imagine* *the jolly scenario*? Some shout ***and***
₁

embrace *on seeing their old friends*, ***while*** others may check out *the*
₂

names ***or*** *words of love they carved on the walls to recapture some of*

the vitality of their youth.

同學會能穿越時空。當你想像這個愉快的場景時，你腦袋裡會出現
1

什麼畫面？有些人一看到老朋友，就抱著對方尖叫，而有些人可能會查
2

看他們刻在牆上的名字或甜言蜜語，以重溫一些年輕的活力。

* reunion⁴ ﹝rɪ'junjən﹞ *n.* 團聚
  class reunion 同學會
  reach across space and time 穿越時空
  pop³ ﹝pɑp﹞ *v.* （突然）出現
  jolly⁵ ﹝'dʒɑlɪ﹞ *adj.* 愉快的；歡樂的
  scenario ﹝sɪ'nɛrɪ,o﹞ *n.* 情景
  shout¹ ﹝ʃaʊt﹞ *v.* 吼叫
  embrace⁵ ﹝ɪm'bres﹞ *v.* 擁抱   ***on + V-ing*** 一…就
  check out 查看   carve⁴ ﹝kɑrv﹞ *v.* 雕刻
  recapture ﹝rɪ'kæptʃə﹞ *v.* 回憶；重溫【capture³ *v.* 抓住】
  vitality⁶ ﹝vaɪ'tælətɪ﹞ *n.* 活力   youth² ﹝juθ﹞ *n.* 年輕

1. (**B**)　(A) image³〔'ɪmɪdʒ〕*n.* 形象
　　　　　(B) ***imagine***²〔ɪ'mædʒɪn〕*v.* 想像
　　　　　(C) imagination³〔ɪ,mædʒə'neʃən〕*n.* 想像力
　　　　　(D) imaginative⁴〔ɪ'mædʒə,netɪv〕*adj.* 有想像力的

2. (**A**)　表「對比」，用 *while*「然而」（= *whereas*），選 (A)。
　　　　　而 (B) since「自從」，(C) at the same time「同時」，
　　　　　(D) on the other hand「另一方面」，則不合句意。

*If this is **what**'s in your mind*, the comments *of Harvard professor*

David E. Bell may cause you to think *otherwise*.　He *once* advised

that *a group of graduating students <u>not</u> attend their reunion.*
　　　　　　　　　　　　　　　　　　　　3

如果你也是這樣想，那麼哈佛大學教授大衛・貝爾的評論，可能會讓你
想得不一樣。他曾經勸告一群畢業生<u>不要</u>參加同學會。
　　　　　　　　　　　　　　　　3

　　　* mind¹〔maɪnd〕*n.* 心智；心　　　comment⁴〔'kɑmɛnt〕*n.* 評論
　　　professor⁴〔prə'fɛsɚ〕*n.* 教授　　cause¹〔kɔz〕*v.* 使
　　　otherwise⁴〔'ʌðɚ,waɪz〕*adv.* 否則；不那樣
　　　advise³〔əd'vaɪz〕*v.* 勸告；建議

> advise 為欲望動詞，其用法為：
> advise that + S. + (should) + 原形動詞

　　　graduate³〔'grædʒʊ,et〕*v.* 畢業　　attend²〔ə'tɛnd〕*v.* 參加

3. (**C**)　依句意，空格前已有關鍵字 otherwise（不那樣），所以可推
　　　　　測教授會勸告一群畢業生「不要」參加同學會，故選 (C) ***not***。

Bell's reason was ***that*** *reunions compel students to face their*

*achievements **or** lack thereof.* ***The moment*** *attendees arrive*, they begin

checking out the model *of the other cars,* *by which* *they assess **how***
4

well their classmates have done since graduation.

　　貝爾的理由是，同學會會強迫學生們，面對自己的成就或是一事無
成。參加同學會的人一抵達現場，就會開始打量其他人的車款，藉此評
估他們的同學在畢業後混得如何。
4

　　* compel[5] (kəm'pɛl) v. 強迫　　face[1] (fes) v. 面對
　　achievements[3] (ə'tʃivmənts) n. pl. 成就
　　lack[1] (læk) n. 缺乏；不足
　　thereof (ˌðɛr'ɔf) adv. 其；在其中；關於那
　　(= of the thing mentioned)
　　the moment 一…就　　attendee (ˌətɛn'di) n. 參加者
　　model[2] ('madl) n. 型；款式　　assess[6] (ə'sɛs) v. 評估
　　graduation[4] (ˌgrædʒʊ'eʃən) n. 畢業

4.(**D**)　依句意，「藉」此來評估，故選 (D) ***by which***。而
　　　　　(A) 關代 that 前面不能有介系詞；(B) then「然後」和
　　　　　(C) in which，皆不合句意。

In his opinion, a reunion underline{triggers} huge anxieties *about one's value as*
5

an individual. The attendees' confidence can be undermined, ***which***

makes them less likely to pursue their true ambitions.

他認為，同學會會<u>引發</u>對自我價值產生極大的焦慮。參加同學會的人可
5
能會逐漸喪失自信，使他們較不可能追求自己真正的抱負。

* opinion² 〔ə'pɪnjən〕 n. 意見　　***in one's opinion*** 依某人之見
huge² 〔hjudʒ〕 adj. 巨大的　　anxiety⁴ 〔æŋ'zaɪətɪ〕 n. 焦慮
value² 〔'væljʊ〕 n. 價值　　individual³ 〔ˏɪndə'vɪdʒʊəl〕 n. 個人
confidence⁴ 〔'kɑnfədəns〕 n. 信心；自信
undermine⁶ 〔ˏʌndə'maɪn〕 v. 逐漸損害
likely¹ 〔'laɪklɪ〕 adj. 可能的
pursue³ 〔pə'su〕 v. 追求
ambition³ 〔æm'bɪʃən〕 n. 抱負

| confidence *n.* 信心 |
| confident *adj.* 有信心的 |
| confidant *n.* 心腹知己 |
| confidential *adj.* 機密的 |

5. (**C**)　(A) recite⁴ 〔rɪ'saɪt〕 v. 背誦
　　　　　(B) repeat² 〔rɪ'pit〕 v. 重複
　　　　　(C) ***trigger***⁶ 〔'trɪgə〕 v. 引發　n. 扳機
　　　　　(D) contribute⁴ 〔kən'trɪbjut〕 v. 貢獻

【劉毅老師的話】

　　要看就要看有詳解的書。只有簡答沒有
詳解，太可怕了！如果答案錯，怎麼辦？句
子分析是本書的特色。分析句子要花很大的
工夫，是為了讓讀者能找出主詞、動詞、修
飾語、子句等。學會分析句子，閱讀速度才
會增快。

TEST 49

Read the following passage and choose the best answer for each blank from the choices below.

Hearing loss is more common than ever before. About 16% of American adults have an impaired ability to hear speech, and more than 30% of Americans over age 20—an ___1___ 55 million people—have lost some high-frequency hearing, according to a new study published in the *Archives of Internal Medicine.*

The finding has made experts and concerned parents wonder about this question: Does listening to loud music through headphones ___2___ long-term hearing loss? Brian Fligor, director of diagnostic audiology at Children's Hospital Boston, explains, "It depends on the person, how long you're listening, and the level ___3___ which you're setting your music device. If you're using the earbuds and you turn the volume up to the maximum and you listen a total of two hours a day, five days a week, our best estimates are that people ___4___ more sensitive ears will develop a rather significant degree of hearing loss. ___5___ is more alarming is that this would happen after about 10 years or so or even more of listening to a personal music device."

1. (A) estimated   (B) estimating   (C) estimate (D) estimation
2. (A) result from   (B) lead to
      (C) bring in   (D) derive from
3. (A) by   (B) for   (C) at   (D) with
4. (A) have   (B) to have   (C) had   (D) having
5. (A) How   (B) It   (C) What   (D) That

TEST 49 詳解

Hearing loss is *more* common *than* ever before. About 16% *of American adults* have an impaired ability *to hear speech*, *and* more than 30% *of Americans over age 20*—*an estimated* 55 million people— have lost some high-frequency hearing, *according to a new study published in the Archives of Internal Medicine.*

　　聽力受損的現象比以往更為常見。根據一份在《內科醫學文獻》中發表的新研究顯示，大約百分之十六的美國成人，聽人說話的能力受損，而超過三成的二十歲以上的美國人——估計為五千五百萬人——已喪失了某些高頻的聽力。

* hearing〔ˋhɪrɪŋ〕n. 聽力；聽覺
　loss²〔lɔs〕n. 喪失；損失；損害
　common¹〔ˋkɑmən〕adj. 常見的；普遍的
　adult¹〔əˋdʌlt〕n. 成人
　impaired〔ɪmˋpɛrd〕adj. 受損的；（能力）衰退的
　speech¹〔spitʃ〕n. 說話；言談
　frequency⁴〔ˋfrikwənsɪ〕n. 頻率
　high-frequency〔ˋhaɪˋfrikwənsɪ〕adj. 高頻的
　according to 根據　　study¹〔ˋstʌdɪ〕n. 研究
　archive〔ˋɑrkaɪv〕n. 文件；檔案
　internal³〔ɪnˋtɜnḷ〕adj. 內部的（↔ *external* adj. 外部的）
　medicine²〔ˋmɛdəsṇ〕n. 醫學　　*internal medicine* 內科
　Archives of Internal Medicine 內科醫學文獻【醫學期刊名稱】

1. (**A**) 依句意，30% of Americans over age 20 which is estimated 55 million people (= *30% of Americans over age 20—an estimated 55 million people*)，這個百分比的人數是「被估計」出來的，故選 (A) ***estimated*** 「估計的；推測的」。estimate[4] 〔'ɛstə,met 〕 *v.* 估計

The finding has made experts *and* concerned parents wonder about this question: Does listening to loud music *through headphones* <u>lead to</u> long-term hearing loss?

2

　　這項研究結果已經使得專家和擔心的父母們，對這個問題感到好奇：用耳機大聲地聽音樂會<u>導致</u>長期的聽力損害嗎？

2

* finding[1] 〔'faɪndɪŋ 〕 *n.* 研究結果
  expert[2] 〔'ɛkspɜt 〕 *n.* 專家
  concerned[3] 〔 kən'sɜnd 〕 *adj.* 關切的；擔心的
  wonder[2] 〔'wʌndə 〕 *v.* 想知道；對…感到好奇
  headphone[4] 〔'hɛd,fon 〕 *n.* 頭戴式耳機
  long-term 〔'lɔŋ,tɜm 〕 *adj.* 長期的

wonder	*v.* 想知道	*n.* 驚奇
w**o**nder		
w**a**nder	*v.* 漫遊；流浪	

2. (**B**)　(A) result from　起因於
　　　　　　(B) ***lead to***　導致
　　　　　　(C) bring in　獲利
　　　　　　(D) derive from　起源於

| lead to　導致 |
| = give rise to |
| = bring about |
| = result in |
| = cause |

Brian Fligor, *director of diagnostic audiology at Children's Hospital Boston*, explains, "It depends on the person, how long you're listening, *and* the level <u>at **which**</u> you're setting your music device.

3

波士頓兒童醫院診斷聽力學主任布萊恩・佛來格解釋說：「這要取決於個人，聽了多久，以及音樂裝置的音量設定<u>在何種程度</u>。
3

* director[2] 〔 dəˈrɛktə 〕 *n.* 主任
  diagnostic 〔 ˌdaɪəgˈnɑstɪk 〕 *adj.* 診斷的
  【diagnose[6] 〔 ˌdaɪəgˈnoz 〕 *v.* 診斷】
  audiology 〔 ˌɔdɪˈɑlədʒɪ 〕 *n.* 聽力學
  Boston 〔 ˈbɔstn̩ 〕 *n.* 波士頓【美國城市名】
  explain[2] 〔 ɪkˈsplen 〕 *v.* 解釋
  depend on 視…而定
  level[1] 〔 ˈlɛvl̩ 〕 *n.* 程度
  set[1] 〔 sɛt 〕 *v.* 設定
  device[4] 〔 dɪˈvaɪs 〕 *n.* 裝置

audio + logy
|　　　|
hear + study

3. (**C**)　依句意，「在…程度」，常與 level 搭配的介系詞為 ***at***，
選 (C)。

[***If*** you're using the earbuds ***and*** you turn the volume up to the

maximum ***and*** you listen a total of two hours a day, five days a

week,] our best estimates are ***that*** people <u>having</u> more sensitive ears
4

will develop a rather significant degree of hearing loss. ***What*** is
5

more alarming is ***that*** this would happen [after about 10 years or so

or even more of listening to a personal music device.]"

如果你正在使用入耳式耳機，並把音量調到最大，一星期聽五天，每天聽整整兩個小時，我們的最佳估計是，有較為靈敏耳朵的人，聽力會受到相當大的損害。而且更令人擔憂的是，如此的聽力損失，會在使用個人音樂裝置大約十年或更久之後才會發生。」

    * earbud〔'ɪr,bʌd〕n.（入耳式）耳機
    turn up 調高（音量）
    volume³〔'vɑljəm〕n. 音量
    maximum⁴〔'mæksəməm〕n. 最大量   total¹〔'totḷ〕n. 總計
    estimate⁴〔'ɛstə,met〕v. 估計
    sensitive³〔'sɛnsətɪv〕adj. 敏感的；靈敏的
    develop²〔dɪ'vɛləp〕v. 發展；形成
    rather²〔'ræðə〕adv. 相當
    significant³〔sɪg'nɪfəkənt〕adj. 顯著的；相當大的
    degree²〔dɪ'gri〕n. 程度
    alarming〔ə'lɑrmɪŋ〕adj. 驚人的；令人擔憂的
    or so 左右；大約   personal²〔'pɝsṇḷ〕adj. 個人的

4. (D)   依句意可知，此句的主要動詞為 will develop，所以「有」較為靈敏耳朵的人的動詞型態應為現在分詞，故選 (D) ***having***。

5. (C)   「而且更…的是」是固定的慣用語，如 what is more「而且」，what is better「更好的是」，what is worse「更糟的是」，這些句子整個當作表累積的連接詞用，故選 (C) ***What***。***what is more alarming is that*** 更令人擔憂的是

─【劉毅老師的話】─
    題目做得越多，知識越豐富、碰到類似的內容，猜也能猜到答案。

TEST 50

Read the following passage and choose the best answer for each blank from the choices below.

If you are a coaster lover, you will not want to miss the king of all coaster theme parks, Cedar Point in Sandusky, Ohio. __1__ seventeen roller coasters in one amusement park, Cedar Point has become a coaster mecca. As the self-proclaimed roller coaster capital of the world, Cedar Point is able __2__ give a thrill ride to everyone. One __3__ coaster at Cedar Point is the 215-foot-high Wicked Twister, the world's tallest and fastest double twisting impulse coaster, which combines two vertical drops with a twist on each end. Reaching a top speed of 72 miles per hour, Wicked Twister is not a(n) __4__ coaster. With one U-shaped twisted track, the train rides on backwards and forwards, increasing in speed as well as in height. For Wicked Twister riders, every seat is a good seat. When the ride moves forward, the front seat goes the highest and when the ride moves backwards the last seat goes the highest, but __5__ you're in the middle, you get height on both sides.

1. (A) With   (B) For   (C) As   (D) On
2. (A) in   (B) of   (C) that   (D) to
3. (A) break-record   (B) record-breaking
   (C) record-broken   (D) breaking-record
4. (A) typical (B) extraordinary (C) optional (D) unusual
5. (A) since   (B) because   (C) if   (D) though

TEST 50 詳解

If you are a coaster lover, you will not want to miss the king *of*

all coaster theme parks, *Cedar Point in Sandusky, Ohio.* <u>With</u>
1

seventeen roller coasters in one amusement park, Cedar Point has

become a coaster mecca. *As the self-proclaimed roller coaster capital*

of the world, Cedar Point is able <u>to</u> give a thrill ride *to everyone*.
2

　　如果你是雲霄飛車的愛好者,你絕對不會想錯過所有雲霄飛車主題
公園中的王者——俄亥俄州桑達斯基市的雪松角主題樂園。雪松角主題
樂園<u>有</u>十七座雲霄飛車,它已經成為雲霄飛車的聖地。雪松角自稱為世
1
界雲霄飛車的首都,而<u>且能夠</u>帶給每個人一趟刺激的旅程。
2

* coaster〔'kostɚ〕*n.* 雲霄飛車 (= *roller coaster* = *switchback*)
miss[1]〔mɪs〕*v.* 錯過　　theme[4]〔θim〕*n.* 主題
theme park 主題樂園　　cedar〔'sidɚ〕*n.* 西洋杉;雪松
point[1]〔pɔɪnt〕*n.* 點;尖端;角　　*Cedar Point* 雲杉角主題樂園
Sandusky〔san'dʌskɪ〕*n.* 桑達斯基【美國俄亥俄州東北部的城市】
Ohio〔o'haɪo〕*n.* 俄亥俄州　　*roller coaster* 雲霄飛車
amusement[4]〔ə'mjuzmənt〕*n.* 娛樂;樂趣
amusement park 遊樂場;遊樂園
mecca〔'mɛkə〕*n.* 聖地;許多人拜訪之地;眾人憧憬之地
Mecca n. 麥加【回教聖地】　　proclaim〔pro'klem〕*v.* 宣稱
self-proclaimed〔'sɛlf,prə'klemd〕*adj.* 自我宣稱的
capital[4]〔'kæpətḷ〕*n.* 首都;中心　　thrill[5]〔θrɪl〕*n.* 刺激;興奮
ride[1]〔raɪd〕*n.* 搭乘;(遊樂場的)乘坐裝置

1. (**A**)　依句意，選 (A) *With*「有」。

2. (**D**)　*be able to* + *V.* 能夠…（ = *be capable of* + *V-ing*）

One <u>record-breaking</u> coaster *at Cedar Point* is the 215-foot-high
     3

Wicked Twister, *the world's tallest **and** fastest double twisting*

impulse coaster, **which** *combines two vertical drops with a twist on*

each end. *Reaching a top speed of 72 miles per hour*, Wicked Twister

is not a <u>typical</u> coaster.
      4

雪松角裡面有一台<u>破紀錄的</u>雲霄飛車，就是兩百一十五呎高的「邪惡旋
               3
風」，它是全世界最高、速度最快的兩倍扭力雲霄飛車，它結合了兩段
垂直下落，每一段最後都有一個大旋轉。最高速度達到每小時七十二
哩，「邪惡旋風」可不是<u>一般的</u>雲霄飛車。
               4

   * foot[1]〔fʊt〕*n.* 呎；腳
    wicked[3]〔'wɪkɪd〕*adj.* 邪惡的
    twister〔'twɪstɚ〕*n.* 旋風
    double[2]〔'dʌbḷ〕*adj.* 兩倍的；雙重的
    twist[3]〔twɪst〕*v.* 扭曲；旋轉
    impulse[5]〔'ɪmpʌls〕*n.*（推進）力；衝擊；衝動
    combine[3]〔kəm'baɪn〕*v.* 結合
    vertical[5]〔'vɝtɪkḷ〕*adj.* 垂直的
    【horizontal[5]〔ˌhɔrə'zɑntḷ〕*adj.* 水平的】
    drop[1]〔drɑp〕*n.* 下降　　top[1]〔tɑp〕*adj.* 最高的
    speed[2]〔spid〕*n.* 速度　　per[2]〔pɚ〕*prep.* 每…

3. (**B**)　依句意，「一台破紀錄的雲霄飛車」One coaster that breaks the record，形容詞子句中的動詞是主動的，所以複合形容詞為 *record-breaking*「破紀錄的」，故選 (B)。

4. (**A**)

(A) *typical*[3] 〔ˋtɪpɪk!〕*adj.* 典型的；一般的
(B) extraordinary[4] 〔ɪkˋstrɔrdn͵ɛrɪ〕*adj.* 不尋常的
(C) optional[6] 〔ˋɑpʃən!〕*adj.* 可選擇的
(D) unusual[1] 〔ʌnˋjuʒʊəl〕*adj.* 不尋常的

With one U-shaped twisted track, the train rides *on backwards and forwards, increasing in speed **as well as** in height.* *For Wicked Twister riders*, every seat is a good seat. ***When** the ride moves forward*, the front seat goes the highest ***and when** the ride moves backwards* the last seat goes the highest, ***but if** you're in the middle*, you get height[5] *on both sides*.

有著 U 型扭曲的軌道，列車會開往後以及往前，同時增加速度跟高度。對乘坐「邪惡旋風」的人而言，每個座位都是好位子。當列車往前開時，前面座位的高度最高，當列車往後開時，後面座位的高度最高，但<u>如果你是坐在中間的乘客，不管往前或往後開，你的高度都很高。</u>[5]

> *　U-shaped *adj.* U 型的　　　track[2] 〔træk〕*n.* 軌道
> backwards[2] 〔ˋbækwɚdz〕*adv.* 往後
> forwards[2] 〔ˋfɔrwɚdz〕*adv.* 往前　　***as well as*** 以及
> move[1] 〔muv〕*v.* 移動　　front[1] 〔frʌnt〕*adj.* 前面的
> go[1] 〔go〕*v.* 變得；處於　　height[2] 〔haɪt〕*n.* 高度

5. (**C**)　依句意，選 (C) *if*「如果」。而 (A) since「因為」，
　　　　　　(B) because「因為」，(D) though「雖然」，皆不合句意。

高三同學要如何準備「升大學考試」

　　考前該如何準備「學測」呢？「劉毅英文」的同學很簡單，只要熟讀每次的模考試題就行了。每一份試題都在7000字範圍內，就不必再背7000字了，從後面往前複習，越後面越重要，一定要把最後10份試題唸得滾瓜爛熟。根據以往的經驗，詞彙題絕對不會超出7000字範圍。每年題型變化不大，只要針對下面幾個大題準備即可。

準備「詞彙題」最佳資料：

背了再背，背到滾瓜爛熟，讓背單字變成樂趣。

考前不斷地做模擬試題就對了！

你做的題目愈多，分數就愈高。不要忘記，每次參加模考前，都要背單字、背自己所喜歡的作文。考壞不難過，勇往直前，必可得高分！

練習「模擬試題」，可參考「學習出版公司」最新出版的「7000字學測試題詳解」。我們試題的特色是：
①以「高中常用7000字」為範圍。 ②經過外籍專家多次校對，不會學錯。③每份試題都有詳細解答，對錯答案均有明確交待。

「克漏字」如何答題

  第二大題綜合測驗（即「克漏字」），不是考句意，就是考簡單的文法。當四個選項都不相同時，就是考句意，就沒有文法的問題；當四個選項單字相同、字群排列不同時，就是考文法，此時就要注意到文法的分析，大多是考連接詞、分詞構句、時態等。「克漏字」是考生最弱的一環，你難，別人也難，只要考前利用這種答題技巧，勤加練習，就容易勝過別人。

準備「綜合測驗」（克漏字）可參考「學習出版公司」最新出版的「7000字克漏字詳解」。

本書特色：

1. 取材自大規模考試，英雄所見略同。
2. 不超出7000字範圍，不會做白工。
3. 每個句子都有文法分析。一目了然。
4. 對錯答案都有明確交待，列出生字，不用查字典。
5. 經過「劉毅英文」同學實際考過，效果極佳。

「文意選填」答題技巧

  在做「文意選填」的時候，一定要冷靜。你要記住，一個空格一個答案，如果你不知道該選哪個才好，不妨先把詞性正確的選項挑出來，如介詞後面一定是名詞，選項裡面只有兩個名詞，再用刪去法，把不可能的選項刪掉。也要特別注意時間的掌控，已經用過的選項就劃掉，以免重複考慮，浪費時間。

準備「文意選填」，可參考「學習出版公司」最新出版的「7000字文意選填詳解」。

特色與「7000字克漏字詳解」相同，不超出7000字的範圍，有詳細解答。

「閱讀測驗」的答題祕訣

① 尋找關鍵字——整篇文章中，最重要就是第一句和最後一句，第一句稱為主題句，最後一句稱為結尾句。每段的第一句和最後一句，第二重要，是該段落的主題句和結尾句。從「主題句」和「結尾句」中，找出相同的關鍵字，就是文章的重點。因為美國人從小被訓練，寫作文要注重主題句，他們給學生一個題目後，要求主題句和結尾句都必須有關鍵字。

② 先看題目、劃線、找出答案、標題號——考試的時候，先把閱讀測驗題目瀏覽一遍，在文章中掃瞄和題幹中相同的關鍵字，把和題目相關的句子，用線畫起來，便可一目了然。通常一句話只會考一題，你畫了線以後，再標上題號，接下來，你找其他題目的答案，就會更快了。

③ 碰到難的單字不要害怕，往往在文章的其他地方，會出現同義字，因為寫文章的人不喜歡重覆，所以才會有難的單字。

④ 如果閱測內容已經知道，像時事等，你就可以直接做答了。

準備「閱讀測驗」，可參考「學習出版公司」最新出版的「7000字閱讀測驗詳解」，本書不超出7000字範圍，每個句子都有文法分析，對錯答案都有明確交待，單字註明級數，不需要再查字典。

「中翻英」如何準備

可參考劉毅老師的「英文翻譯句型講座實況DVD」，以及「文法句型180」和「翻譯句型800」。考前不停地練習中翻英，翻完之後，要給外籍老師改。翻譯題做得越多，越熟練。

「英文作文」怎樣寫才能得高分？

① 字體要寫整齊，最好是印刷體，工工整整，不要塗改。

② 文章不可離題，尤其是每段的第一句和最後一句，最好要有題目所說的關鍵字。

③ 不要全部用簡單句，句子最好要有各種變化，單句、複句、合句、形容詞片語、分詞構句等，混合使用。

④ 不要忘記多使用轉承語，像*at present*（現在），*generally speaking*（一般說來），*in other words*（換句話說），*in particular*（特別地），*all in all*（總而言之）等。

⑤ 拿到考題，最好先寫作文，很多同學考試時，作文來不及寫，吃虧很大。但是，如果看到作文題目不會寫，就先寫測驗題，這個時候，可將題目中作文可使用的單字、成語圈起來，寫作文時就有東西寫了。但千萬記住，絕對不可以抄考卷中的句子，一旦被發現，就會以零分計算。

⑥ 試卷有規定標題，就要寫標題。記住，每段一開始，要內縮5或7個字母。

⑦ 可多引用諺語或名言，並注意標點符號的使用。文章中有各種標點符號，會使文章變得更美。

⑧ 整體的美觀也很重要，段落的最後一行字數不能太少，也不能太多。段落的字數要平均分配，不能第一段只有一、兩句，第二段一大堆。第一段可以比第二段少一點。

準備「英文作文」，可參考「學習出版公司」出版的：